13852

GW00670528

ST. LOUIS
Library
13852
s/563669

ANGLO-NORMAN
ULSTER

Published for
The Institute of Irish Studies
The Queen's University of Belfast
by
John Donald Publishers

ANGLO-NORMAN ULSTER

The History and Archaeology of an Irish Barony, 1177-1400

T. E. McNEILL

Department of Archaeology
The Queen's University of Belfast

ST. LOUISE'S
Library.....
563669

JOHN DONALD PUBLISHERS LTD.
EDINBURGH

© T. E. McNeill, 1980

All rights reserved. No part of this publication may
be reproduced in any form or by any means without
the prior permission of the publishers, John Donald
Publishers Ltd., 138 St. Stephen Street, Edinburgh.

ISBN 0 85976 057 X

Printed in Great Britain by Bell & Bain Ltd., Glasgow
Phototypesetting by Wright Printers, Dundee

Preface

THIS book is based on a doctoral thesis for the Queen's University of Belfast, and so my thanks must first go to those who helped me in that work, above all Professor E. M. Jope, my supervisor. The references show my debts to printed works of scholars before me; G. H. Orpen's work on the Inquisitions Post Mortem of the Earl of Ulster's lands in 1333 providing the starting point, followed by the *Ecclesiastical Antiquities* of W. Reeves. The same position in the field of archaeology is occupied by the late D. M. Waterman with his series of excavations and surveys of many of the key sites for this work. I would like to record my indebtedness to the many people with whom I discussed the problems of the study, professional colleagues or not, and most importantly those who told me of the results of their work, particularly the late T. G. Delaney of the Ulster Museum and C. J. Lynn of the Historic Monuments Branch, Department of the Environment with their excavations. The information may be theirs but the views, and mistakes, are mine. I am grateful to others for photographs: plates 3A & B, 4A, 5A, 6A, 7B and 8A were taken by Mr B. N. Hartwell; plate 2A was taken by Mr B. C. S. Wilson, both of Queen's University Archaeology Department; plate 5B was taken by the Ulster Museum, and plate 6B by Professor St. Joseph of Cambridge University: the rest were taken by myself. The production of the whole would have been made much worse without the secretarial help of Mrs R. Swindall, while I owe more than gratitude to my parents and my wife for their support over the years. Last, but not least, thanks are owing to the Institute of Irish Studies at the Queen's University of Belfast, who made a generous grant towards publication of this book.

I have used certain conventions and abbreviations in the work which should be explained. For both Irish personal names and place names I have followed Orpen in his spelling: for the identification of place-names in nearly every case I have followed him or Bishop Reeves. The nomenclature of counties provides a problem with both a modern and an Anglo-Norman county of Down and Antrim. To make it clear which I mean, I have used the abbreviated 'Co.' before the name (i.e. Co. Antrim) for the modern county, the unabbreviated 'County' after it (i.e. Antrim County) for the Anglo-Norman counties. The maps are based on lists of sites which are given in my thesis, where not otherwise stated, in the footnotes. In both these last and the Bibliography I have used the following abbreviations (for all details, see the Bibliography):-

A.S.C.D.	– *An Archaeological Survey of Co. Down.*
C.D.I.	– *Calendar of documents relating to Ireland.*
C.D.S.	– *Calendar of documents relating to Scotland.*
Clyn's Annals	– *The Annals of Friar John Clyn and Thady Dowling.*

De l'Isle and Dudley mss.	– Royal Commission òn Historical Manuscripts: *Report on the papers of Lord de L'Isle and Dudley.*
J.R.S.A.I.	– *Journal of the Royal Society of Antiquaries of Ireland:* the volumes are cited according to the continuous series of numbering.
Patent and Close Rolls, Ireland	– *Rotulorum Patentium et Clausorum Cancellariae Hiberniae Calendarium* (ed. E. Tresham).
Reports of the Deputy Keeper, P.R.I.	– *The Reports of the Deputy Keeper of the Public Records of Ireland.*
U.J.A.	– *Ulster Journal of Archaeology:* unless otherwise stated, references are to the Third Series (starting in 1938).

T. E. McNeill.

Contents

List of Figures

List of Plates

Introduction

WHEN Robert Guiscard conquered southern Italy he did so to establish a hereditary lordship there for himself and his family. He may have admitted a respect for his former feudal superior, the Duke of Normandy, a respect the greater for the Duke's absence, but he never acknowledged any superior from France in his conquests. After Cortes had conquered Mexico he did not establish himself as hereditary Duke there: he was succeeded by a governor appointed by Charles V back in Spain. Mediaeval conquests were not made as state expeditions by appointed officials; they were the result of private ventures by individuals intending to carve out estates for themselves and their families in the new land. They did not mean to return, their duty done, to be replaced by others, while they retired to a mediaeval equivalent of Bournemouth. It is true that the classic statement of this commitment to the new country, Maurice FitzGerald's speech at the siege of Dublin in 1171, was said at a particularly tense moment for the Anglo-Norman invaders of Ireland. However, Giraldus Cambrensis thought it worth repeating (or inventing?) later and so must have considered the sentiment a true one: 'to the Irish we are English, and to the English, Irishmen.' This was alleged to have been said only just over two years from the first arrival of the Anglo-Normans in Ireland. The result of this enterprise and commitment is well known. Over about two-thirds of Ireland the Anglo-Normans established themselves in baronies, settling down to exploit the land in their own interests and partly in the interests of the King of England.

The general history of this settlement has been recounted, with different emphases, several times: the basic political framework of the story has been clear since Orpen. This present study sets out not to trace the general history of Ireland but to look at one of the baronies which composed the Anglo-Norman colony of Ireland. The Earldom of Ulster is particularly susceptible to being picked out for a specific study. It was unrivalled in the north on the Anglo-Norman side as a Liberty with little or no royal land and, except for the short-lived grants to the de Galloways, no other Anglo-Norman barony was concerned. The northern part of Ireland, which was the setting within which the Earldom had to live, was itself also an isolated world, in part cut off from the rest of Ireland by the difficult country of the present counties of Armagh, Monaghan and Cavan. The former Irish kingdoms of Breffny or Connacht which had been the northern kingdoms' rivals and neighbours became involved in their own struggles against the Anglo-Normans of Meath, Oriel and Connacht and were less and less concerned with the north. Because this is the study of how one particular barony functioned in mediaeval Ireland, the evidence used must be derived from it. It is not the aim of this work to compare the Earldom of Ulster with other baronies, for this can lead all too easily to assumptions that what prevailed elsewhere happened in Ulster. It is a study of an Anglo-Norman barony and the information is derived largely from the Anglo-Norman side. The clearest example of this can be seen in the discussion of the organisation of the agricultural settlement, where the evidence from pre-Norman Ireland is not brought into the discussion. This is in part, of course, because it is a large and tangled subject which the writer is not competent to handle, but also because too fixed an idea must prejudice our reading of the actual position of the thirteenth century Anglo-Norman barony. On the other hand it is a study which attempts to use the physical evidence from archaeology as much as the documentary evidence, not just because the latter is thin but because it can give us a different range of evidence.

What we will look at, then, is one social unit at the edge of the feudal world, at the other end of mediaeval Europe's frontier from the Kingdom of Jerusalem. This may seem a comparison which attempts to drag in an impossible glamour to bestow on a very small and unimportant part but it does provide us with a setting in which we can pose questions of the evidence: whether they are answered is a judgement that must lie with the reader not the writer. The first and most basic is where did the Anglo-Normans actually settle in Ulster, and when, as opposed to where did they claim to, or where have later writers assumed that they did? What resources did they exploit and how did they do this? How was the Earldom organised and how much did it succeed in establishing a little part of the English way of life in Ulster, always assuming that this was the aim? The corollary of this question is to ask what the impact of this settlement was on the Irish, so far as we can judge. These questions form the framework of this work. 'Coacervavi omne quod inveni': it is to be hoped that the answers will emerge from the heap.

BELFAST PUBLIC LIBRARIES SCHOOLS

1
The Initial Settlement, 1177-1226

HOWEVER much a ruler may or may not succeed in subordinating himself to economic or social forces operating in his society, there are times when his personality matters. With an invasion or colonisation this is particularly true, and so in discussing the Anglo-Normans in Ulster, we must start with one man, John de Courcy. He did not come from a great aristocratic family, unlike the later de Lacy and de Burgh earls who succeeded him, but was a relative (though not the heir) of a county family from Stoke Courcy in Somerset. In spite of this he founded a lordship in which he was able to give himself the trappings of independent kingship, household officers like seneschal and chamberlain, coinage and the title *princeps*. All our views of him are for ever coloured by the pen portrait that Giraldus Cambrensis gives, and historians from Goddard Orpen[1] to Lydon[2] have been seduced by his glamour: 'John was fair-haired and tall with bony and sinewy limbs. His frame was lanky and he had a very strong physique, immense bodily strength, and an extraordinarily bold temperament. From his youth he was a man of courage and a born fighter, always in the front line, always taking upon himself the greatest share of the danger . . . Although in war he was impetuous, and had about him the air of an ordinary soldier rather than that of a leader, yet away from the battlefield he was modest and restrained, and gave the church of Christ that honour which is its due . . . Twin blemishes of excessive meanness and unreliability stained the gleaming purity of a character in other respects so worthy of praise.'[3]

This is the basis of his legend which we must analyse. His love of fighting is clear enough and the grants to the church and monastic foundations bear out Giraldus' verdict. What we must examine, of course, is how far he was successful behind the picture of the hefty blonde soldier, and it is here that the reference to his meanness is significant. Behind the facade, as seen for example in his castle at Carrickfergus, he was not a great conqueror, certainly not to the extent of controlling Cos. Antrim and Down as he is often credited with: his meanness may reflect the fact that after he had given himself the trappings of lordship and the church what it considered its due share (Giraldus was a cleric) there was little left for his men.

When John de Courcy invaded the north of Ireland in 1177 he was faced with a complex political situation, with three dominant powers (fig. 1). In the west, the Cenel Conaill controlled most of Co. Donegal and were pressing eastwards on to the main power bloc in the north, the Cenel Eoghain. These latter were now centred on Tir Eoghain (west of Lough Neagh) and had established themselves as overlords of the O Cahans whose lands lay in north Co. Londonderry and also of the various tribes of the Airgialla south of Lough Neagh between Lough Erne and Louth. Although dominant in the north in the eleventh and twelfth centuries, providing two high kings in the latter, they were losing ground to the Cenel Conaill in Inishowen and the middle Foyle valley and were to lose these by the early thirteenth

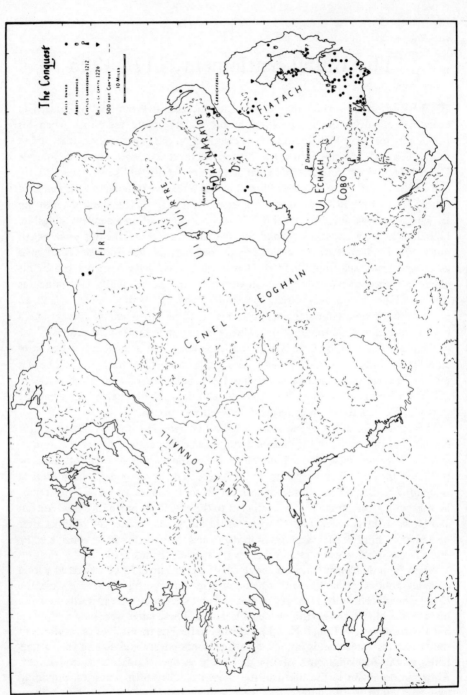

century.[4] Internally their position was also weakened between 1177 and 1241 by internal rivalry for the kingship between Aedh O'Neill, briefly king in 1177,[5] and the MacLochlainn line of succession who had previously controlled it. Just as they lost ground to the eastward movement of the Cenel Conaill, so they had been moving steadily to the east throughout the historic period at the expense of the Ulaid who had been, since the eighth century at least, confined east of the river Bann.[6]

By the later twelfth century there were four kingdoms involved in this area, the modern Cos. Antrim and Down. Central and west Co. Down were the lands of the Ui Echach Cobo, who had two families involved in the kingship, the MacCartains[7] and the MacOenghusa or Magennises.[8] They were clearly a vigorous kingdom, raiding to Armagh, for example, in 1173.[9] East and north of them in coastal Co. Down and in south Co. Antrim were the lands of Dal Fiatach who had controlled the kingship of Ulaid since the tenth century.[10] In doing so they had taken the south Antrim lands, where they established their inauguration place at Craebh Tulcha, from the Dal nAraide who had also shared the kingship of Ulaid. These last were clearly declining in power, partly as a result of Dal Fiatach but more seriously because of the invasion of Co. Antrim by Ui Tuirtre. These last had been pushed out from their former lands west of Lough Neagh by the Cenel Eoghain probably some time after 919 when the last Ui Tuirtre king of Airgialla died. A hundred years later however their former home, Tullahogue, was in Cenel Eoghain hands[11] while in 1016 the Ui Tuirtre are allied with Dal nAraide in a defeat by Dal Fiatach,[12] and so are probably settled in some part of Co. Antrim: their relationship with Dal nAraide then is unknown. Involved with the Ui Tuirtre from early times[13] were the Fir Li who seem also to move from west to east of the river Bann. From 1059 the family of O Flainn (O'Flynn) controlled the kingship of Ui Tuirtre according to the Annals of Ulster. By the time of John de Courcy, the Ui Tuirtre had replaced Dal nAraide as the dominant tribe of Co. Antrim and in fact may have conquered them, for in 1176 Cu-maighi Ua Flainn is described in the Annals of Ulster as king of Ui Tuirtre, Fir Li and Dal nAraide. If so it must have been a recent conquest because Ua Loingsigh kings or Lords of Dal nAraide are recorded in the Annals of Ulster down to 1128 and in the Annals of the Four Masters (the Annals of Ulster are missing for 1131-55) as late as 1141, 1156 and 1166. They must, however, have been confined to their centre in the valley of the Six Mile Water (e.g. Annals of Ulster, 1030 – 'Ua Loingsigh's house . . . in the middle of Oentruimh').[14] John de Courcy, when he attacked the Ulaid, faced two stronger tribes, the Ui Tuirtre and Ui Echach Cobo, a weak one Dal nAraide and Dal Fiatach. All had been attacked recently by Cenel Eoghain or its subjects but especially Dal Fiatach as kings of Ulaid, particularly in 1165-6 when Muircetach Ua Lochlainn had divided the kingdom and then blinded Eochadh MacDonnsleibhe against his word, an action which led to Muircetach's fall. Ulaid hardly gained however from this respite, with Eochadh's brother and successor Magnus being killed in 1171 by his brother Donnsleibhe, who was himself replaced by a third brother Rory by 1177. Ui Tuirtre may not have been stabilised by Cu-maighi Ua Flainn's killing of his brother for the kingship in 1176.

John de Courcy must have known much of this when he left Dublin for the north in 1177. He knew where to go: to arrive in Downpatrick to catch the king by surprise he must have moved very fast and with secrecy through Co. Down. He had, according to Giraldus,[15] twenty-two knights but some three hundred footmen; he arrived on the morning of the fourth day of his march from Dublin: to accomplish night marches or find safe camp-site (it was January or the first days of February) he would have needed local help. Orpen[16] postulates that some of his three hundred were Irish: at least one must have been from Dal Fiatach. John de Courcy had to fight hard for his conquest in the first five years against both Ulaid and Cenel Eoghain.[17] The turning point came in 1181-2: in the first of these years the alliance against him broke down with a raid by Cenel Eoghain against Ulaid, Ui Tuirtre and Fir Li, while O Cahan raided Ui Tuirtre and Fir Li as well. The next year Cenel Eoghain raided into Dal Riata (i.e. north Antrim) only to be defeated by the Anglo-Normans.[18] After this there is no more fighting recorded between John de Courcy and Ulaid: we even find Rory MacDunlevy raiding Tir Eoghain as an Anglo-Norman ally in 1196.[19] By 1185, when he was appointed Justiciar in Ireland by Henry II, de Courcy must have regularised his position with the English king.[20] He had further secured his position by marrying about the year 1180 Affreca, daughter of Godred, King of Man, a man with Ulster connections (he had married Muircetach MacLochlainn's daughter) but, more importantly, a fleet. John de Courcy had clearly arrived within six or seven years of his attack on Downpatrick.

The story of the rest of John de Courcy's political and military activity can be told quickly. He was not a successful Justiciar and returned within a few years to Ulster. He founded an outpost castle at Maycove (probably Ballyroney, Co. Down) in Ui Echach Cobo by 1188,[21] and in 1197[22] one at Cill Santain (probably Mount Sandel near Coleraine): from the latter in particular he raided north Co. Londonderry or Inishowen annually to 1200. These raids were inconclusive, as is shown by the events of 1199 when he raided via Ardstraw and Derry to Inishowen but was forced to return by Aedh Ua Neill, king of Cenel Eoghain, who raided Larne and the Six Mile Water valley by sea from five ships. The forces were highly mobile but small and the damage they did short-lived. His principality was not conquered by this sort of traditional Irish hosting. John did not die in Ulster but was expelled in 1204-5, in a confused intrigue and campaign by Hugh de Lacy, second son of the man who had set himself up, under Henry II, as Lord of Meath. The causes of the quarrel and whether King John encouraged it or not are unknown as are the details of the fighting.[23] Hugh de Lacy was created Earl of Ulster on the 29th of May 1205, and John de Courcy in effect vanishes from history although not from legend.

The reasons which brought King John to Ireland in 1210 need not be discussed here, but the consequences of his visit affected both the history of the new Earldom and our knowledge of it. He pursued Hugh de Lacy to Carrickfergus and expelled him from his Earldom. Any further expansion of the Earldom by itself was halted, to be subordinated to royal policy, as for example in 1211-12 when the Justiciar organised an attack on the Cenel Eoghain from Meath via Clones. Royal policy also introduced a second British element to Ulster in the grants made along the north coast to the de Galloway, or MacUchtred, family from south-west Scotland. By taking the Earldom into his hands John also ensured that documentation should survive in the royal archives for historians, which allow us to look at the settlement of John de Courcy and Hugh de Lacy (before his return in 1226) in much more detail than we otherwise might, in particular as a result of the survival of an Irish Pipe Roll for the year 1211-12.[24] These documents allow us to ask where the Anglo-Normans had settled by 1226 and how they had ordered these lands. They were conquered by force and depended ultimately on force for their administration.

The key military bases were the two castles of Carrickfergus and Dundrum, both stone-built and both ports: Antrim whose garrison equalled Dundrum's in 1211-12[25] seems always to have been a motte and bailey. It was in these two castles that Hugh de Lacy's men stood siege against King John in 1205.[26] Dundrum guards the southern approaches by land into east Co. Down: whether a traveller takes the route over the Newry pass and then skirts north of the Mournes between them and Slieve Croob, or crosses Carlingford Lough by ferry – as existed in the 1180's[27] – and then round south of the Mournes, he must pass the rock on which Dundrum castle is sited. Its physical appearance has been well described already (fig. 2).[28] Excavation in 1950[29] showed that the castle first consisted of a multangular enclosure of stone and mortar on the hill top. This, with its slightly fortified entrance and wall only four feet thick, appears weak but on the south-west side there are preserved the holes for timbers projecting out on both sides at the wall-head, to widen the wall-walk on the inside and provide machicolations on the outside. The whole may have been covered by a wall-top roofed passage. At this period, presumably built by John de Courcy, there was at least one major timber building in the enclosure. At the south, at a point nearest the keep, there is a double latrine recess in the curtain with the offset for a gable end over it, yet no signs of toothing on either side. The floor of the recess is about four or five feet above the original courtyard level: it could only be reached from there by means of gratuitously difficult manoeuvres. It must have been part of a major building stretching off into the courtyard, which at least at this point had a low first floor. Whatever this can be (and it is very tempting to postulate an early timber hall here), the building must have been demolished when the keep was built. When exactly this happened is not clear, but the present massive round keep must be identified with the 'magne turris' of the Irish Pipe Roll in 1211-12.[30] Here a small sum is recorded as spent on work on it, either repairs to it, a few finishing touches or expenses connected with suspending work on it. Whichever it be, there can be little doubt that the round keep at Dundrum was in existence in 1211, and, given political vicissitudes, probably before 1205. It could well be the work of Hugh de Lacy with his cousins in the south Welsh Marches, where the experimental round keep was most popular.[31] The Pipe Roll also records expenditure on a hall at Dundrum as well as the keep which allows us to hazard an account as to how these buildings were used. The keep was originally of at least three stories: the flue of the fireplace and the spiral staircase both extend above the sockets of the second floor, although the bulk of the existing second floor is to be attributed to the fifteenth century.[32] The ground floor or basement (the original entrance was into the first floor) was clearly for storage and access to the well below, for it has no fireplace or latrine and only two

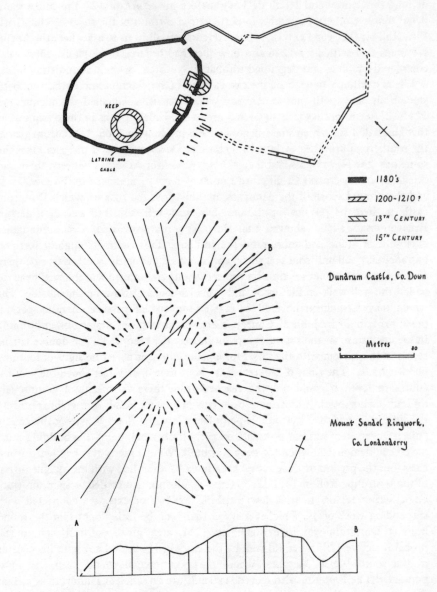

2. Plans of Dundrum castle (after A.S.C.D., fig. 133) and Mount Sandel ringwork.

narrow slit windows. The first, or entry, floor has a large fireplace and handsome windows with window-seats. Because of the Pipe Roll we can see that this was not the hall but presumably the great chamber of the castle, the place where the lord's semi-public and private life went on. The second floor would have housed the private chambers of the lord, where he slept. The site of a timber hall might be marked by a secondary skin of masonry at the north-east side of the ward: it has a chase and offset for a first floor.

The second and more important of John de Courcy's two castles of stone was at Carrickfergus (fig. 3), built at the end of a peninsula of rock flanking the harbour (Plate 1). It has been much altered and added to since the twelfth century as a result of its continuous occupation down to the present day but remains the most complete example of an early castle in Ireland.[33] The castle seems to have been built in part at least in 1178 when Giraldus[34] refers to John de Courcy retreating from a defeat in Fir Li to it. His castle (the first period in the castle's sequence of construction) consisted of a polygonal enclosure of stone, the present inner curtain, with a large stone keep attached, intended from the first and started in the second building campaign (plate 2B). This is the castle in which King John stayed from 19th to 28th July 1210,[35] either during or after a siege of Hugh de Lacy's followers there – after Dublin his longest stay in any place in Ireland. The pre-eminence of this castle within Ulster is shown in the 1211-12 Pipe Roll[36] where the garrison at its height (during a wartime winter) with its ten knights, sixteen soldiers, five bowmen, a chaplain and eight non-combatants was twice as large as that of any other castle in Ulster. The amount of flour sent there was four times that sent to Dundrum, nearly ten times that sent to any other castle. The Pipe Roll also mentions a chamber, whose windows needed repair, a kitchen and a barn at the castle. The present fabric shows the position of two of the buildings in the courtyard. The position of the hall is marked by two fine original windows with window-seats on the inner splays, set at first-floor level in the eastern curtain wall. On the south side there are the remains of two windows, also at first-floor level, which appear to be those of the chapel. The keep has three floors (fig. 8) providing accommodation. The key to understanding the roles that each floor played is given by the fireplaces and latrines provided. The entry floor is a public room, with a double latrine, but is poorly lit and has access to the well but no fireplace. The second floor is also poorly lit, but has a fireplace; the latrine is a single, private one: the floor above, with an impressive display of windows in all four walls and a fireplace, has only a single, private latrine. The arrangement of the accommodation is reasonably to be interpreted as a guard-room on the entry floor; a room above for the members of John de Courcy's curia, more comfortable and private; and a third floor marked out by its luxurious lighting as an important room but by its latrine as a private one. The third floor should be identified as the principal chamber of the castle, protected from the public in the entry floor by the lesser chamber between. Thanks to its documentation and the survival of much of its fabric, we can see at Carrickfergus the key castle of John de Courcy's principality, captured in 1205 and 1210, and make a reasonable reconstruction of its appearance and use, the most complete example possible in Ireland of a castle of the Anglo-Norman conquest period (fig. 4).

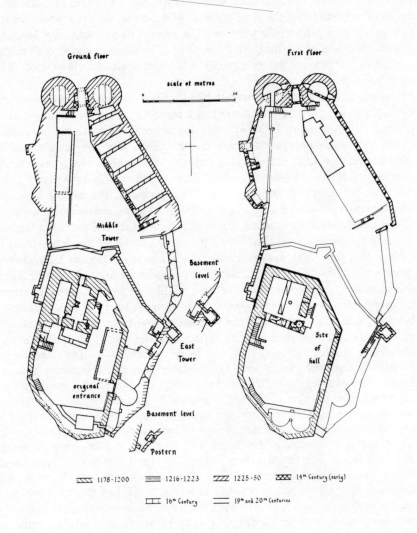

3. Carrickfergus castle: simplified plans at ground and first-floor levels.

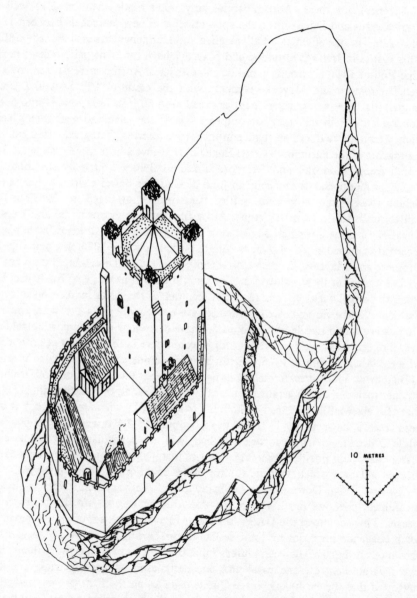

4. Carrickfergus castle: reconstruction as it might have been in 1200.

To back up these two major castles were other, lesser ones of earth and timber. Three others had garrisons in 1211-12, Antrim, Dromore and Maycove (Ballyroney). Of these, Antrim is the only other castle mentioned as well as Carrickfergus and Dundrum in the appointments of new seneschals between 1215 and 1226,[37] in one of which[38] Ballymaghan and Dundonald are also named. Unlike other castles in Ireland, Dromore and Maycove have garrisons paid in cows in the Pipe Roll of 1211-12; troops guarding the district of Antrim were paid in cows as well.[39] Dromore and Maycove compare with the castle of Cill Santain (Mount Sandel) (fig. 2) – whose garrison, after it had been built in 1197, raided into north Londonderry – in that they are outposts against the Irish and near them, bases from which to raid rather than administrative centres. They are sited on the approaches of the Earldom to Cenel Eoghain, Maycove a little more than ten miles' march from Dundrum, and Dromore linked to Belfast Lough by the motte at Duneight mentioned as Dunechti in John de Courcy's dower charter to his wife.[40] Behind these outposts were the settled lands proper, arranged in 1226 into five bailiwicks:[41] Antrim, Carrickfergus, Ards, Blathewic (Newtownards) and Lecale. These cover quite a restricted area, as confirmed by putting all identifiable places recorded as owned or given away by Anglo-Normans before 1226 on a map (fig. 1): Dromore and Maycove have no close neighbours, except Duneight, and do not fit easily into any of these bailiwicks. They might be within range of Blathewic, but when these bailiwicks re-emerge as the counties of the 1333 inquisition into the Earldom, Blathewic and Ards bailiwicks are one county on a par with Antrim, Carrickfergus and Lecale. This would not have been done had Blathewic stretched over into central or west Co. Down, for it would have been quite out of proportion with the others. Again in 1226, Antrim bailiwick renders more than twice as much as Blathewic, and Carrickfergus about half as much again. The diocese of Dromore was not included in the arrangements of either the synod of Rathbreasil (1111) or that of Kells/Mellifont (1152), although Connor and Down were in both.[42] It had been created, however, by 1197 and probably by 1191-2.[43] It was always a poor see while Down, from which it was detached, was not particularly large. The only reason that seems possible for its creation was that it should cater for the areas of the diocese of Down which John de Courcy either could or would not conquer.

The rest of Co. Down was in the bailiwicks of Blathewic and Ards, as already mentioned, covering north Down and the Ards peninsula, and the bailiwick of Lecale. This contained the Dal Fiatach centre and bishop's see of Down, renamed for propaganda purposes by John de Courcy as Downpatrick. Mrs Flanagan has shown on the basis of the Irish sources[44] that by the later twelfth century there were two separate centres, óne royal and one ecclesiastic, at Downpatrick, and has suggested that the earthwork in the Quoile marshes north of the present cathedral might be the royal one. This earthwork has usually been called a motte and bailey and attributed to the Anglo-Normans.[45] The first problem in this Anglo-Norman attribution is the earthwork itself: the motte appears uncomfortably sited in the pear-shaped bailey, against the tail of the latter's bank which runs into the motte ditch. The bailey bank at the point nearest the motte is the same height as the motte which nullifies the use of height on which the military strength of a motte depended. The motte has a deep cleft in it and may not have been finished. The other problem is that there is no evidence that there was a castle of the Earl in Downpatrick. In 1210 King John stayed at the meadows below Down ('apud pratum subtus Dun'), [46] not at Down. Again there is no mention of Downpatrick in either the Irish Pipe Roll or the four lists of castles handed over by seneschals. Yet Downpatrick was an important place; if it had a castle it must have been an important one and the documents would surely mention it, but even in the 1333 inquisition into the lands of the Earldom [47] there is no mention of a castle there. This leaves the 'motte and bailey' without an archaeological or historical basis, and the earthwork must be attributed to MacDunlevy before 1177, with an attempted fortification by the Anglo-Normans, abandoned before it was finished.

The reason why John de Courcy decided not to put a castle there must lie in the role of the church. The centre of power of Dal Fiatach was there and in Lecale. Giraldus records that he was generous to the church, and in Lecale we can see it. There are three grants recorded which give us the information: lands granted by John de Courcy to Randulph bishop of Down, [48] by Malachy, also bishop of Down to the cathedral church of St. Patrick, [49] and from John de Courcy to Christchurch, Dublin: [50] these are gathered with others by MacNiocaill, [51] with textual emendations but no other comment. All simply give lists of placenames without further definition, but about half of these names can be identified with modern townlands (a factor which will be commented on later for its implications for the origin of townlands). When the townlands concerned are marked out on a map (fig. 16), they delineate large blocks of Lecale. Add to them the unidentified names and the few that are added by 1305, when we have a detailed escheator's account of the bishop's land [52] (but which may, of course have been acquired in the interval), and it can be seen that much of the present barony and ancient bailiwick of Lecale was in church hands. John de Courcy chose the time-honoured way (compare Muirchetach O Brien's gift of Cashel in 1101) of neutralising the main centre of potential Irish disaffection by giving it to the church. It is not surprising that the bailiwick of Lecale rendered by far the smallest proportion of the bailiwicks in 1226.

Apart from these grants which put the bishopric of Down on its feet for the mediaeval period, John de Courcy made many others to the church. He was a true man of the twelfth century in his patronage of monasteries. He was not a great benefactor of the Benedictines, for their day was over, but he founded one cell, St. Andrew in Ards or Black Abbey, of which there are now no remains: [53] it was a cell of his home abbey at Stoke Courcy and also Lonlay in Normandy. He refounded the pre-Norman abbey of Nendrum as a cell of St. Bees in Cumberland and St. Mary's abbey, York: neither house was large. To replace the abbey of Erenagh, in an unknown place in Down, which he had burned, John founded the Cistercian abbey of Inch, daughter of Furness. His wife, Affreca, also founded a Cistercian house, Grey abbey, a daughter of Holm Cultram. Inch [54] is a fine building, aisled with well moulded piers: with its tiered, pointed lancets in the chancel and rib vaulting of its transept chapels it is the earliest surviving Gothic building in Ireland. On the other hand Grey abbey [55] is aisleless and much less elaborate; it also took much longer to finish – the west door does not appear to have been finished until about the 1220's.

The answer to this disparity must lie in the dates and circumstances of their foundation. Inch was founded before 1188[56] from a pre-existing house's lands. It had a firm economic base and perhaps twenty years of John de Courcy's patronage, while Grey was founded from nothing in 1193, to be overtaken in ten years by the troubles of de Courcy's expulsion. John also patronised the canons. He founded an Augustinian house in Downpatrick and one for the Fratres Cruciferi.[57] With his barons he founded another Augustinian house at Muckamore in Co. Antrim, again like Nendrum a re-foundation of a defunct Celtic house.[58] There remains one more, the Premonstratensian house at Carrickfergus, White Abbey or Woodburn, all names which appear. The question is how many of these had an independent existence. Gwynn and Hadcock[59] propose that the first two were amalgamated between 1306 and 1326 (when they record the first mention of it) into Woodburn, and attribute references to the abbey of Dieulacresse[60] to White Abbey. In this they disagree with Reeves,[61] who equates Dieulacresse with Down Cathedral, and indeed Gywnn and Hadcock's reasoning would leave the cathedral to be equated with St. Patrick's church, valued at only five marks. Dieulacresse is valued at £41. 5. 5. and would need to have been very badly ruined by Bruce to need refoundation on a new site by 1326 after such a valuation. The house of Carrickfergus, whose prior witnessed a Downpatrick grant in the 1180's[62] after its foundation by de Courcy, was so poor in c.1224 that it could only support three canons,[63] after de Lacy's attacks: it was dedicated to St. Mary. St. Mary's in Carrickfergus was parochial in the 1306 Taxation, valued at £3. 11. 4. (vicarage 14/8):[64] the house seems to have collapsed as an institution. Stones from the site of Woodburn Abbey, however, are preserved in St. Nicholas' church to the present day, and with their heavy roll mouldings and dog-tooth, some must date to the mid-thirteenth century at least: a double cloister arcade base must be fourteenth century or later. The church seems therefore to date back further than the date of the earliest documentary reference. The former Premonstratensian abbey of St. Mary's, Carrickfergus, which had lapsed to parochial status, may well have been revived as the new abbey of Woodburn in the 1320's. If so it may have absorbed the endowments of White Abbey, if any, which had escaped taxation in 1306.

Our conclusions about the extent of settlement in Co. Antrim by the 1220's depend on our evaluation of grants made along the coast of the county, and in particular around Coleraine, under King John. John de Courcy founded a castle at Kil Santain, in 1197,[65] almost certainly the ringwork at Mount Sandel about two miles south of Coleraine. This seems to be isolated except for John de Courcy's grant in his dower charter to Affreca of a third part of 'Culintheskert' (Culrathain in Twescard, i.e. Coleraine), which apparently included two vills, neither now identified. King John brought in a new factor however in the politics of the area, the family from south-west Scotland known in Anglo-Norman documents as Fitz Roland or de Galloway, in Irish ones as MacUchtred: there were two brothers involved, Alan and Thomas, sons of Roland and grandsons of Uhtred, and their uncle Duncan, son of Uhtred's brother, Gilbert.[66] The grants made to them ranged from realistic ones which they took up, held and settled to wildly speculative ones, lands which they might have if they could conquer them. Both elements are present in the grant in 1212 to Alan.[67] To Alan was granted all of north Co. Antrim, Dalriada, Rathlin, Twescard (the north in Irish), the region around Larne and two cantreds across the Bann, one of them (Kunnoch = Ciannachta) the lands of the O Cahans, for the service of 140 knights. This is pure speculation but reserved from it are lands already given to Duncan, who had captured Matilda de Braose in 1210. In 1215 these, again being excepted from grants to Alan, are recorded precisely as two carucates and eight acres.[68] In 1224 Hugh de Lacy attacked Duncan's lands at Ballygalley, near Larne,[69] so we may conclude that he had found tenants to hold them from, and for, him. Alan's grant in 1212 is shown to be speculative by its repetition in 1215 as before,[70] except that it is now to be held for ten not 140 knights' service: by easing the terms so drastically King John hopes that Alan will take it up seriously. To Thomas was made the most speculative of these grants: O Neill's part of Derry and the 'cantred of Talachot' (Tullahogue – the centre of Cenel Eoghain) in 1213. In that year, however, he was granted three knights' fees on each side of the Bann,[71] presumably part of those reserved from Alan's grant in 1212 of Twescard and Ciannachta, the first described as near Mount Sandel. Thomas founded the castle of Coleraine in 1214, using material derived from 'all the cemeteries, fences and buildings of that town, save the church alone':[72] it must have been at least partly of stone. In 1215 he is granted[73] custody of Coleraine and Mount Sandel castles and ten fees on either side of the Bann, near the castles, in place of his earlier three. There seems to be evidence in all this for settlement up to about five miles north of Larne on the one hand, and on the other a nucleus at Coleraine and Mount Sandel of unknown size but hardly surrounded by much of a hinterland. In the rest of the county, the Six Mile Water valley and Belfast Lough shores are the centres of settlement: Robert de Vallibus' two most productive bailiwicks in 1226 are those of Antrim and Carrickfergus.[74] There is no mention of lands in north Antrim (they were in Scottish hands), but there is none in the Pipe Roll of 1211-12 either.

The initial settlement of Ulster by the Anglo-Normans was over by 1226, largely the work of John de Courcy in 25-30 years. He did not immediately create a sharply demarcated Anglo-Norman unit over against the Irish world around him. We have seen how his initial campaign owed much to Irish help, as soldiers and guides. In the Pipe Roll of 1211-12 the military forces recorded in Ulster are different from those of other areas: only in Ulster are there payments in cows to bands of soldiers guarding places. The best example is that of the 40 men who guarded Antrim against Ui Tuirtre, who were given two cows a day between them for food and pay and ten cows to help their wounded and to pay for their lost cloaks.[75] These men must have been Irish foot-soldiers of a tribe loyal to the Anglo-Normans, at least as against Ui Tuirtre: they might even have been men of Dal nAraide from the immediate vicinity. The area settled at this time reflects Irish divisions at John de Courcy's time. The lands he conquered were in east Co. Down and south Co. Antrim, with outposts in Mount Sandal/Coleraine and west Down. These are the lands of the tribes he is known to have defeated, Dal Fiatach and Dal nAraide, while he left alone the Ui Echach Cobo and Ui Tuirtre: the latter, at least, are known to have beaten him in battle. He was himself conscious of the Irish ancestry of the principality he ruled. In two charters he refers to his lands as 'ab aqua de Lenart ad austrum'[76] and 'from the water of Danart to the water of Carlingford',[77] traditional definitions of the limits of the Ulaid kingdom. Again he fostered Irish links in religion, prompting Jocelin of Furness to write a life of Patrick and, in a famous ceremony in 1186, in the presence of the Papal legate Vivian, translating into Down cathedral the bodies of no less than St. Patrick, St. Columba and St. Brigid. The appeal to traditional formulae and to those saints shows him either attuned to Irish ways or well able to exploit them.

This much said, the Anglo-Normans were not Irish nor was the Earldom an Irish kingdom after fifty years of their rule. The administrative units found in 1226 were the basis of the counties of 1333 as pointed out above, just as Carrickfergus castle remained the main English base in Ulster into the seventeenth century. The new organisation and stability is best seen in the Pipe Roll of 1211-12, where the settled land is divided up in English fashion into manors which are carrying on English farming with barns, mills, ploughs, etc. producing large quantities of corn. The land was productive, too, for Robert de Vallibus accounted for over £900 from Ulster in 1226. The royal government had no intention of letting go of this land in the fifteen years after 1210. Under King John, his Justiciar attempted to use Ulster as a base for the conquest of Cenel Eoghain in 1212, as well as fighting Ui Tuirtre in Co. Antrim. The result was negligible, for although the Justiciar could mobilise considerable forces, they were not sufficiently united or persistent to hold the land they raided: it was a pattern to be repeated again (see Chapter Six). There was, however, little danger of Cenel Eoghain attacking the Anglo-Normans in these years: de Galloway pressure and the threat of more action by the Justiciar ensured that. The problem that the Crown had to face in Ulster was that of Anglo-Norman political disaffection centred on the exiled Hugh de Lacy. He had gone to France after his expulsion from Ulster and joined Simon de Montfort fighting the Albigenses, a fairly typical recruit to this distinctly worldly Crusade: he was with Simon in 1211 and stayed on in the Crusade until 1219.[78] His brother Walter, Earl of Meath, was pardoned by King John before his death in 1216. The men captured at Carrickfergus in 1210 were also released by then: as John's position grew worse in his struggle with the barons, they were set free: two in 1212, five in 1213, one in 1214 and twelve in 1215.[79] John kept in touch with Ulster closely;[80] by this time he had become worried about its safety and ordered new defences at Carrickfergus castle. The constable of the castle was William de Serlande (who had succeeded Geoffrey de Serlande by February 1212), and in January 1216 he was ordered to admit the Justiciar, Geoffrey de Mariscis, with a force to the castle for the defence of the country.[81] Later in the same year an outer curtain was ordered, and in 1217 William de Serlande was assigned £100 per year to carry it out: in 1224 the constable's salary was £20, while he united command of Dundrum and Carrickfergus.[82] The result of this royal concern and expenditure was the present middle curtain at Carrickfergus, datable to within the years 1216-24, and the only royal work identifiable in Ulster (fig. 5).

Its aim seems to have been to protect the eastern approaches of the castle over the sand exposed at low tide, and the approach along the rock from the town to the

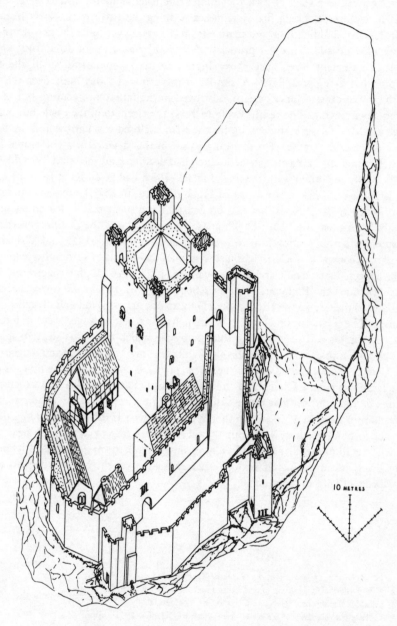

5. Carrickfergus castle: reconstruction as it might have been in 1225.

north as well as a shelf of rock above high tide level along the eastern side. To do this it deployed flanking fire systematically along the two fronts, partly from the now levelled middle tower, but mainly from the east tower set at the new north-east angle of the castle. This was primarily defended by an array of three triple arrow-slits at basement level, just above high tide mark, commanding all the tidal approaches along that flank. A similar triple arrow-slit was built over the gate through the present inner curtain, destroyed in the nineteenth century but known from an engraving. The result was to increase the strength of the castle but not the area available for accommodation, for the strip enclosed was narrow and needed to be kept clear for traffic. It is tempting to see in this defence of a vulnerable flank which contained the castle gate and which had dead ground sheltered from the keep in front of the curtain wall, the line of attack which had given King John the castle in 1210. If so, it did its work against Hugh de Lacy. In 1223 he returned to Ulster and joined Aedh O Neill in a raid on Meath and a successful attack on Coleraine castle.[83] This had been built by Thomas de Galloway, and the Dublin government responded by appointing him constable of Antrim against Hugh and William de Serlande, constable of Carrickfergus, with men and provisions from the Justiciar.[84] The expected attack on Carrickfergus came in 1224 when Hugh besieged the castle and despoiled the Premonstratensian Abbey of St. Mary's in the town because it supported the Crown: he also attacked Duncan of Carrick's land at Ballygalley, near Larne. The Justiciar in Dublin, William Marshal the younger, sent a force of twenty knights and twenty other soldiers by sea which raised the siege in spite of Hugh's attempts, with eight boats to stop him landing.[85] This force and the garrison of 31 in 1212 give a good idea of the forces involved in warfare of the time, as does the raiding of enemies' lands and church buildings. The result was inconclusive, for Hugh de Lacy did not give up his attempts, and the Crown was forced to return his Earldom to him. In 1226 his brother Walter received Hugh's lands and castles in Ulster to hold for three years but they were transferred to him in the next year, 1227.[86] In all probability the Dublin government realised the weakness of its power in Ulster, when compared with the determination of Hugh, who had no other prospects of land in front of him.

NOTES

1. G. H. Orpen: *Ireland under the Normans,* II, chapter 1.
2. J. F. Lydon: *The Lordship of Ireland in the Middle Ages,* pp. 56-7.
3. Giraldus Cambrensis: *Expugnatio Hiberniae,* chapter 18.
4. J. Hogan: *Proceedings of the Royal Irish Academy,* XL (C), 1931-2, pp. 222-4.
5. *Annals of Ulster,* 1177.
6. F. J. Byrne: *Irish Kings and high Kings,* chapter 7.
7. *Annals of Ulster,* 1165.
8. *Ibid.,* 1172.
9. *Ibid.,* 1173.
10. F. J. Byrne: *Irish Kings and high Kings,* p. 126.
11. *Annals of Ulster,* 1012.

12. *Ibid.*, 1016.
13. J. Hogan: *Feil-Sgribhinn Eoin Mhic Neill* (ed. J. Ryan), p. 4.
14. D. Flanagan, *U.J.A.*, XXXII, 1969, pp. 98-9.
15. *Expugnatio Hiberniae*, chapter 17.
16. *Ireland under the Normans*, II, p. 10.
17. *Ibid.*, pp. 10-18.
18. *Annals of Ulster*, 1181, 1182.
19. *Ibid.*, 1196.
20. G. H. Orpen: *Ireland under the Normans*, II, p. 110.
21. *Annals of Ulster*, 1188: H. C. Lawlor; *U.J.A.*, I, 1938, pp. 84-9.
22. *Ibid.*, 1197.
23. G. H. Orpen: *Ireland under the Normans*, II, pp. 138-42.
24. O. Davies & D. B. Quinn: *U.J.A.*, IV, 1941, supplement.
25. *Ibid.*, pp. 55 & 58.
26. *Rotuli de Liberate et Misis et Praestitis regnante Johanne*, (ed. T. D. Hardy), pp. 196-208.
27. W. Dugdale: *Monasticon Anglicanum*, VI (2), p. 1124.
28. *A.S.C.D.*, pp. 207-10: the plan in fig. 2 is based on this.
29. D. M. Waterman: *U.J.A.*, XIV, 1951.
30. O. Davies & D. B. Quinn: *U.J.A.*, IV, 1941, p. 59.
31. D. F. Renn: *Norman Castles in Britain*, pp. 64-5.
32. *A.S.C.D.*, p. 10.
33. Surprisingly the castle has not been described in print except for the short and preliminary Official Guide. A full account of the fabric and history has now been prepared by T. E. McNeill *et. al.* which will be published in the near future.
34. Giraldus Cambrensis: *Expugnatio Hiberniae*, chapter 17. De Courcy is described as retreating thirty miles, on foot, for two days and nights, from his battle in north Co. Antrim, to an unnamed castle. Dundrum and Downpatrick are both too far and there is no evidence for an important castle at the latter: Carrickfergus is much more plausible.
35. *Rotuli de Liberate et Misis et Praestitis regnante Johanne*, (ed. T. D. Hardy), pp. 196-208.
36. O. Davies & D. B. Quinn: *U.J.A.*, IV, 1941, pp. 54-65.
37. *C.D.I.*, I., no.'s 611, 1015, 1167 & 1371.
38. *Ibid.*, no. 1015.
39. O. Davies & D. B. Quinn: *U.J.A.*, IV, 1941, pp. 61-3.
40. E. Curtis: *Proceedings of the Belfast Natural History and Philosophical Society*, 1928-9, pp. 2-10; A. J. Otway-Ruthven: *U.J.A.*, XII, 1949, pp. 77-81; D. M. Waterman: *U.J.A.*, XXVI, 1963, pp. 55-78.
41. *C.D.I.*, I, no. 1488.
42. J. A. Watt: *The Church in medieval Ireland*, pp. 24-5.
43. W. Reeves: *Ecclesiastical Antiquities*, pp. 190ff. & 307; A. Gwynn & R. N. Hadcock: *Medieval Religious Houses, Ireland*, pp. 69-70.
44. D. E. Flanagan: *Dinnseanchas*, V, 1973, pp. 65-71.
45. Most recently *A.S.C.D.*, p. 203.
46. *Rotuli de Liberate et Misis et Praestitis*, (ed. T. D. Hardy), p. 196.
47. G. H. Orpen: *J.R.S.A.I.*, XLIV, 1914, pp. 51-66.
48. *Calendar of Patent Rolls*, 1340-3, p. 509.
49. W. Dugdale: *Monasticon Anglicanum*, VI (2), p. 1124.
50. W. Reeves: *Ecclesiastical Antiquities*, p. 211.
51. G. MacNiocaill: *Seanchas Ardmacha*, V, 1970, pp. 418-28.
52. W. Reeves: *Ecclesiastical Antiquities*, pp. 167-8.
53. *A.S.C.D.*, p. 289.
54. *Ibid.*, pp. 279-81.
55. *Ibid.*, pp. 275-9.
56. A. Gwynn & R. N. Hadcock: *Medieval Religious Houses, Ireland*, p. 135.
57. W. Reeves: *Ecclesiastical Antiquities*, pp. 229ff.
58. L. McKeown: *Journal of the Down and Connor Historical Society*, IX, 1938, pp. 64-6.

59. *Medieval Religious Houses, Ireland,* pp. 204-6.

60. E.g. L. McKeown: *Journal of the Down and Connor Historical Society,* IX, 1938, p. 66; *C.D.I.,* I, no. 2734.

61. W. Reeves: *Ecclesiastical Antiquities,* pp. 90-1.

62. W. Dugdale: *Monasticon Anglicanum,* VI (2), p. 1125.

63. *C.D.I.,* I, no. 1225.

64. W. Reeves: *Ecclesiastical Antiquities,* p. 61.

65. *Annals of Ulster,* 1197.

66. G. W. S. Barrow: *Feudal Britain,* pp. 245-6.

67. *C.D.I.,* I, no. 427.

68. *Ibid.,* no. 564.

69. *Ibid.,* no's 1200 & 1201.

70. *Ibid.,* no. 468.

71. *Ibid.,* no. 474.

72. *Annals of Ulster,* 1214.

73. *C.D.I.,* I, no. 565.

74. *Ibid.,* no. 1468.

75. O. Davies & D. B. Quinn: *U.J.A.,* IV, 1941, p. 63.

76. Dugdale: *Monasticon Anglicanum,* VI (2), p. 1124.

77. G. H. Orpen: *J.R.S.A.I.,* XLIV, 1914, p. 52.

78. *Dictionary of National Biography.*

79. *C.D.I.,* I, no.'s 426, 447, 453-4, 460, 476, 485-7, 491, 522, 534-5, 539, 551, 553, 575, 582, 625, 834.

80. The Misae Roll of 14 John records visits of messengers from Carrickfergus to the King on 2 June 1211, 1 July 1211, 9 October 1211, 3 & 12 February 1212: *Documents illustrative of English history in the 13th and 14th centuries,* (ed. H. Cole), pp. 233-65. A further message reached the King on 30 October 1212: *C.D.I.,* I, no. 445.

81. *C.D.I.,* I, no. 674.

82. *Ibid.,* no.'s 760, 1167.

83. *Annals of Ulster,* 1222 − see G. H. Orpen: *Ireland under the Normans,* III, p. 38.

84. *C.D.I.,* I, no.'s 1110, 1111, 1126.

85. *Ibid.,* no.'s 1200, 1201, 1203, 1225.

86. *Ibid.,* no.'s 1371-4, 1385-6, 1498.

2
The Later Earldom, 1227-1333

IT is one of the matters for regret in the history of Anglo-Norman Ulster that we have not more direct evidence on Hugh de Lacy's second tenure of the Earldom, from 1227 to his death in 1243. It forms a transitional period between the earlier and later Earldom, just as he personally was a transitional figure, born at the very start of the Anglo-Norman adventure in Ireland and yet of the second generation of its leaders: his brother retained the family estates in Herefordshire until his death in 1242. His stepmother was Rory O Connor's daughter and his daughter married the last of the Lords of Galloway: during his lifetime he saw all the major Anglo-Norman expansion in Ireland. His career was dominated by English royal policies, however, from his acquisition of Ulster to the manner of its disposal on his death. At the same time the power of the Scottish kings was being enforced in Galloway and the Isles. The freedom of action that John de Courcy had possessed was gradually eliminated between the spheres of power based on Dublin, Westminster and Edinburgh. The de Burgh Earls of Ulster who succeeded Hugh after twenty years of royal control had a more circumscribed world in which to work as a result. They were Irish barons with few immediate interests outside the island: their principal involvement outside Ulster was as Lords of Connacht. They had to face a complex position of Irish power equal to theirs in war and then the problems created by the Scottish wars of independence dividing the later thirteenth century unity of the north Irish Sea area, personified in Robert Bruce's marriage to Richard de Burgh's daughter.[1]

Hugh de Lacy had been helped to this restoration by Aedh O Neill, and so until Aedh's death in 1230[2] he seems to have been little concerned with threats from Cenel Eoghain: Aedh was succeeded by Domnall MacLochlainn[3] who was dethroned by Hugh in 1238[4] when Brian son of Aedh was installed, only to be ejected again in the next year, but returning permanently in 1241. Hugh's work of securing his position in Ulster was directed more at his fellow Anglo-Normans and the Scottish grantees of Co. Antrim. He had attacked them, as we saw, in 1223-4, and their grants were specifically excluded from his Earldom in 1227 as being held direct from the Crown,[5] and Hugh must have seen them as clear rivals for power in Ulster. As discussed in the previous chapter, the lands which they had settled and controlled were probably limited to an area north of Larne held by Duncan of Carrick and around Coleraine held by Thomas de Galloway, and so it is not to be wondered at that we hear nothing of their conquest by de Lacy. Alan de Galloway married Hugh de Lacy's daughter Margaret,[6] so he seems to have been reconciled to his loss — his grants had been entirely speculative anyway. Thomas lost custody of Antrim castle in 1226: Coleraine castle was rebuilt in 1228.[7] It seems unlikely, perhaps, that Thomas could muster strength enough to do so in the face of opposition from Hugh de Lacy and Aedh O Neill, and this may mark his expulsion from Ulster. For Duncan of Carrick's lands, Hugh adopted a different strategy. When we next hear of them, in 1279, they are in the hands of one John Byset, and are described as coming into the King's hands (because of a minority?) on his father's death in 1260.[8] The Earl of Ulster, presumably Walter de Burgh, Earl from 1264, had held an inquisition to sort out conflicting claims of Byset and the Bishop of Connor. The lands must have been in Byset hands some time for the need for clarification to arise: there is no mention of a claim from the Earl of Carrick. There was bad blood between Bysets and de Galloways since at least 1242 when Patrick (Thomas de Galloway's son) was killed by Walter and John Byset who fled to Ireland.[9] Alan, Patrick's half-brother, was pardoned in 1252[10] for killing some of John Byset's men at Dunaverdum castle (to be identified with Doonavernon motte, Co. Antrim): in 1257 John Byset died.[11] Hugh de Lacy probably granted the Bysets Duncan of Carrick's lands before he died in 1243, for he could rely on their hostility to the de Galloways.

It was almost certainly under Hugh de Lacy that north Co. Antrim was conquered and settled by the Anglo-Normans. After 1228, the next mention we have of this area is in 1248[12] when the Justiciar of Ireland built a castle over the Bann at Coleraine and a castle at Drumtarsy. The base from which this was built is described in two consecutive accounts of the 'custos' of Twescard, for the years 1260-62.[13] The area, known from now on as Twescard county, is divided into stable manors; the list of names is the same in both accounts and the money produced in each is also the same. The area covered by the accounts runs from Coleraine in the west to Dunseverick and Armoy in the east, but only as far as Loughguile in the south. The lands were rich as well as stable, producing some £240 per annum, and we may confidently conclude that they had been conquered before 1243 when the Earldom came into the King's hands: such a conquest would have left some trace in royal documents.

At the other end of his Earldom Hugh de Lacy was also worried about security. King John had been able to expel him in 1210 because he had been able to surround Dundrum castle by enveloping it from Lecale (reached by sea) and from the Mournes. Hugh de Lacy was probably responsible for the strengthening of Dundrum castle by adding a new, more powerful gatehouse[14] (fig. 2); this was probably referred to as being repaired in the account of Robert Gelous in 1260.[15] It was not a large undertaking but one which in its asymmetrical design cleverly and economically exploits its position. It has only one projecting tower which enfilades the line of approach along a ramp up the rock. The design is probably derived from that of the gatehouse at Pembroke castle. This strengthened the southern approaches of the Earldom, but they were made much stronger by the construction of Greencastle in Co. Down (fig. 7). The Archaeological Survey of Co. Down records that it was 'approaching completion, at least in part, in 1261'.[16] The source quoted to support this, however, is the account of Robert Gelous, for money received early in 1260, and spent by 1261, which is clearly stated to be for repairs to the castles of Carrickfergus, Dundrum and Greencastle ('Idem Robertus reddit compotum de xx marcis receptis de thesauro . . . ad praedicta castra emendanda').[17] The sums involved are very small − 20 marks, of which some £11 are spent at

Greencastle: only minor works are involved. The accounts included money spent on taking tools, wood, sand and water to the castle: if works had been going on immediately before this, these things would have been there. There are other, earlier references to the castle: in the Pipe Roll 38 and 39 Henry III, 1254-6,[18] when corn is sent to it. It appears as 'destroyed by the Irish' in the fighting of 1260,[19] while the army of Greencastle is mentioned twice, in the same years as the accounts for the repairs.[20] The castle, therefore, was in existence by 1254-6, was repaired and damaged in 1260 and served as a military base the next year against Cenel Eoghain. It was not mentioned in the documents of 1210-26, when a stone castle would have been conspicuous: again expenditure of this order should leave some record if it were built after 1243. The main period of construction at Greencastle can probably be dated between 1227 and 1242.

X The design of Hugh de Lacy's castle is of considerable interest. It consists of a quadrilateral curtain-wall with three-quarter round towers probably at three corners (plate 3A). Excavation of the east ditch in 1970-71[21] uncovered at the south end a narrow wall across the ditch which in all probability was meant to be a dam to retain water. If so it failed, for it was built over highly porous rock. As excavated, this ditch was found to have been left choked with masonry, among which complete chunks of fallen embrasures were shown to have come from the curtain wall (cf. the section excavated in 1952);[22] the significance of this for dating the ditch contents will be discussed later. The south-west tower (fig.7; plate 3B) is the most puzzling feature of the standing remains. It seems to be a simple D-shaped tower but it neither has an axis projecting at 45° to the lines of the curtain walls, nor is it three-quarters round like the other two surviving examples, but continues along the east wall for some 15-20 feet. It is divided by a cross wall into a western room, semi-circular or polygonal in plan and an eastern, rectangular room. The existence of the eastern room is shown by east/west doors at ground and first-floor levels and a door from the mural stair east of them; these must all have led somewhere. The western half is three-storied (marked by an offset and a line of joist holes), and has access to roof level from the curtain wall to the east. The ground floor was entered direct from the courtyard. The first floor was presumably reached via a quarter round stair, where there is ragged walling below it, from the door halfway up the mural stair, while the second floor was reached through a short vaulted passage direct from the wall-walk. The eastern room was probably less important: certainly at the ground floor, thanks to the rising slope of the rock eastwards it can only have been for storage, or possibly a prison entered from the western room. The first floor was reached from the mural stair: the narrowing of the curtain precludes its going further east up to wall-walk level. The wall-walk has no remaining wall or parapet to north or south at the second-floor level, which would mean that a second floor over the eastern room would be open to the elements: presumably it must have been roofed at this level, one floor below the western room. The whole is most peculiar, with a large apsidal tower (presumably it was rectangular to the east) projecting out parallel to the south face of the curtain. Thanks to the rock it was hardly vulnerable to mining, but the differing levels and angles must have made defence very awkward. Why it was put there seems to be in part a need for one larger tower at

C

this angle (presumably because the entrance lay to the north of it, on the side towards the church and ferry) and partly to provide in this complex way more private lodgings.

The main feature of the castle now – and when it was built – is the great rectangular central block. This is called a keep in the Archaeological Survey of Co. Down, which would imply an anachronistic element in the design, even for the 1230's. It was entered on the first floor and, although much rebuilt in the fifteenth and sixteenth centuries, enough remains to show how it originally was laid out at this level. There are two doors at the west end, the southern one the main entrance, marked by a roll-moulding,[23] the northern leading to a small building beyond. Along the north wall there are the remains of three original windows, probably out of four: the easternmost one is raised two feet over the others. There are probably the remains of one window in the south wall, but it has been much rebuilt. However, at the eastern end of the south wall is preserved part of an original fireplace, cut by both fifteenth and sixteenth century windows. There is a small latrine in the north-east angle. All these features can be explained if we are dealing not with a keep but with a first-floor hall. The opposed doors at one end imply a screens passage with the northern door leading to the service block or kitchen. The rest must have been a fine room, 27' 6" wide and about 40 feet long, lit by high windows on three sides. At the east end the raised window implies a dais for Hugh de Lacy to sit on with his tenants in the body of the hall below. Significantly the fireplace and the private latrine are at his end. Linked to this hall arrangement must be the north-west corner tower. Here there are two private chambers, at ground and first floor, marked by a private latrine at each level. Slightly later than the original building, the rear of the tower was angled to fit with a wall built parallel to the east curtain, with a large projection into the courtyard. Although, when excavated in 1951, the southern wall was not found (nor was the curtain wall surviving at this point),[24] it may be assumed to have existed. This addition may be linked with the latrine chute to the north, found in 1952 to be an addition to the tower. What we have here must again be a first-floor arrangement of a chamber block, reached by a stair on the projection, from the courtyard. It would have led to a lobby over the entrance to the ground-floor chamber in the tower. There to the left would have been the latrine, to the right a great chamber, and in front the door to the smaller private chamber.

The castle as described here is a fine example of the domestic ideas of the early thirteenth century. Its social role as providing accommodation for Hugh de Lacy and the later earls, conveniently on their way to Dublin, will be discussed in comparison with contemporary English standards, in Chapter Four. Defensively the castle is sited to control this route, via the ferry to Carlingford. It is there to reinforce, and indeed replace, Dundrum, to prevent a manoeuvre like King John's in 1210, by denying him a landfall in Ulster at all. The tactics of the defence reflect the latest ideas, in particular those close to the de Lacy barony in the Welsh march. Hubert de Burgh (himself a man with Irish baronial connections)[25] largely rebuilt the castle of Skenfrith in Gwent during the 1220's[26] (fig. 7). Not only is its overall plan of a trapezoidal curtain wall and angle towers very similar, it also has no

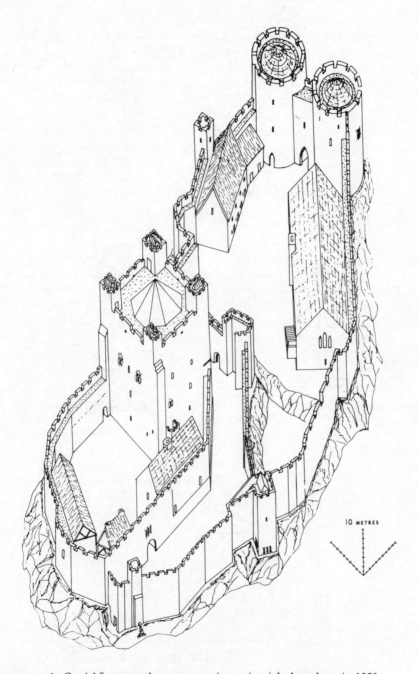

6. Carrickfergus castle: reconstruction as it might have been in 1250.

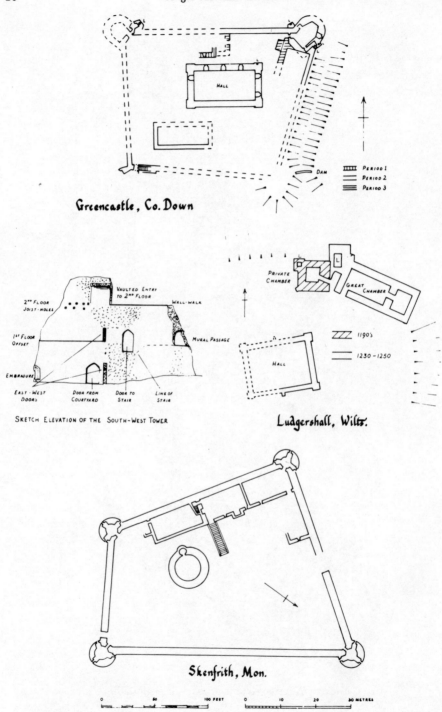

7. Simplified plans of Greencastle, Co. Down (after A.S.C.D., fig. 136); Ludgershall castle, Wiltshire (after Addyman); Skenfrith castle, Monmouth (after D.o.E. guide).

powerful gatehouse. Outside the walls it depended on a water-filled ditch as Greencastle seems to have tried to do and as proved so successful at Kenilworth on a major scale in the siege of 1265-6. As originally built, Skenfrith like Greencastle followed the latest ideas in not having a keep but relying on the curtain and its towers for its defence.

Hugh de Lacy is also the most likely man to have built the present outer ward at Carrickfergus castle (figs. 3 and 6). It may possibly be the one referred to in 1216, but its design would be remarkably advanced for that time and its construction before 1223 unlikely. It consists not only of the curtain wall, which doubles the area of the castle and denies any of the rock to an attacker, but also of the twin-towered gatehouse as well. This has the interesting feature of originally having its towers completely circular in plan, joined by a shorter gate passage than now exists: the towers were cut in half in the later sixteenth century. This, like Hugh's other work, must be related to work in south Wales. The only other castle gatehouse with this design of circular towers, as opposed to the usual D-shaped ones, or ones like Ballyloughan, Co. Carlow or even Caernarvon which only become round or polygonal from the first floor, is the gatehouse of Chepstow castle. This was added by one of the Marshal brothers who owned the castle in succession between 1225 and 1245. Both have been much rebuilt but the Carrickfergus one has one other feature of note, in the second-floor room of the east tower. Here there is a fine double window of Transitional style, round-arched with attached ringed shafts and vaguely foliate capitals (fig. 8). It fits very awkwardly into the curved tower wall but there are no signs of its being inserted at a later date. What seems most likely is that it has been transposed into its present position from its original one in a straight wall. The window faces east and the room is traditionally known as the castle chapel: when **the outer** curtain was built, the opportunity may have been taken to demolish the original chapel in the cramped inner ward. The east window was preserved and put in the new gatehouse.

Hugh de Lacy could present good credentials as a castle-builder, contributing to the Earldom's security and his own comfort. As we have already seen, the security problems he countered with these castles were not with the Irish so much as with the royal authority. He played a greater role outside Ulster than de Courcy had been able to, as a result: intervening in Connacht to help Richard de Burgh's campaigns, and being rewarded with five cantreds for his help.[27] He showed his contacts with Galloway politics in his grants to the Bysets but also in organising an expedition in 1234 to intervene there after Alan de Galloway's death.[28] His exploitation of royal power in 1203-5 against de Courcy was hardly honourable and in fact rebounded in 1210, while his part in the murder of Richard Marshal is another indication of his tolerance of the dishonest.[29] Unlike John de Courcy, he founded no monasteries: although friaries were founded in his time in Ulster, their founders are unknown and they were the cheapest form of religious house. To Downpatrick Cathedral he gave permission to have one boat and one net at the Bann fisheries[30] and 5 carucates in the Ards to the bishop.[31] He cannot be accused of weakening his Earldom by excessive grants to the church. The lands of north Antrim, Twescard county, are remarkable for their large manors and large parishes in 1306.[32] In 1333 there are

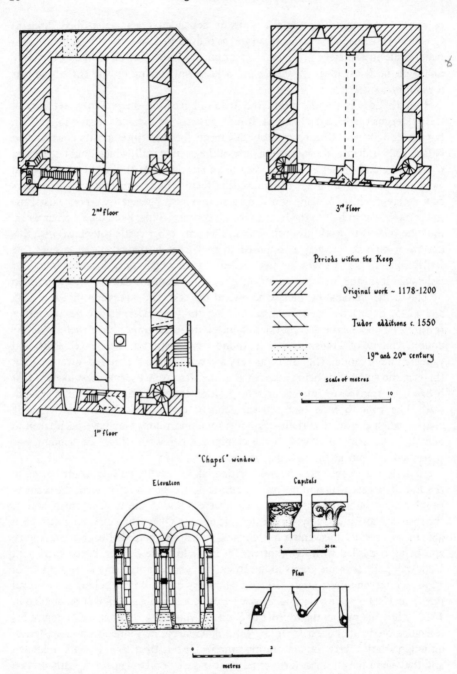

2nd floor

3rd floor

1st floor

Periods within the Keep

Original work ~ 1178-1200

Tudor additions c. 1550

19th and 20th century

scale of metres

0   10

"Chapel" window

Elevation

Capitals

0   30 cm.

Plan

0   2

metres

8. Carrickfergus castle: plans of the 1st, 2nd and 3rd floors of the keep; plan and elevation of the east window of the second floor of the east tower of the gatehouse.

very few lands recorded as subinfeuded out of the Earl's demesne or not let on subordinate tenure (much of the demesne was granted as appanage to John de Burgh and held by his widow – see below). When Hugh de Lacy conquered it he did not enrich his followers unduly either: it is clear why he was able to build at home but fight abroad. In some ways he seems to have given reality to John de Courcy's claims of power.

Hugh died in 1243 and his Earldom escheated to the crown: he had heirs but, as Orpen pointed out,[33] it was probably part of the conditions of his grant of 1227. It was held directly by the Crown until 1254 when it was granted, with the lordship of Ireland, to Prince Edward who, in turn, granted it to Walter de Burgh of Connacht in 1264. This royal interlude was much taken up with the growing power of Cenel Eoghain. In 1241 Brian O Neill, who had been installed by de Lacy and the Justiciar in 1238[34] only to be ejected again, returned with Cenel Connaill help and completely defeated his rival, Domnhall MacLochlainn, at the battle of Cameirghe. So many MacLochlainn kin fell in the battle that the family was never able to mount a successful challenge for the kingship of Cenel Eoghain again.[35] As a result Cenel Eoghain were bound to grow stronger and, either as a result of this or greater Anglo-Norman pressure (or, most likely, both), there is inaugurated a period when there is normally direct confrontation between the Earldom and Cenel Eoghain. The opening moves in the tension came from the Anglo-Norman side, led by the Justiciar. John FitzGeoffrey attacked Cenel Eoghain from Ulster while Maurice FitzGerald attacked Cenel Connaill from Connacht, invading Co. Donegal repeatedly from 1245 on.[36] We have seen that in 1248 FitzGeoffrey built a bridge over the Bann at Coleraine and the castle of Drumtarsy at the other side,[37] as a ready base for attacks into Co. Londonderry. In 1252 he attacked Cenel Eoghain more directly: he built the castle of Magh Cobha in west Co. Down,[38] and raided to Armagh, using the new castle as his base when he returned to Ui Echach Cobo.[39] Brian O Neill submitted then and gave his brother as hostage, but when the Justiciar raided again in 1253, Brian defeated him and counter-attacked, destroying Magh Cobha castle. FitzGeoffrey probably re-established it in 1254, however, with a grant of £100 or 100 marks,[40] while scutage was levied for rebuilding it.[41]

There the matter rested for a few years while O Neill made a spirited attempt to gain other Irish support. At a meeting by the Erne at Ballyshannon, he was recognised as High King of Ireland by O Connor and O Brien, the two principal Irish kings outside the north. He attempted to force the Cenel Connaill to give allegiance but was defeated at the battle of Credran. In 1259 O Donnell, with Brian's cousin Aedh Buidhe O Neill, raided into Tir Eoghain.[42] The climax of all this came in 1260 when Brian O Neill raided into the Earldom and was killed in a battle outside Downpatrick by the local levies led by the mayor of Down and one Sir Roger des Auters.[43] We have seen how Greencastle was damaged in the same year, although the repairs paid for by Robert Gelous, being done with money received in Hilary 1260 (i.e. before Easter), may not have anything to do with this. There were follow-up raids into Cenel Eoghain lands after the battle, recorded in scutages owed for service on the Bann, Magh Cobha, Cenel Eoghain or Greencastle from Carlow, Oriel and Wexford in 1261-2 Pipe Rolls.[44] On an Irish scale this war culminating in the battle of Down is considered important as marking the collapse of Brian's (afterwards called Brian 'Battle of Down') attempts to revive the Irish high kingship. From this and his son's 'Remonstrance' to the Pope can be seen the start of a nationalistic spirit, on the Irish side at least, in wars with Anglo-Normans. In the history of the Earldom of Ulster, it can be seen as interesting in that it marks the start of a period when relations with Cenel Eoghain dominated relations between the Earldom and the northern Irish kingdoms, and also for the way in which the policy of confrontation was carried out. With its raids based on frontier castles, in particular that of Magh Cobha, and the defence resting on the local levies of Down, it was very much that of 1211-12 and the twelfth century. The castle of Magh Cobha was indeed rebuilt to a new design but that was all. This can probably be identified as the two sites, Ballyroney motte and bailey and Seafin castle, close together on the Upper Bann.[45] The new castle of Seafin, found on excavation to be of two periods, probably to be equated with the castle-building of 1252 and 1254, was not an earthwork but a small polygonal enclosure with an attached tower. Its use and those like it will be discussed later, in Chapter Four.

The personnel on both sides changed after the battle of Down – of necessity on the Cenel Eoghain side. There Brian's cousin Aedh Buidhe who had attacked him in 1259 became king, but for the two years 1261-3 was expelled in favour of his brother, Niall Culanach.[46] But from then until 1283 he was king of Cenel Eoghain. In 1264 the Earldom of Ulster was revived for Walter de Burgh, Lord of Connacht, who acquired it from Edward as Lord of Ireland, in return for some Munster manors.[47] This is probably not a consideration of its true worth; as Orpen pointed out,[48] he owed a debt to Walter. It was also probably an acceptance of a devolutionary solution for the north of Ireland. Anglo-Norman security depended on control of Cenel Connaill from Connacht and Cenel Eoghain from Ulster, in both cases requiring steady pressure and lordship. The Justiciar could not spend every summer campaigning in the north, and so logic demanded the revival of the Earldom: to do so and unite it with Anglo-Norman Connacht must have seemed the obvious solution. With Walter de Burgh and Aedh Buidhe O Neill it succeeded well. Aedh Buidhe married Walter's second cousin[49] and promised cows and hostages, as well as to treat his wife well and honourably (an interesting clause), under pain of forfeiting his kingdom. In the contract he calls Walter his lord and there seems to have been a real subservience in their relationship. This lasted for the lifetimes of the two principals: Walter de Burgh died in 1271, leaving as his heir his under-age son, Richard, while Aedh Buidhe O Neill died in 1283, by which time Richard had been invested with the Earldom in 1280.[50] Richard's policy towards Cenel Eoghain followed his father's in avoiding direct confrontation and relying instead on having a friendly king in power. The workings of this policy in detail will be examined later.

The documents from the minority of Richard de Burgh are dominated by a dispute between the families of FitzWarin and de Mandeville over the control of the Earldom under the King. The details of the dispute are of less interest than the light they shed on the Earldom at the time. The position of Twescard county seems to have started the fighting. Henry de Mandeville had been sheriff since 1260 at least:

(1) Carrickfergus: the caput of the Earldom. The car park occupies the site of the mediaeval harbour; the market place can be seen to the left of the castle; the spire marks St. Nicholas' parish church.

(2) A. Carrickfergus castle: the interior of the third floor of the keep, John de Courcy's chamber, before the installation of the present disfiguring museum cases.

B. Carrickfergus castle: keep and curtain from the south-west. The original third-floor chamber windows are prominent, with the latrine chutes of the second and first floors below (all in white Cultra stone). The latter rest on the keep offsets (in red sandstone) which terminate there, showing the original intention to build the keep there. The south-west latrine tower and quoin of the middle curtain (1216–24) can be seen built against the keep with the outer curtain built on to the north. The gun ports date to c.1560.

(3) A. Greencastle, Co. Down from the south-east. The ditch and ruined curtain can be seen in the centre with the hall (the upper parts rebuilt later) prominent behind; to the left, among the farm buildings can be seen the south-west tower.

B. Greencastle, Co. Down: the south-west corner tower. For an explanation, see fig. 7.

(4) A. Greencastle, Co. Donegal: the gatehouse from the south. The polygonal towers are emphasised by the lighter stone of the quoins; the latrine tower at its east angle lies in the bushes to the right; behind, high on the rock, the wall is part of the east curtain of the courtyard.

B. Harry Avery's castle, Co. Tyrone, from the south. The gatehouse, with its first floor-chamber windows, can be seen in front of the courtyard, cut out of the hilltop and surrounded by the ruined curtain.

(8) A. Doonbought fort, Co. Antrim from the south-east. The site is made prominent by the rough grazing on the rock spur overlooking the valley; the inner and outer enclosures appear as platforms on the hill.

B. Dunluce castle, Co. Antrim from the south-east. The towers are those usually attributed to John de Burgh, c. 1300, but here argued to be work of a century later. The other buildings are work of the MacDonnells in the sixteenth and early seventeenth centuries.

(7) A. St. Nicholas' parish church, Carrickfergus: the exterior of the chancel from the south-east. The window tracery is seventeenth century except for the nineteenth century east window. The low buttress along the south wall may mark the beginning of the early fourteenth century extension with the moulded angle buttresses.

B. St. Nicholas' parish church, Carrickfergus: the nave and south transept from the north-east. The arcades of the twelfth and fourteenth centuries are cut by the seventeenth century windows and door.

(6) A. Inch abbey, Co. Down: the early Gothic lancets of the east end of the choir.

B. Grey abbey, Co. Down: the Cistercian house from the air. The rectangular cloister may be the result of leaving room for the addition of aisles to the church, whose nave is also short, hardly projecting west of the frater (Cambridge University Collection: copyright reserved).

(5) A. Dungiven priory, Co. Londonderry. The early thirteenth century chancel with twin lancets above a splayed plinth and moulding was built on to the nave, almost obliterating the strip-work of its east wall.

B. Pottery from Downpatrick kiln, and Carrickfergus castle (the two jug fragments to the left): Ulster Museum.

when Walter de Burgh died in 1271, he seems to have refused to surrender it to William FitzWarin, the King's nominee as seneschal,[51] perhaps invoking a memory of its more recent conquest than the rest of the Earldom.[52] The dispute dragged on until Richard de Burgh became Earl in 1280, when William FitzWarin appealed to the King's court, in 1282, against his conviction in the earl's court of the murder of Henry de Mandeville some time before, perhaps before 1277, when William de Mandeville witnesses a charter as seneschal of Ulster.[53] FitzWarin was sheriff of Down, Newtownards and Antrim until 6th January 1276.[54] Both sides involved Irishmen: in 1273 Aedh O Neill and O Cahan invaded to help de Mandeville, but were met by Hugh Byset and FitzWarin assisted by many of the Irish kings of Ulster.[55] The situation must have been complicated by Walter de Burgh's leaving to his widow five castles on the march of Ulster, which weakened the Earldom.[56] The two main documents about the dispute[57] give us many details of topography, land ownership and administration, to which we will refer often again.

When he had settled this essentially private war (although it overlapped into Irish relationships), Richard de Burgh was able to concentrate most of his effort on problems outside his Earldom: with his Lordship of Connacht, he was recognised as the most powerful man in Ireland. In 1260 Henry de Mandeville accounted for no lands in Twescard west of the Bann, except for Drumtarsy just over the river from Coleraine. Under the de Burghs the Anglo-Norman Earldom was pushed into Co. Londonderry; for information on this we depend on five documents and one castle. In 1277 Dermot O Cahan, King of Ferncrewe, granted Richard de Burgh the as yet unidentified Glen Oconcahil; this was of course during Richard's minority and may have been a penalty as a result of O Cahan's invasion of the Earldom in 1272, or a result of a revenge expedition.[58] It must, however, as O Cahan land, relate to Richard de Burgh's granting his sister Egidia and James, the Steward of Scotland, on the occasion of their marriage in 1296, the Manor of Le Roo (Limavady) with its borough and demesne.[59] In the 1290's, or shortly after 1300, Richard extended his interest into Inishowen. In 1305 the Annals of Ulster record the building (presumably the start) of the castle of Inishowen, known in Anglo-Norman documents as Northburgh, now Greencastle in Co. Donegal. It is now sadly neglected but much is still there, well described by Waterman in 1958.[60] It is a major building mostly of one period, except for a tower added probably in the fifteenth century (fig. 17). It has a magnificent twin-towered gatehouse (plate 4A) at one end of the rock-built courtyard: at the other a large polygonal tower. It provides the whole array of accommodation of a high mediaeval magnate's castle, which we will discuss in Chapter Four. Here the point to notice is the position of the castle at the narrow mouth of Lough Foyle, with Coleraine commanding the coastal communications of the whole region. Richard exploited this position and the rivalries of the Irish of the area. In 1310 he obtained the King's pardon[61] for accepting without royal leave land at Derry and Port Lough from the Bishop of Raphoe (the Cenel Connaill bishop) and other lands in Derry, Moville, Fahan and Inch from the Cenel Eoghain Bishop of Derry. In 1333, the position was summed up in the Inquisitions after Earl William's death:[62] Roo was productive and settled before the murder, but the lands dependent on Greencastle were let to Irishmen.

Richard had acquired rights and rents in Inishowen but there had been no Anglo-Norman settlement much beyond Limavady.

The marriage of 1296 between Richard de Burgh's sister and James the Steward arose from the involvement of the Irish baronage in Edward I's campaigns in Scotland. In that year the first of a series of Irish armies[63] crossed to Scotland: nearly half of this army of just over 3,000 men was contributed by Richard de Burgh, a striking illustration of his power. He did not join the armies of 1298 or 1300; a big effort was made to involve him in 1301, but he refused, although he sent a contingent under Thomas de Mandeville.[64] In 1315 the Scottish wars came to Ireland in the person of Edward Bruce, who landed in May near Carrickfergus[65] to stop the Irish help to the English war effort in Scotland. The campaign itself has been well-discussed and need not concern us here except in the light it sheds on the Earldom. The key to the campaigns in Ulster was the castle of Carrickfergus which controlled the harbour the Scots most needed to preserve their communications. They started the siege in September 1315 after defeating the Earl at the battle of Connor. It continued, in spite of a seaborne relief expedition by Thomas de Mandeville who died in the streetfighting,[66] and the collecting of a second convoy of grain-ships which however Richard de Burgh used to ransom his cousin,[67] until September 1316. The garrison surrendered for lack of food, in spite of allegedly eating eight Scottish prisoners.[68] There was a definite feeling that the Anglo-Normans of Ulster were sympathetic to Bruce, culminating in the arrest of the Earl of Ulster in Dublin.[69] Robert Bruce had married Elizabeth de Burgh, the Earl's daughter, in 1302:[70] the Bysets had Scottish links as well and owned Rathlin island where it is alleged that Bruce took refuge in 1307 while John Byset was commissioned to look for him.[71] Hugh Byset fought with success against Bruce in 1316[72] but his lands were granted to John de Athy in 1319 because he joined the Scots.[73] Presumably after Carrickfergus and Greencastle, Inishowen were captured, the position for Ulster tenants was resolved into a choice between joining the Scots or the Earl wandering around Ireland with 2,000 Ulstermen[74] but no home. Byset's treachery must have been worse than that of others who were pardoned for joining the Scots. The Irish of Ulster, in particular Domnall O Neill, the son of Brian 'Battle of Down', were Edward Bruce's main support: the Remonstrance to the Pope in which O Neill sought to justify his support and widen the conflict on a nationalistic basis has been noted.

Edward Bruce was killed in 1318 and the colony in Ulster settled back somewhat to repair the damage done by the wars: some of the damage was still to be mended in 1333 (e.g. Dundonald castle, Co. Down).[75] The old Earl Richard (he was about 67) died in 1326 at Athassel in Co. Tipperary after attending a Parliament in Kilkenny. His heir was his grandson William, who was a minor at the time but who came over to Ireland in 1328.[76] He was the son of John de Burgh, Richard's second son, who had died in 1313, and Elizabeth de Clare, the sister of the Earl of Gloucester. His main activities were in his lordship of Connacht trying to restore order: one of his acts was to imprison his cousin Walter in Greencastle, Inishowen where he died in 1331. William de Burgh was himself killed by his barons on 6 June 1333 at the ford, between Newtowards and Carrickfergus,[77] usually identified as Belfast. The murderers are named by Friar Clyn[78] as John de Logan and Robert and Richard de Mandeville: he blames the murder on Richard de Mandeville's wife, Gyle, who was the dead William de Burgh's sister. The affair has never been adequately explained: Clyn's reason seems a bit far-fetched; murdering one's lord seems extreme revenge for a brother-in-law. Orpen attributed it to dislike of William's attempts to impose order on his tenants:[79] again, resistance or rebellion would seem the normal method of proceeding. No evidence exists, and presumably whatever was planned may have got out of hand. The result is clear. William's heir was his two-year old daughter Elizabeth: her mother Matilda fled with her to England. Absentee little girls make poor marcher barons and the Earldom of Ulster began to decline to its fifteenth century boundaries from then on. This decline can be considered in Chapter Seven only after discussing the Earldom in the days of its health.

The first question to be answered has been dealt with in these first two chapters: what land did the Anglo-Normans hold and settle in Ulster, as opposed to claim to own? The evidence comes from mapping (fig. 9) all the documentary references to specific identifiable mentions, either from major sources such as those mentioned so far, or from lesser incidental notices: the whole is made much more solid by the preservation of the inquisition *post mortem* carried out on the Earl's lands in 1333, and incorporating valuations made on the death of Richard in 1326: they have been published with extensive notes by Orpen.[80] The answer to the question is often given as Counties Antrim and Down and north Londonderry, but as we have seen it was really less than this area. The early Earldom did not include mid or west Co. Down, nor, for all the revival of interest in Magh Cobha castle in the 1250's, is there any evidence that it was more than an outpost throughout the Earldom's life. In Co. Antrim, Hugh de Lacy added the county of Twescard, as far south as the Cloughwater river, to the Earldom, while Richard de Burgh was able to settle the lower Roe valley but not exploit his vaguer claims in Inishowen more than to exact rent from some Irish. If this pattern is compared with a map of the parishes of Ulster dioceses in 1306, with their values (fig. 10),[81] the same pattern can be seen. It has been shown how,[82] in the deanery of Skreen, the Anglo-Norman settlement resulted in a proliferation of smaller parishes as each principal tenant set up one of his own. The result can be seen in Ulster in the number of parishes in the area of the Earldom's nucleus, south Antrim and east Down. The greater contrast, however, lies in the parish values themselves: in the areas known to be occupied by Anglo-Normans they are much higher. The single parish of Billy is valued at £36; the parishes of the Irish diocese of Clogher total a little over £32. The church divisions and organisation reflect the boundaries of the Earldom proposed here. The diocese of Dromore has been noted, detached for the Irish parts of Down, while the deanery of Turtrye (from the Irish Ui Tuirtre) is clearly for those parts of Connor held by the Irish, the valley of the river Main and the glens of Antrim north of Glenarm, Glencloy and Glenarriff, 'waste and inhabited by Irish' in 1278.[83] It is even listed out of the geographical order of the list of deaneries, after Twescard. The Earldom before 1226 could be described in terms of the Irish kingdoms occupied, Dal Fiatach and Dal nAraide, and the later expansion of Twescard seems to have been at the expense of Fir Li, the subordinate sept of Ui Tuirtre. Two

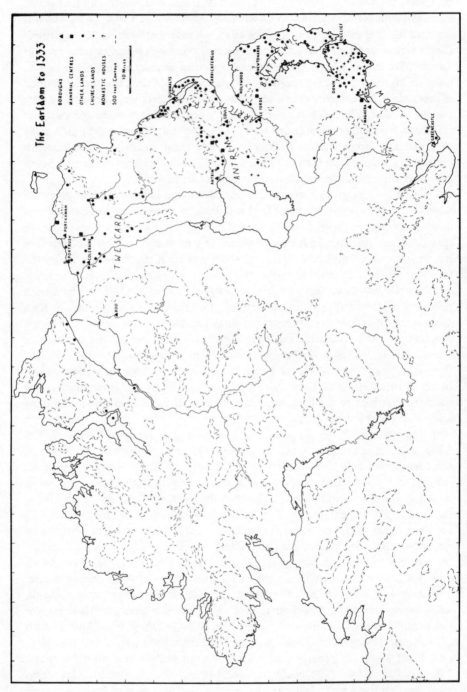

9. Map of Ulster showing places held by Anglo-Normans, 1177-1333.

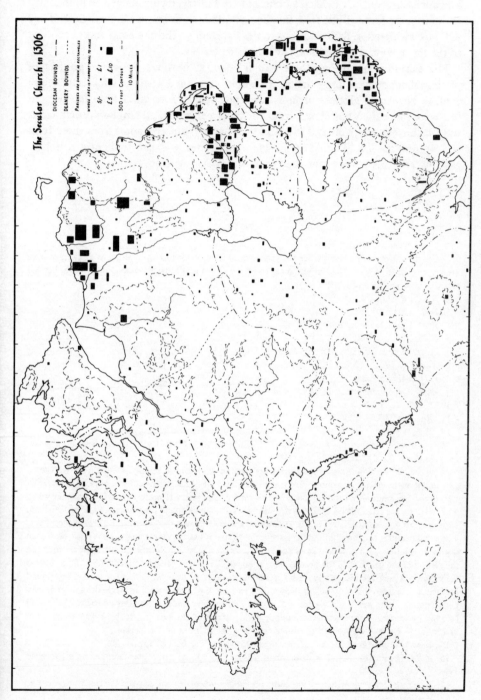

10. The Secular Church in Ulster in 1306.

kingdoms survived, Ui Echach Cobha and Ui Tuirtre, owing allegiance to the Earl, as did in some sense all the Irish kingdoms [84] although in essence independent. They will be considered in their relations to the Earldom on the one hand and in contrast to the more westerly kingdoms later, in Chapter Six.

The Earldom as outlined here had no natural frontiers. It was a product of piecemeal conquest of pre-existing Irish units combined with the vital factor of sea control. No Anglo-Norman manor was more than twenty miles from the sea and few were more than ten. Apart from the Ards peninsula, all Anglo-Norman lands were within ten miles of land still occupied by an Irish sept, apart from those Irish still within the Earldom. The Earldom of Ulster was pre-eminently a border earldom and this border must be constantly borne in mind.

NOTES

1. For the various relationships, see the genealogical trees, Appendix One. Hugh de Lacy must have been born about 1170-75: his father 'married' Rory O Connor's daughter in 1180; Hugh himself married between 1191 and 1199.

2. *Annals of Ulster*, 1230.

3. *Ibid.*, 1231.

4. *Ibid.*, 1238, *Annals of Loch Cé*, 1238.

5. *C.D.I.*, I, no. 1498.

6. G. H. Orpen: *Ireland under the Normans*, III, p. 255.

7. *Annals of Ulster*, 1228.

8. *C.D.I.*, II, no. 1500.

9. G. H. Orpen: *Ireland under the Normans*, III, p. 256.

10. *C.D.I.*, II, no. 2.

11. *Annals of Ulster*, 1257.

12. *Ibid.*, 1248.

13. *National manuscripts of Ireland*, (ed. J. T. Gilbert), plate 73; E. Curtis: *Proceedings of the Royal Irish Academy*, XXXIX (C), 1929, pp. 1-17.

14. *A.S.C.D.*, p. 208. This work is probably the last work before the late mediaeval period to be carried out at the castle. The outer ward is considered by the Archaeological Survey of Co. Down (Fig. 133) to be 13th century but the evidence for this rests on the dating of pottery found in the outer ward. The stratigraphic relationship of this to the outer curtain is unclear and the distinguishing of 13th from 15th century pottery in Ulster, in the absence of sealed late mediaeval groups, is a dubious exercise. The curtain wall is thin and built along a rock step so that it has re-entrant angles and shows no sign of towers; it is unlike 13th century ideas of defence. Late mediaeval double-splayed gunloops are found in the section of the gate beside the post-mediaeval house. They have been described (A.S.C.D. p. 210) as belonging to a later rebuild clearly visible in the upper parts of the outer face of the wall. They extend however down into the lower part of the walling (and are of one build with it) while the apparent two-period nature of the wall is not visible on the inner face or core. It seems unnecessary to divide this wall into two periods but rather to treat it as of one build, datable by the gate and double-splayed loops both of 15th century type, and regard the outer curtain as an addition of that period.

15. *Reports of the Commissioners Respecting Public Records of Ireland*, I, plate 2.

16. *A.S.C.D.*, p. 211. Fig. 7 is based on *A.S.C.D.*, fig. 133 with additions from excavations since 1966.

17. *Reports of the Commissioners Respecting Public Records of Ireland*, I, plate 2.

18. *Analecta Hibernica*, II, p. 255.

19. *Annals of Ireland*, (ed. J. T. Gilbert), 1260.

20. E. St. John: *J.R.S.A.I.*, LXII, 1933, p. 209; *35th Report of the Deputy Keeper*, P.R.I., p. 43.
21. By C. Lynn; unpublished, but vid. *Excavation* 1971, pp. 10-11, *U.J.A.*, XXXIX, 1976, p. 52.
22. D. M. Waterman & A. E. P. Collins: *U.J.A.*, XV, 1952, fig. 2 opposite p. 91.
23. *A.S.C.D.*, p. 115.
24. D. M. Waterman & A. E. P. Collins: *U.J.A.*, XV, 1952, p. 88.
25. His brother was the first Lord of Connacht.
26. Dept. of the Environment: *Guide to Skenfrith Castle.*
27. G. H. Orpen: *Ireland under the Normans*, III, pp. 182 & 257.
28. *Ibid.*, pp. 255-6.
29. *Ibid.*, pp. 62-3.
30. W. Dugdale: *Monasticon Anglicanum*, VI (2), p. 1125.
31. *Calendar of Patent Rolls, 1340-3*, pp. 508-9.
32. W. Reeves: *Ecclesiastical Antiquities.*
33. G. H. Orpen: *Ireland under the Normans*, III, pp. 264-5.
34. *Annals of Loch Cé*, 1238.
35. J. Hogan: *Proceedings of the Royal Irish Academy*, XL (C), 1932, p. 217.
36. G. H. Orpen: *Ireland under the Normans*, III, p. 268.
37. *Annals of Ulster*, 1248.
38. *C.D.I.*, II, no.'s 32 & 124.
39. *Annals of Ulster*, 1252; E. St. John: *J.R.S.A.I.*, LXII, 1933, p. 209.
40. *C.D.I.*, II, no. 124.
41. *Analecta Hibernica*, II, pp. 262f.
42. *Annals of the Four Masters*, 1259.
43. *C.D.I.*, II, no. 661.
44. *35th Report of Deputy Keeper*, P.R.I., pp. 38-9, 43, 45.
45. H. C. Lawlor: *U.J.A.*, I, 1938, pp. 84-9; D. M. Waterman: *U.J.A.*, XVIII, 1955, pp. 83-104.
46. *Annals of Ulster; Annals of Loch Cé*, 1261-3.
47. G. H. Orpen: *Ireland under the Normans*, III, pp. 265-7.
48. *Ibid.*, pp. 280-1.
49. *De l'Isle and Dudley mss.*, I, pp. 31-2.
50. *C.D.I.*, II, no. 1632.
51. *Ibid.*, no. 941.
52. *Ibid.*, no. 929.
53. *De l'Isle and Dudley mss.*, I, p. 32.
54. *C.D.I.*, II, no. 2073.
55. *Ibid.*, no.'s 952 & 953.
56. *Ibid.*, no. 950.
57. *Ibid.*, no.'s 929 & 1918.
58. *De l'Isle and Dudley mss.*, I, p. 32.
59. *C.D.I.*, IV, no. 338.
60. D. M. Waterman: *U.J.A.*, XXI, pp. 74-88.
61. *Calendar of Patent Rolls, 1307-13*, p. 292.
62. G. H. Orpen: *J.R.S.A.I.*, XLV, 1915, p. 127.
63. J. Lydon: *Irish Sword*, V, 1962, pp. 184-90, 207-17.
64. *Ibid.*, pp. 212-3.
65. *Annals of Ireland*, (ed. J. T. Gilbert), p. 344.
66. *Ibid.*, p. 350.
67. *Ibid.*, p. 296.
68. *Ibid.*, p. 352.
69. *Ibid.*, p. 352.
70. *Ibid.*, p. 331.
71. *C.D.I.*, V, no.'s 610 & 627.
72. *Annals of Ireland*, (ed. J. T. Gilbert), p. 298.
73. *Calendar of Patent Rolls, 1317-21*, pp. 217, 313.

74. *Annals of Ireland,* (ed. J. T. Gilbert), p. 300.

75. G. H. Orpen: *J.R.S.A.I.,* XLIV, 1914, p. 63.

76. *Clyn's Annals,* p. 367.

77. *Annals of Ireland,* (ed. J. T. Gilbert), p. 378.

78. *Annals,* 1333.

79. G. H. Orpen: *Ireland under the Normans,* IV, pp. 247-9.

80. G. H. Orpen: *J.R.S.A.I.,* XLIII, 1913, pp. 30-46, 133-43; XLIV, 1914, pp. 51-66; XLV, 1915, pp. 123-42.

81. Reeves: *Ecclesiastical Antiquities; C.D.I.,* V, no.'s 693-702. William Reeves left a transcript of the dioceses not covered by his *Ecclesiastical Antiquities* in Armagh Public Library, which is invaluable for the identifications of parish names that he makes: these have been followed here.

82. A. J. Otway-Ruthven: *J.R.S.A.I.,* XCIV, 1964, pp. 111-22.

83. *C.D.I.,* II, no. 1500.

84. G. H. Orpen: *J.R.S.A.I.,* XLV, 1915, p. 141.

3

The Economy of the Earldom

IT is clear that the Earldom produced money for the Earls: buildings were put up, soldiers paid and the state maintained. How much income the Earl might expect in a year is nearly impossible to estimate although we have several accounts or valuations. Roger Pipard received some £230 from Ulster lands in two years, September 1210 to September 1212.[1] Robert de Vallibus accounted for £936 in 1226: we do not know his position or how long a period this sum covered. William Serland was seneschal probably from 1217, certainly 1223-24; Roger Waspail became seneschal in March 1224,[2] while Ulster was granted to de Lacy in May 1226. Either de Vallibus was seneschal and the account is for only 1224-6 at most, or he was treasurer in which case it could be from 1216 to 1226. Nicholas Dunheved, the seneschal, farmed Ulster, apart from Twescard county, for £200 in 1260-1, while Henry de Mandeville received some £240 a year from Twescard[3]: in all some £440 per annum. A similar sum was received by William FitzWarin for 21 months in 1273 to 1275, approximately £500 a year, or £440 without the 'farm of Ulster'.[4] The 1333 inquisition *post mortem* includes two valuations of the lands, one in 1326 when Richard de Burgh died and one in 1333. In 1326 the value of his lands is given at about £650 but this excluded lands (most of Twescard county) granted by him to his son John and held in 1333 by his widow Elizabeth of Clare.[5] In addition, there was an item of military service owed by Irish kings, valued at £355 per annum, which would bring the Earl's annual income (if it could be levied) up to £1,000. In 1333, after the last effective Earl's death, the valuation was about £100, with the Irish services valued at nil. Whatever these absolute figures mean, and they must be at best approximate, to work out their real value would require a knowledge of prices prevailing in Ulster in each year, and more yearly incomes (to even out bad years): then we might assess it properly or compare it with other baronial incomes. The rising trend must be real, however, with the access of Twescard and then the lands west of the Bann.

The best indication we have of the Earldom's resources, as compared to other parts of the north of Ireland, comes in the valuation of parishes made in 1306.[6] This has already been used in the discussion of the Earldom's area, but the values themselves are of interest. They are best illustrated in a map (fig. 10), with each parish represented by a rectangle whose size is relative to its value. The contrast of values between the Anglo-Norman parishes and those in Irish lands is striking: the values of an Anglo-Norman parish can be as high as an Irish diocese. It is possible that the reason for this discrepancy is a formal one, deriving from a different means of providing parish income or assessing it between the two nations: a different attitude to paying tithes, for example. This might be thought to receive support from valuations given for papal records when annates were paid in the fifteenth century.[7] Here, for example, in the diocese of Derry the values of Irish parishes which had been very low in 1306 are anything up to 16 times as high (e.g. Leckpatrick: ¼ mark in 1306, 4 marks in 1413).[8] Two objections must be made to this, however. Firstly, where there are three or more values given, the values rise until mid-century and then level off, or even fall, as can be seen in a list of three parishes:

Clonca rectory:	1427 - 15 mks	Donaghmore vicarage:	1420 - 10 mks
	1463 - 10 mks		1429 - 8 mks
	1470 - 10 mks		1440 - 9 mks
Clonca vicarage:	1419 - 7 mks		1464 - 8 mks
	1429 - 9 mks	Moville rectory:	1412 - 10 mks
	1431 - 12 mks		1478 - 20 mks
	1492 - 8 mks	Moville vicarage:	1419 - 10 mks
Donaghmore rectory:	1422 - 8 mks		1429 - 16 mks
	1442 - 10 mks		1430 - 16 mks
			1431 - 20 mks
			1459 - 16 mks

The 1306 values (Clonca, 14/4; Donaghmore, 1 mark, Moville, £2) are by no means too low to be accommodated in this rising trend. Secondly, the absolute parish values still remain low. If parishes of high value in Anglo-Norman areas in 1306 (e.g. £10-20) had increased, they would have been split: these Irish values were still only making the parishes just viable. In the diocese of Meath, the parish of Trim, valued at £40-9-2 (just over 60½ mks) in 1306,[9] was valued at 100 mks in 1425, 150 mks in 1428, 120 mks in 1450 and 100 mks in 1497:[10] here is an Anglo-Norman parish also sharing this increase. These 1306 parish values therefore appear to be reliable and comparable.

The differences in value across the borders cannot be explained by geographical variation. The soils of the valley of the river Main are fertile, certainly not markedly poorer than those of north Antrim or the Six Mile Water, yet the values in the deanery of Turtrye are much lower. Again the fertile lands of the Clogher valley and east Co. Tyrone are not reflected in the parish values. These figures, and the generalities behind them, must indicate a genuine prosperity in the Earldom which was not shared by the Irish kingdoms. What must principally supply these parish values are the tithes paid to them, and these depend on the agricultural strength of the communities. The basis of the wealth of the Earldom as opposed to the Irish kingdoms lay in its more profitable practice of agriculture. We have no detailed extents of manors from Ulster to give us a real picture of actual practice, but some features can be sketched in. Most accounts of manorial receipts include figures derived from the profits of mills. As well as this there are references to ploughteams and barns in the Pipe Roll of 1212. The mills of Twescard produce the largest part of the income in the de Mandeville accounts. Again in 1282 damage done to FitzWarin's lands included the burning of barns and corn in sheaf and the killing of working horses.[11] There are as many references to cattle, sheep and pigs in the same sources, while FitzWarin is recorded as losing 2,000 two-year old hogs and goats:

the presence of large flocks of goats is a problem to be borne in mind by the identifiers of bones from excavations. This mixture of arable and pastoral farming is hardly surprising either in relation to English farming or in comparison to what we know of Irish agriculture. The Irish use of cattle as units of account has tended to emphasise the pastoral side of Irish farming, yet it is quite clear from references to grain and mills[12] that the Irish had a mixed agriculture as well. A neat example comes from the 1211-12 Pipe Roll: the men of Ballymaghan were compensated in cows for destruction of their corn.[13] The contrast between the Earldom's farming and that of the Irish kingdoms is not really to be explained by a difference of kind but by one of degree. The Anglo-Norman farmers had access to markets outside Ireland with both their shipping and mercantile structure. Some direct evidence of grain exports exists: the Abbot of Grey abbey and the Bishop of Down were given licences in 1223 and 1226;[14] provisions for English armies were sent from Carrickfergus in 1245;[15] and Walter Byset provisioned a Scottish castle from Ulster in 1248.[16] There is better evidence for the export of pastoral produce from the Earldom in the receipts of the Customs levied on hides, wool and sheepskins (Appendix Two). The Ulster ports, Coleraine, Carrickfergus, Strangford, Carlingford and Dundalk,[17] were usually lumped together, although it appears that Carrickfergus was the chief.[18] They do not appear high among the lists of exporting ports, being comparable with those of Connacht, and far behind the major ports of Waterford and Ross: the highest yield from Ulster in one year was £39-17 in 1279 out of an Irish total of £1,285-15; overall Ulster contributed between 1.5 and 2%. Like the Earl's income in 1326, the Ulster customs receipts, from the few years available, do not show much long-term sign of the Bruce wars.

From agriculture it is easy to move to fishing. This was a steady source of income for the Earldom, especially the fisheries of the Bann. Between 1226 and 1243, Hugh de Lacy gave the monks of St. Patrick's, Down the right to have a boat and a net there.[19] The fisheries produced £20-3-4 per year, the third largest item in the de Mandeville accounts of Twescard.[20] In 1409 David Archer and others were licensed to import cloth, wine, salt, beer, and food to the Bann fisheries.[21] There were other, lesser fishing centres: Holywood, Co. Down was listed in 1333,[22] and Rossglass, in Lecale, had fisheries belonging to the Bishop of Down in 1305.[23] One centre of a different kind is recorded in the Pipe Roll of 1337,[24] where the Abbot of Inch is recorded as having a court at Munkhille, near the shore in Tevere tenement for herring fishers in the season. This presumably is a place (perhaps Tara in the Ards peninsula) where herring fishermen traditionally came ashore for food, to cure their catch, or to dry nets. Where their home port was is of course unknown.

More directly extractive industry existed in a small way. A somewhat unexpected one, perhaps, was the production of salt. The Pipe Roll of 1211-12 records the expenditure of £2-1-8 on a saltpan at Dundrum.[25] In 1282 the de Mandevilles are recorded[26] as destroying a saltpan worth £1-6-8 at 'Lerges' (Loughinisland, Co. Down?). Neither of these can have been large concerns, supplying no more than very local needs. A regular item of expenditure in the 1211-12 Pipe Roll is for salt, appearing linked with iron purchases for plough teams, more often than is recorded for other areas: where these supplies came from we do not know, but not, by

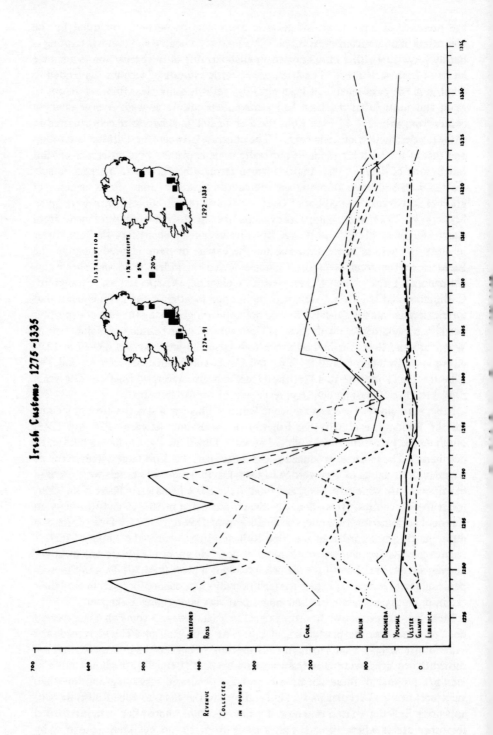

Irish Customs 1275–1335

DISTRIBUTION

• 1% or receipts
■ 5%
■ 20%

1276–91

1292–1335

REVENUE COLLECTED IN POUNDS

700
600
500
400
300
200
100
0

WATERFORD
ROSS
CORK
DUBLIN
DROGHEDA
YOUGHAL
ULSTER
GALWAY
LIMERICK

1275 1280 1285 1290 1295 1300 1305 1310 1315 1320 1325 1330 1335

definition, from within the manors. A bigger industry must have been that of stone quarrying. This was always a fair part of the mediaeval economy with its big building industry. There is no sign of the import of building stone into Ulster, unlike south-east Ireland,[27] although many large buildings have lost the freestones for their dressings. The best example of the opening up of a stone source is the replacement of the very local red sandstone at Carrickfergus castle by the creamy-white limestone from Cultra, Co. Down. This happened early on, during the first building period, probably in the 1180's, and it was taken over Belfast Lough up to the fourteenth century. This Cultra stone was also used for the early thirteenth century Holywood church, which was largely built from it, while it was also used for dressings at Ardkeen and Ballywalter churches in the Ards.[28] It does not appear in the churches attributable to post-Norman times in Co. Down[29] where Castle Espie limestone appears to replace it. The castles of Dundrum and Greencastle both use local calcareous tufa: in Dundrum, the gatehouse has dressings of sandstone probably from Scrabo hill at the head of Strangford Lough.[30] It is possible that this latter is the freestone bought at Downpatrick by Robert Gelous in 1260;[31] he also bought chalk at Carlingford.

We can study one stone-using industry fairly completely: the small-scale production of stone grave markers or coffin-lids (fig. 12). These are the slabs of stone – of which 42 survive – carved with simple foliate designs, which must have been cheaper than the elaborate stone effigies of the thirteenth century upper classes. The designs carved on them are of two main kinds, both based on a long cross. The first of these (e.g. Movilla lid 4) is one where the fleur-de-lis terminals of the cross-head are expanded so that the head looks composed of four horseshoe motifs set diagonally. In the second main design an element like a St. Andrew's cross is added to the first kind either overtly (as on the lid from Holywood) or else integrated into the design (as Movilla lid 2). The stem of this second kind of cross is sometimes decorated with foliate stems sprouting from it on alternate sides. Both kinds usually have a plain, stepped base, traditionally said to represent Calvary. Apart from these two main designs, there are three plain crosses and four simple variants of the first design: seven have lost their heads. On many of them a sword or a pair of shears is carved, as an indication of the sex of the person buried. They have been dated in the past to the fifteenth century,[32] on the grounds that their distribution corresponds to the restricted Earldom of that time. The argument is doubly erroneous. Firstly there is no reason why the distribution of these slabs should coincide with political boundaries: as we shall see, no archaeological distribution map reflects the Earldom's political extent. Secondly, it assumes that all Co. Down was held by the Anglo-Normans in the thirteenth century, which we have seen is an overstatement. The swords, with their lobed pommels, are of thirteenth century type, survivals of Viking types.[33] The stone built into the fifteenth century tower house at Kilclief should date from before then.[34] The source of the first design outlined above lies in the north of England in the thirteenth century. Similar designs come from thirteenth century contexts in Cheshire (Runcorn abbey has several, Chester cathedral one), Westmorland,[35] Northumberland and Durham.[36]

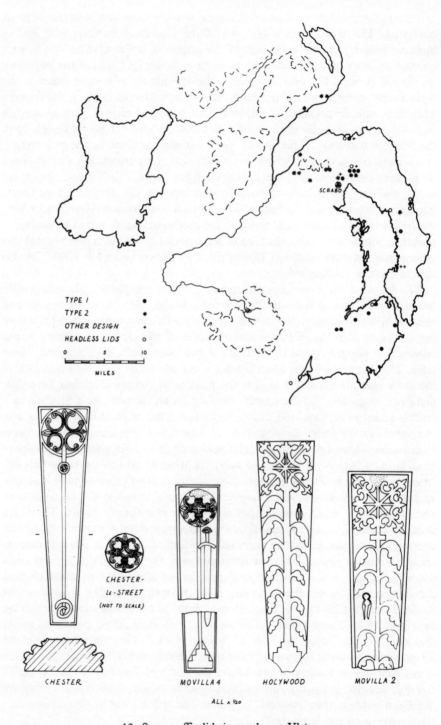

12. Stone coffin-lids in south-east Ulster.

The distribution of these coffin-lids in Ulster is restricted to the coasts of Co. Down and the Belfast Lough. From the similarity to northern English slabs, we may confidently assume that the carver of the first group of slabs came from there, perhaps from Cheshire, to open up the Scrabo resources. The marketing structure he set up was based on water transport, for the slabs are heavy. These did not, apparently, reach all the Anglo-Norman population in Ulster, for there were none found away from the coast in south Antrim or Twescard county: the limiting factor is economic – a question of transport. Within this general pattern there is another modifying factor operating. Curiously, the two main designs are found in different areas, overlapping somewhat but distinct. The first kind reaches from the southern shore of Belfast Lough to Lecale, while the second kind is found in north Down and south Antrim: except for the example from Black abbey,[37] in the Ards peninsula, they all lie north of Scrabo hill. Why this should be is inexplicable. The second design, which seems to be an addition by the Ulster masons (for it has no English parallels), does not seem to have been saleable in the southern part of the distribution area. The answer might lie in a very curious discrimination among the customers: the families in the southern part who bought these slabs were reluctant to buy the second design. Alternatively, we may emphasise the hypothesis that the second design is a development from the first: in this case the reason for the distinctive distributions would lie with the man who developed the design. If this is so, we would postulate that he either had his contacts in the north, or else that he was 'given' this area to market his produce. Both designs were made in the same place, apparently of Scrabo stone where it has been examined. It was a small-scale industry, and it is easy to postulate mechanisms when probably what we are dealing with is a single family's output.

The questions raised by this small industry of monumental masons leads us on to discuss the larger building industry. As in everything we must not forget the Irish background when the Anglo-Normans arrived. With the Savignac house of Erenagh founded in 1127, Ulster had been in the forefront of the movement of reformed Benedictine monasticism.[38] This not only involved questions of religious discipline but also a whole new design for church building. It involved taking individual skills in carving and building, as witnessed by high crosses and round towers, and creating whole buildings and groups of buildings from the parts. The presence of institutions like Erenagh or Newry, and such typically Irish Romanesque details as chevrons with ornamented spandrels from Downpatrick or Killyleagh,[39] show that there was a developed industry of some sort before 1177. The best surviving example of this is the most enigmatic, the nave of the Augustinian priory of Dungiven, Co. Londonderry (plate 5A). The east wall of this building was originally the end of the church, and sports the main ornament. On the inside are the remains, cut by the later chancel arches, of a row of blank arcading with scalloped capitals and reeded bases which would fit well with the date generally given for the building of the early twelfth century. The outside of the east wall is decorated with a vertical projection at each corner with three horizontals presumably originally linking the uprights. These have been called antae but are too small: 10″ wide and projecting only about 2″. These projecting strips could be taken as evidence of another influence from England as well as those visible at Cormac's chapel at Cashel. [40] This second line of communication with Anglo-Saxon work, considering Dungiven's decoration as derived from pilaster strips, did not catch on however: Ulster, like the rest of Ireland, followed the lines of Irish Romanesque style in the twelfth century.

The most obvious change in the industry, as a result of the Anglo-Norman conquest, was its involvement not only in church building, but castle building as well. This may not have involved the decorative work and complex detail of a church but it also needed men, stone, money and organisation. In the castles there seems always to have been an outside mason in charge of the major pieces of work. At Carrickfergus John de Courcy must have brought in an outsider: no native Irishman could have controlled the building of the massive keep of the first period. Again the similarities of its gatehouse and the keep and gatehouse at Dundrum to contemporary work in south Wales must imply that Hugh de Lacy also brought in a master mason to design his works. It is possible, of course, that in cases like the design of the defences at Greencastle, Co. Down, Hugh himself might have laid down the lines to be followed, but it seems unlikely. He would have been able to appreciate a castle's design, from the point of view of its usefulness in war and as an expression of his status and comfort, but he would probably have needed more than simply a straightforward builder to translate his wishes to the workmen. Richard de Burgh, as we shall see, seems to have employed a master-mason who had worked in Wales or Scotland for Master James of St. George and Edward I. Behind these men however lay local resources: we have noted their exploitation of quarries. There are signs of both continuity and local workmanship in the castles. Doors and arches with shouldered lintels appear in all the first three periods at Carrickfergus. At Greencastle, Co. Donegal, one of the recesses of the great polygonal east tower shows that it was vaulted on wicker centring. This was to become almost universal practice in the Irish tower-houses of the fifteenth century. Its appearance here, at the start of the fourteenth, again implies local labour at least to foreman level using this method. It is known outside Ireland very rarely: Dunollie castle, Argyll, and Lancaster castle [41] are two cases. The smaller, polygonal enclosure castles like Doonbought or Seafin are very simple (fig. 16), but apart from that share several characteristics. They all have a simple chamfered plinth on the exterior: in the case of Doonbought, Connor and Seafin tower this is contrived by the easy method of tipping the facing stones over against the core to produce the required slope. The castles of Ulster seem to have been built by local labour using local stone, but under expert guidance from outside the Earldom, to design the larger ones.

We have lost most of the finest products of the mediaeval church-building industry. This means that we must be very reserved in our judgements. What is clear at first is the prestige, in architectural terms, of the Cistercian order in Ulster churches (plate 6). The key building is that of Inch abbey, founded by John de Courcy. Richardson has drawn attention [42] to a letter from Bishop Malachy of Down confirming a grant of 'Venseris island' to Abbot Adam, to build the abbey. Adam thus had a community (he witnessed a charter of Jordan de Courcy c.1181) but was about to build a new house in the early 1180's. Inch arose from Erenagh and, as already mentioned, one of the reasons why Inch was so well built is that it had a ready-made economic base. The church Adam erected was a true Gothic building with its subtle verticality, achieved at the east end with graduated lancets and emphasised by using pointed bowtell mouldings, and its rib vaulting in the eastern chapels (plate 6B). In this building, contemporary with Christchurch, Dublin in full Romanesque style, Gothic came to Ulster and Ireland.[43] However, it is not the source of all Gothic in Ireland, any more than the later nave at Christchurch was. What it did was to provide a definite Cistercian model for Gothic style in thirteenth century Ulster. The first example of this trend is to be found at the parish church of St. Nicholas, Carrickfergus (figs. 13 and 14; plate 7). This church has suffered many vicissitudes in the post-mediaeval centuries, not least at the hands of 'restorers' in the last fifty years. As a result, only fragments survive of the work of the first period, dating to about 1200. There are two piers surviving on either side of the nave and most of the north-east crossing pier, but more may be deduced from later remains, although this is not helped by the irregular setting-out of what there is. The two pairs of nave piers (plate 7B) allow us to work out the bay intervals and the width which, combined with the crossing details, can give us a reasonable idea of the overall plan. From the measured elevation of the north wall (fig. 14), we can see that the stones that appear to be part of the crossing arch are now set out of line in the wall, but the ones of the nave arcade are still in position, so it had a round arcade. The north-east pier is composite, unlike the plain drums of the nave, and the outside of the angle between the modern chancel and transept is built over its base. This gives us the level of the original floor but also, because it is clearly round to the north, it shows that there was an open arch on this side. From this arch we can deduce that there was an eastern chapel in the north transept. Preserved in the south wall of the south transept is a piscina with a bluntly pointed arch and heavy roll moulding on the arris, which may have been reset in the seventeenth century rebuilding from a southern chapel to the east. The west wall of the southern transept is now taken up by a large fourteenth century double arch, where a second south aisle was added. We may assume that this repeated the dimensions of the west wall of the transept: from this we have the size of the whole transept and crossing. We have seen that there is certainly evidence for an original eastern chapel close to the chancel, and some evidence for the reasonable hypothesis of two chapels to each transept. The midway pier of the double arch in the south transept presumably would have been aligned on the original south aisle wall, which gives us the combined nave and aisle width. The nave was originally longer, for the present west wall is not a bay length from the westernmost piers, but there is no way of telling how much longer it was, as there is no indication of the original chancel length.

This can be reconstructed as a Cistercian plan and indeed elevation, with the drums of the nave arcade like Boyle or Buildwas. Using the proportional system worked out by Hanno Hahn[44] is a dubious exercise, because of the lack of remains, but, given its application in Ireland from Mellifont onwards, it is worth trying. It is based on two squares in the proportion of 3:4. The smaller of these has a side length equal to the width of the nave and one aisle. This at Carrickfergus is 46 feet, and double this equals approximately the width of the two transepts and crossing, at 94

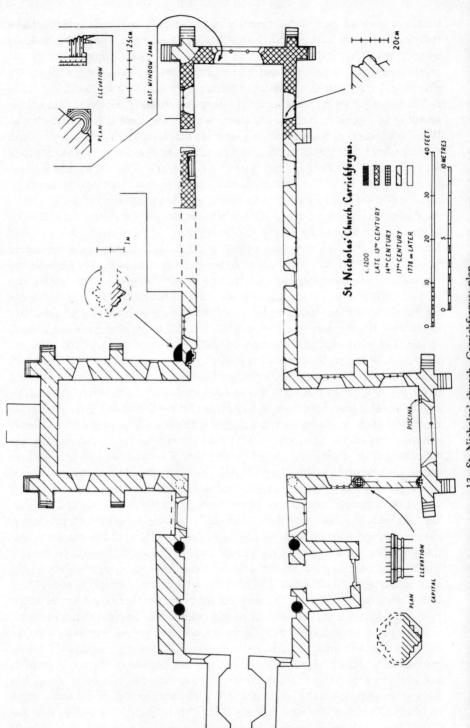

St. Nicholas' Church, Carrickfergus.

c. 1200
LATE 13TH CENTURY
14TH CENTURY
17TH CENTURY
1778 or LATER

EAST WINDOW JAMB

ELEVATION

PLAN

PISCINA

CAPITAL

PLAN

ELEVATION

13. St. Nicholas' church, Carrickfergus: plan

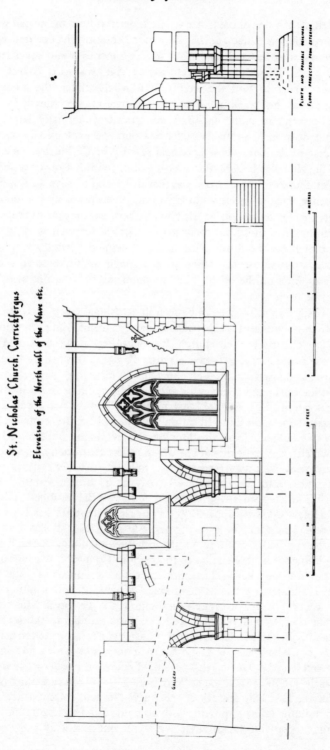

14. St. Nicholas' church, Carrickfergus: elevation of the north wall of the nave and crossing.

feet. The length of a side of the larger square is derived from the overall width of the nave, at Carrickfergus 62 feet, or the width of the crossing and one transept, here 63 feet. Three times 62 feet and four times 46 feet 6 inches would equal 186 feet, the theoretical overall length of the church: were a trial excavation 70 feet west of the present west tower to find the west wall it would clinch the argument. It is interesting to see this possible Cistercian influence in this church, for it is not a Cistercian or even a monastic one. Its status was always formally parochial, but its aggrandisement so early, probably under de Courcy, is explained by the geography of the diocese of Connor, whose episcopal seat lay in Ui Tuirtre. As a result, the church of St. Nicholas became the pro-cathedral. John de Courcy wished to build up the chief church of the diocese, the first in Ireland to have an English bishop, and apparently chose a Cistercian to lay it out. It was probably not totally built by Cistercians, for the decoration on the two southern nave arcade capitals, a debased foliate pattern and scallops, is surely too ill-matched for their work, although the scalloped capital on the drum pillar and the pointed bowtell mouldings of the crossing pier are reminiscent of their work at Boyle or Buildwas on the one hand and Roche or Inch on the other. The last point might be a hint as to where the designer came from.

Further Cistercian influence can be seen in occasional places in Ulster churches. In the early thirteenth century the Augustinian canons of Dungiven priory added a small but fine chancel to their church. It was vaulted in two bays, and at the east end it has two lancets (reconstructed as pointed), whose sills rest on a keel-mounted string course, as do two aumbries on either side. This string course steps up a short way before the north and south walls and cuts the vaulting shafts in the angles at two rings: it can just be traced for most of the length of the north wall. Outside, on the east wall, there is a weathered plinth surmounted by projecting keel moulding defined by two hollows. In all this Dungiven is like Ballintubber or other western houses,[45] which are Augustininian but which reflect Cistercian ideas: the moulding of the vault ribs, with two three-quarter rolls on each arris and a soffit quirk between, comes from the Cistercian repertoire, as do the external plinth and moulding.[46] The stepped string course is found at Ballintubber. The parochial church of Holywood (later apparently a Franciscan church)[47] has been mentioned for its use of Cultra stone, for it has the best ashlar in Ulster. It also has a weathered plinth on the east with a projecting roll and hollow moulding above.[48] This strong Cistercian influence is very similar to the story in Connacht, where the masons of the late twelfth and early thirteenth centuries produced a local school of Transitional architecture.[49] The mouldings of this school, running round the window without a break for capitals, is found at the Teampull Mor on Devenish and the chancel of Banagher church, near Dungiven: similar mouldings are found at Inishkeel and Killaghtee in Co. Donegal.[50] Ulster can thus be seen to correspond to other parts of Ireland where Anglo-Norman influence was weak, in taking to Cistercian architecture. During this period, of course, the order itself was building from the early 1180's at Inch and at Grey from 1193, to the fine frater of about the 1230's. For the first half century of the Anglo-Norman colony, there was steady Cistercian building effort to provide both a standard and an inspiration, but also at Carrickfergus to provide expert advice on laying out new work.

The rest of the building effort in the Earldom seems to have been handled mostly by local men. The largest operations were the re-building of Armagh and Down cathedrals: of the first very little survives and only decorated fragments from Down. These last are of two dates: carved capitals and arch mouldings of the early thirteenth century, and fragments of a large traceried window of about a century later. The capitals [51] have been much patched, but are still recognisable. They can be lively on occasions [52] but on the whole are poorly executed and designed. They cannot compare with the work around Kilkenny, [53] either in their polished details or in their ability to fit the design to the awkward part-conical shape of a capital. Nothing here looks of more than local standard. The same can be said of the later additions to St. Nicholas' church in Carrickfergus (plate 7A), where the chancel was lengthened about 1303 when John Cantock leased the church to Robert le Mercer, on condition that the chancel was completed. [54] The east end (fig. 13) survives with salient buttresses on the exterior, while of the rear arches of the three eastern windows, one in each wall is also original, although the tracery is of the seventeenth and nineteenth centuries. The low buttresses are decorated with weathered plinths and attached shafts at the angles and culminate in gables which perhaps supported small finial crosses. The rear arches of the windows have attached shafts with rings and plain capitals just within the splay: in the north and south windows these are filleted and are flanked by a hollow on the outer side but have no bases. The east window shafts are unfilleted and rest on triple ringed bases: they are flanked by a double hollow. Thanks to savage 'restoration', including the re-facing of the outer face of the walls, in 1973-74, there is now no sign of joins in the chancel walls, but a small buttress on the south wall might mark the halfway point between the east wall and its junction with the first period chancel. As already mentioned, the west wall of the south transept contains a walled-up double arch. This has a central octagonal pier with octagonal capital; the attached shaft on the south wall has a similar profile. The capitals are simply moulded and the arches are of three plain orders: the inner one plain chamfered, the middle one square, and the outer one hollow chamfered. This work must be the result of adding a second aisle on the south side in the fourteenth century, to make the church a large one if somewhat gloomy inside, unless the nave clerestory was large.

Two of Ulster's six friaries survive in parts. The church of the Franciscans at Armagh founded in 1263 is a plain rectangle, with a later inserted tower. There was a south arcade for the length of the nave, whose mouldings have mostly been robbed, but some have been uncovered in recent excavations. [55] There were attached, filleted shafts resting on ringed bases, similar to the work in Carrickfergus chancel in their simple use of thirteenth century motifs. At Newtownards, the Dominicans added a north aisle about 1300 to their church, also a plain rectangle until then; [56] general chapters of the order were held there in 1298 and 1312. [57] This arcade is carried on plain round piers with moulded capitals: the arches are of two plain chamfered orders. It compares well with the Carrickfergus south aisle. To these can be added other fragments: the east window of Movilla, [58] the mouldings from Woodburn discussed in Chapter One, or the window tracery from Downpatrick.

It is all very plain by any standards except those of the parish churches of Ulster. Before the Anglo-Normans arrived, the normal church had been a small rectangular building, with the only relieving feature projecting antae on occasions (e.g. Derry churches).[59] Both windows and doors were extremely plain. This tradition continued into the Anglo-Norman period, and the normal parish church until the seventeenth century seems to have been a straightforward box with no structural division between nave and chancel. Even large examples, like Ballywillin, Co. Antrim, which is as large as any at 82 × 22 feet and with fine lancet windows, are as simple as this structurally, as are Augustinian churches at Kells, Co. Antrim or Devenish: even the new monastery at Muckamore was very simple structurally.[60] The result can be seen at Loughinisland, Co. Down, where there are three plain, rectangular churches.[61] An inscription shows one to be seventeenth century, but the others are in effect undatable for they have no distinctive features.

The building industry in Ulster cannot be considered a large one. It was adequate, for there seems to have been little need to bring in masons who would have put up more exotic buildings. It was not unaware of fashion, either in mouldings on churches or the more interesting examples of the bonding timbers used to strengthen the walls of Maghera and Derry south churches.[62] These are humble examples of a technique used in Britain from the late eleventh century into the thirteenth century, mainly in castles, although used often for churches in Burgundy in particular.[63] The aim is to strengthen walls while the mortar sets: it is used elsewhere in Ireland in Rindown castle, Co. Roscommon which is built on marshy ground. Neither of the two Co. Down churches are, and Derry church does not even use mortar, which is usually taken to mean a pre-Norman date. The Ulster masons, however, seem to have been essentially men who could build a wall or a simple arcade with some carving. When elaborate designs were needed it was necessary to bring in master-masons, whether Cistercians for the churches or men for the Earl's castles. When they arrived there would have been enough trained men in Ulster to follow their directions, and the knowledge of exploiting quarries to sustain a large building effort. It is symptomatic that, unlike the west of Ireland about 1200, there is no local Ulster style in mediaeval Ulster, for neither the steady patronage of consecutive large building projects nor the master-masons existed. The only mason we know of, John le Masoun who held 10 acres at Doagh in 1333, by suit of the fortnight court and one shilling a year, was not an important man in society, but he was probably typical of the building industry of the Earldom of Ulster in his time.

The building industry involves a complex of trades culminating in the masons themselves, all based on extraction of stone. One step further away from the land is a manufacturing industry. The one which we can study best, the pottery industry, is not necessarily the largest or in contemporary terms the most important. Its products survive, however, unlike those of the cloth or leather industries for example, and, as we have no documents, this is what counts. We can, by studying the pottery found on sites, hazard answers to several questions: was it new to Ulster? Where did the workers come from and when? How was it marketed? And did it supply all Ulster's needs?

It is unlikely that he noticed it, but John de Courcy was the only Anglo-Norman to invade a part of Ireland with a native pottery industry. This had produced the undistinguished souterrain ware for several centuries, coil-built bucket-shaped cooking pots. The pots are remarkably uniform in their shape (and ugliness), varying only in whether they have some slight decoration like an applied cordon or not, and usually well made out of quite carefully prepared clay. The clay, however, is very varied and seems to be exploited only on a very local scale. The pots are poorly fired, almost certainly in bonfires rather than kilns. The evidence of the stability of the design and execution seems to indicate professional manufacture, but on a very small scale at any time and very locally. Perhaps they were made at small local clay pits by itinerant potters, without equipment such as kilns or wheels, like the proposal for metalworkers made by Collins.[64] The potters of the Anglo-Norman Earldom seem to have had no contact with the native craftsmen, except to teach them English ways. They used wheels and kilns and produced glazed jugs as well as different types of cooking pots in their industry: the effect of its arrival on the Irish potter we must leave to Chapter Six.

There are numbers of problems hampering a full description of Ulster pottery of the Anglo-Norman period. There are few dated contexts as yet, certainly few that have a *terminus ante quem* attached: the mediaeval pottery tradition in Ulster continued without drastic change into the sixteenth century. The vagaries of excavation create problems: thanks to the efforts of the Archaeological Survey in the 1950's, south-east Co. Down is well covered, but mediaeval sites from Co. Antrim, especially the north of the county, are much less so. Major sites like Greencastle, Co. Down and the town excavations in Carrickfergus and Armagh are unpublished. This said by way of warning to the reader, we must attempt at least an interim statement. The obvious starting point is with the glazed jugs and the only known kiln in Ireland, that excavated at Downpatrick in 1960[65] (plate 5B). These jugs are wheel-thrown and barrel-, not baluster-shaped, sometimes with finger pinching at the base angle. The neck has a ridge externally to which the handle is attached: the latter is a pulled strap handle with a heavy longitudinal thumb channel down the middle and thumb impressions at the body junction but otherwise normally undecorated. The rims often have a slight internal bevel but also a fairly large amount of clay rolled over to give a rather heavy rim: spouts are simply pinched out. The clay was well mixed with only fine grits (less than 1 mm. across) and fired to produce an oxidised surface (usually red or buff) with a reduced, or unoxidised grey core: this was probably the result of firing to a temperature (c.750°C?)[66] not far above that at which oxidation occurred and then letting it drop quite soon, allowing no opportunity to complete oxidation but saving fuel. The result is often rather soft, not so much at the kiln site, where over-fired wasters are common, but at other sites in Co. Down where similar pots have been found. These are not necessarily supplied with jugs from the actual kiln excavated in 1960, for the distinctive white spots[67] are often absent. The bulk of the jugs from Ballynarry,[68] the later levels of Clough[69] and, to a certain extent, Lismahon[70] are products of the Downpatrick industry; all these sites are in Lecale.

Similar to these are the jugs from Carrickfergus castle[71] (plate 5B) and from the town excavations. The overall forms are very much the same as those from Co. Down, with barrel-shaped bodies, pulled strap handles and ridged necks. The rims tend to have less clay turned over and to be more sharply bevelled internally or flattened off. The fabric of the pots differs, being less well mixed with clear vesicles of air visible in the fractures, and containing more grit. These features combine with the harder firing they have been given to produce sherds noticeably harsher and stronger than those from Co. Down. The firing resulted in oxidised red surfaces over a grey core, the result of using different clays, more refractory and with more iron than in Co. Down, but using a similar technique of only a short period at oxidising temperatures. In the summer of 1979 a kiln has actually been found in Carrickfergus.

There is a third type of jug found in Ulster, principally at Greencastle, Co. Down, Muckamore abbey and Armagh friary.[72] This is of very high quality, in the preparation of a fine clay almost without any grit for potting, and in the use of a fast wheel to produce a thin body. This pottery shares several traits with the pottery of Leinster, although it lacks the mica content of the latter: footrings at the base angle flattened and finger moulded; strap handles not pulled as in the Downpatrick industry but cut and often very wide and quite thin; the occasional use of applied pinched rings on the neck below the rim; and a tendency not to have the well-marked ridge on the neck clear of the rim. Where these were made is a puzzle: they occur at Carrickfergus in lesser numbers than the local products but not in Lecale. The most likely centre perhaps to supply Muckamore and Armagh is Antrim, where reasonable potting clay occurs to the north-east of the town at Rathenraw and, if water-sorted, might give good deposits in the Six Mile Water bed. The distribution problems from there to Armagh and Greencastle would be interesting for the role of the Irish if this were the centre.

The Ulster pottery industry therefore had at least three centres, at Downpatrick, Carrickfergus and one other. Their marketing areas were extremely limited, Lecale for one, but not Greencastle, and the Carrickfergus pottery hardly reaching Muckamore only fifteen miles away.

The date at which these centres begin producing is difficult to fix accurately. On the one hand we have the lack of close dating for sites, on the other really firm identification of individual sherds is needed. These problems combine: in Lecale we have the two early periods, and Clough and Lismahon, both with stratified coins of King John and John de Courcy respectively,[73] which should be of about 1200, but the problem lies in identifying certain examples of local ware, when the actual kiln products are rare, as already noted. The excavator considered that the pottery from the bottom of the ditch at Greencastle sealed beneath the layer of rubble derived from the destruction of the curtain wall dated from before 1260 when the castle was damaged.[74] The ditch had only a little quick silt below the rubble and so the suggestion is reasonable, but it runs counter to two other arguments. Firstly, there were no jugs but only native wares in the deposits above the rubble and secondly, of course, the rubble was never cleared from the ditch. The castle was occupied intensely under Richard de Burgh: he stayed there in 1306,[75] he saw his two daughters married there in 1312, and it figured in the Bruce invasion, being captured and recaptured in 1315 and figuring in 1327 peace negotiations.[76] It seems most unlikely that throughout this period Richard allowed the ditch to lie choked with masonry (although the curtain was rebuilt) and used no jugs which could find their way into it, although native wares did. The ditch has more probably been cleaned out at some time after its digging, perhaps in the early fourteenth century. There are other 'destruction dates' for Greencastle: it was unsuccessfully besieged in 1333-4,[77] 'destroyed' in 1343[78] and 1375,[79] and repaired in 1381-2.[80] The result is that we cannot use the evidence of Greencastle to date the third class of pottery to before 1260; it could well be fourteenth century. On general grounds the earlier date would also cause difficulty to other dating. These pots were made after the Leinster industry had been established, itself an offshoot from Bristol; it would be difficult to complete the chain by 1260.

The origins of the potters' training is betrayed in their work. The shapes of the first two groups of jugs are those of Cheshire. There the potters used the same barrel shapes, ridged necks with pulled strap handles, and simple turned-over rims for their jugs. The preparation of the clays, choosing those with little grit, and the firing are very similar also, as is the near total lack of decoration on the pots except for a simple lead glaze and some incisions on the handle or a thumbed base. It is almost certain that the potters who set up business in thirteenth century Carrickfergus and Lecale came from either Cheshire where the kilns of Audlem and Ashton produced very similar pots,[81] or the offshoot at Rhuddlan.[82] The third group, as already pointed out, were made by men who had worked in Leinster, perhaps Meath where similar material has been found but in a different, micaceous fabric.

Besides these local supplies there was a sale in Ulster of other pots, derived from outside. So similar is Cheshire ware to Ulster wares that it is difficult to point to imports from there, but Leinster products did find their way north, for example to Carrickfergus.[83] There are found at most sites sherds of rough white fabrics often rather gritty and harsh which may well be from anywhere between the Midlands of England and eastern Scotland, from the kilns of Sneyd Green, Staffordshire to Colstoun. Again the tradition, if not the actual pots, with two-colour glaze painting, must have its origins in the same large area. The problem is not simple, however. On the one hand the white fabrics are in themselves not exclusive to any one area and may even occur in Ulster if iron-free clays were used. One pot from Doonbought[84] is so badly made that it could hardly be an import; its base is so poorly fixed to the body that it looks as though it would fall off if the jug were full, let alone if it travelled, yet its fabric is white. Again, it is the idea alone of glaze painting which may be travelling. Another common occurrence is sherds of reduced, grey ware. These might be from south-west Scotland or Carlisle, where they became the norm in the fourteenth and fifteenth centuries and were frequent earlier.[85] They might, however, be from an unknown local source (Coleraine and Twescard are *terra incognita*) or simply slight accidents in local firings. It is a brave man who attributes sources to individual sherds.

E

Apart from these north Irish Sea contacts, there were two other areas involved in the pottery trade to Ulster: Bristol and south-western France. In southern and eastern Ireland these sources are strongly represented in the pottery record, but not so much in the north. Bristol imports, either from kilns like Ham Green[86] or St. Peter's,[87] remain almost unknown. Traits derived from this tradition are there, as with the frilled neck rings or the slashed and grooved strap handles, but they are imitations not imports, derived not even directly from Bristol but from the Leinster potteries established from Bristol. In the pottery trade, at least, there was apparently little direct contact between the Bristol Channel and the Earldom of Ulster. French pottery was of a much higher standard in some respects than that produced in Ireland. The use of white, iron-free clays gave a fine body which the potters decorated with either a bright green glaze made by staining the lead glaze with copper or else motifs painted in brown, green and yellow under a clear glaze, the so-called polychrome ware. Green-glazed pottery from France occurs from early on in the Earldom, being imported to Clough during its first period of occupation.[88] The polychrome ware, which was produced for about twenty-five years on either side of 1300, is rarer in Ulster. In any such collection of pottery a rough guess would be that something less than 10% is from France. This contrasts with the southern evidence. There, during the thirteenth century in Dublin, perhaps 50% of pottery is imported, 25% from Bristol and 25% from France; in Cork the proportions are even higher.

We must not read too much into this sort of evidence, and take it to apply necessarily to more than the pottery trade. Some archaeologists would be inclined to use these pottery figures as a straightforward index of Franco-Irish trade in the thirteenth century. If we look at the English situation we can see the problems. There is equal disparity between coastal towns such as Southampton,[89] with many imported pots, and inland ones like Oxford where they are much rarer. Assuming, as must be the case, that the French trade was in imported wine, to use the pottery evidence as an index of trade would be to imply that Oxford provided a smaller market for wine than Southampton. There are other factors at work here: the strength of the local potteries' control of the market or the practice of trans-shipping. Both of these could have operated in the Irish Sea. The Anglo-Normans of Ireland had other priorities on their minds in Leinster or Munster than setting up a pottery industry after the invasion, so they imported their fine ware until, later, Bristol potters came over to start one: imports therefore figure largely until the local industry is established.

We have considered only the top end of the market, the glazed jugs: it is time to look at the lower end, the cooking pots. There are two points to be made. Firstly, the range of products in Ulster is smaller than that produced by the industry of southern England. The Downpatrick kiln potter was making a number of types other than the ordinary globular cooking pot. Only the pipkins, round vessels with hooked handles (referred to by Pollock and Waterman as skillets), occur on other sites, as for example Castlescreen.[90] The wide open bowls and pans did not seem to have much sale, and forms like flat skillets, comparable to a modern frying-pan, seem unknown. Some meat-dishes occur at Carrickfergus, but otherwise cooking in

Ulster seems only to have involved various types of narrow-necked cooking pots. These also differ from some found in England in their size: large ones more than eight inches in diameter seem unknown. The second point involves their distribution. Both Carrickfergus and Lecale used cooking pots of English type. We are hampered by a lack of excavated sites in Co. Antrim, but it would seem that these English cooking pots had no market in the district round Antrim (none occurs at Muckamore[91] or among the lesser amount of pots from Dunsilly motte),[92] or Twescard (there are none from Doonbought).[93] Here the cooking pottery was supplied by the native industry.

As well as evidence of the movement of individual commodities, there is also evidence of unspecified trade between Ulster and other areas, usually casual references arising from other circumstances. The fourteenth century wars with Scotland, for example, provide several. There is the levy of corn and barley exacted by Bruce in 1327,[94] which can hardly be cited as trade in itself but indicates that the capacity to trade was there. As one might expect from geographical proximity, trade between Ulster and Scotland appears to have been continuous through the thirteenth and fourteenth centuries. In 1237 Hugh de Lacy was ordered to release Scottish merchants arrested in Ulster ports on suspicion of piracy.[95] The problems of the wars are shown by the constable of Carrickfergus arresting merchants, presumably of that port, for trading with the Scots, the King's enemies, in 1338 and 1340.[96] Even wine from the castle there was sold, illicitly, to the Scots.[97] Licences to export corn, flour, beer and salt meat to the Scots were issued to a Carrickfergus merchant in 1403 and 1404.[98] Similar licences were issued in 1338 and 1357 to Portrush merchants to allow them to trade into the Hebrides, because the Lord of the Isles was supporting the King of England.[99] Trade to the southern parts of the Irish Sea is evidenced, in spite of the absence of pottery from there, in 1340 by the protests of merchants at being asked to pay customs on hides in Bristol, after they had paid at their ports of export in Ireland: Carrickfergus is one of the latter.[100] A Carrickfergus boat took supplies for Mortimer, King's Lieutenant, from Bristol to Ireland in 1374.[101] Trade with Chester, however, unmentioned in the documents, cannot be ignored, on the evidence of craftsmen in clay and stone coming from the region: the settlers cannot have been taking routes untouched by other trade. Commerce with Gascony is referred to in 1308: Thomas Mercer of Carrickfergus was joint-owner (with a Drogheda man and two Gascons) of a ship wrecked at Beaumaris on its journey from France.[102] In 1317 the *Grace Deu* of Coleraine was arrested at Falmouth on its way to Gascony.[103] There is evidence, on the other hand, of indirect trading with France or Spain. William Symcock of Drogheda was licensed to import wine into London in 1390; a similar licence was issued to an Englishman to ship Spanish wine to Coleraine in 1409.[104]

This survey of the economy has been made complex by the evidence, which is never directly presented in contemporary records, either physical or literary. To summarise the results depends on the point of view taken, whether we compare the economy of the Earldom with the economy of the Irish world or with its English or Anglo-Irish contemporaries. The result of the Anglo-Normans' arrival in Ulster in the later twelfth century was undoubtedly to increase both the volume and variety of economic activity. The evidence from the 1306 Taxation makes it clear that they were able to produce more from the land, presumably because of their commercial contacts. These contacts meant that agriculture could be practised for more than subsistence and could be part of a whole economic system. Agriculture was the only major export and had to support the Earl's income and state as well as attracting in the silver for the currency that circulated in Ulster and paying for the industries we have discussed. These industries were either new, like the pottery industry, or greatly expanded, like the building industry. An illustration of this change can be seen in the iron industry. Before the Anglo-Normans came, most raths, to judge from excavations, had iron working carried on on occasions.[105] Only Lismahon motte in its earlier period has produced this evidence out of the excavations in the rural society of the Earldom. The iron industry seems to have become concentrated, presumably in towns, as the furnace bottoms found in Market Place, Carrickfergus,[106] might indicate; for his work on Greencastle, Co. Down, Robert Gelous bought iron in Drogheda.[107]

The main emphasis must, however, be laid on the slenderness of the resources of the Earldom, just as the lesson of examining the area settled is the same. Agriculture was its base, and for all its mills Ulster cannot have been good grain country compared to south-east Ireland. From the customs revenue we can see that its pastoral exports were small too. We would not expect to find Ulster a centre of manufacture like the Low Countries, but what industries or trade we do know of are very limited. Pottery and stone are the only commodities whose marketing we can study and they are quite restricted. The industries do not so much appear to be slow in being established as hampered by poor communications or small markets. The tradition of the pottery of Lecale seems to go back to at least early in the second generation of the settlement, to judge from Clough and Lismahon. The Irish evidence, where no Anglo-Norman sites without glazed high jugs or using tripod pitchers have been found, would seem to prove that the English pottery industry had established its production of jugs some time before 1200. With pottery and stone, however, in Ulster, the story always seems to be a very local one, not involving the whole Earldom: it may be that the reason was as simple as bad roads. It is the same with the building industry: the effort is limited to local resources, without importing outside freestone, and the design is simple. The exceptions occur only when the Earl is directly concerned: either churches built under his patronage like Inch, or else castles built for his use, and the Earl usually had resources other than Ulster to produce money.

NOTES

1. O. Davies & D. B. Quinn: *U.J.A.*, IV, 1941, p. 55. This is the total accounted for, less arrears and an advance from the Treasurer.

2. The seneschal's dates come from *C.D.I.*, I, no.'s 760, 1126, 1167.

3. *National Manuscripts of Ireland*, (ed. J. T. Gilbert), plate 73; E. Curtis: *Proceedings of the Royal Irish Academy*, XXXIX (C), 1929, pp. 1-17.

4. *36th Report of the Deputy Keeper, P.R.I.*, p. 54.

5. *45th Report of the Deputy Keeper, P.R.I.*, p. 22; *Calendar of Close Rolls 1349-54*, p. 442.

6. W. Reeves: *Ecclesiastical Antiquities; C.D.I.*, V, no.'s 893-902; the parishes in the latter have been identified by referring to Reeves' ms. notes in Armagh Public Library.

7. M. A. Costello: *De Annatis Hiberniae*, I.

8. *Ibid.*, p. 187.

9. *C.D.I.*,V, p. 265.

10. M. A. Costello: *De Annatis Hiberniae*, pp. 61, 62, 99, 103.

11. *C.D.I.*, II, no. 1918.

12. For a recent mill in pre-Norman Ulster, see M. Baillie: *U.J.A.*, XXXVIII, 1975, pp. 25-33.

13. O. Davies & D. B. Quinn: *U.J.A.*, IV, 1941, p. 63.

14. *C.D.I.*, I, no.'s 1131, 1377.

15. *Ibid.*, no. 2768.

16. *Ibid.*, no. 2925.

17. *C.D.I.*, II, no. 1902.

18. *39th Report of the Deputy Keeper, P.R.I.*, p. 38.

19. W. Dugdale: *Monasticon Anglicanum*, VI (2), p. 1125.

20. *National Manuscripts of Ireland*, (ed. J. T. Gilbert), plate 73; E. Curtis: *Proceedings of the Royal Irish Academy*, XXXIX (C), 1929, pp. 1-17.

21. *Patent and Close Rolls Ireland*, (ed. E. Tresham), p. 193.

22. G. H. Orpen: *J.R.S.A.I.*, XLIV, 1914, p. 66.

23. W. Reeves: *Ecclesiastical Antiquities*, p. 168.

24. *45th Report of the Deputy Keeper, P.R.I.*, p. 48.

25. O. Davies & D. B. Quinn: *U.J.A.*, IV, 1941, p. 59.

26. *C.D.I.*, II, no. 1918.

27. D. M. Waterman: *U.J.A.*, XXXIII, 1970, pp. 63-77.

28. *A.S.C.D.*, pp. 282, 297, 300.

29. *Ibid.*, pp. 297-312.

30. *Ibid.*, pp. 208, 215.

31. *Reports of the Commissioners Respecting the Public Records of Ireland*, I, plate 2.

32. O. Davies & A. H. George: *U.J.A.*, IX, 1946, pp. 37-44.

33. *A.S.C.D.*, p. 231.

34. *Ibid.*, p. 235.

35. R.C.H.M: *Westmorland*, plate 32.

36. D. R. Fyson: *Archaeologia Aeliana*, XXXIV, 1956, pp. 213-8; L.A.S. Butler: *Ibid.* XXXVI, 1958, pp. 207-20.

37. *A.S.C.D.*, plate 111.

38. J. G. Richardson, in *Medieval Studies presented to Aubrey Gwynn*, (ed. J. A. Watt, *et al.*), pp. 29-43.

39. *A.S.C.D.*, plate 91; D. M. Waterman: *U.J.A.*, XXXIV, 1971, p. 110.

40. L. de Paor, in *North Munster Studies* (ed. E. Rynne), pp. 133-45.

41. *A.S.C.D.*, p. 132.

42. J. G. Richardson, in *Medieval Studies presented to Aubrey Gwynn*, (ed. J. A. Watt, *et al.*), pp. 29-43.

43. R. A. Stalley: *Architecture and sculpture in Ireland*, pp. 58-63.

44. R. A. Stalley: *Studies*, 1975, pp. 347-67.

45. R. A. Stalley: *Architecture and sculpture in Ireland*, pp. 110-116.

46. J. Bilson: *Archaeological Journal*, LXVI, 1909, fig. 15.

47. *A.S.C.D.*, p. 282.

48. *Ibid.*, plate 103.

49. H. G. Leask: *Irish Churches and monastic buildings*, II, chapter 4.

50. D. M. Waterman: *U.J.A.*, XXVII, 1964, pp. 133-6.

51. *A.S.C.D.*, plates 89-91.

52. E.g. *Ibid.*, plate 89, no. 11.

53. R. A. Stalley: *Architecture and sculpture in Ireland*, plates 33-7.

54. W. Reeves: *Ecclesiastical Antiquities*, p. 62.

55. C. J. Lynn: *U.J.A.*, XXXVIII, 1975, pp. 61-80.

56. *A.S.C.D.*, pp. 284-7.

57. A. Gwynn & R. N. Hadcock: *Medieval Religious houses: Ireland*, p. 228.

58. *A.S.C.D.*, pp. 283-4.

59. D. M. Waterman: *U.J.A.*, XXX, 1967, pp. 53-75.

60. C. J. Lynn: *Excavations*, 1973, p. 5.

61. *A.S.C.D.*, pp. 305-6.

62. *Ibid.*, pp. 290-1, 306-7.

63. R. J. Wilcox: *Chateau Gaillard*, V, 1972, pp. 193-202; R. J. Wilcox: unpublished Ph.D. thesis, *Timber and iron reinforcement in medieval churches*, Queen's University, Belfast.

64. A. E. P. Collins: *U.J.A.*, XXXI, 1968, p. 57.

65. A. J. Pollock & D. M. Waterman: *U.J.A.*, XXVI, 1963, pp. 79-104.

66. The temperature of mediaeval pottery firings has not often been investigated by experimental re-firings, and is probably consistently over-estimated. The fuel consumption in a kiln rises sharply above c.750°C – G. F. Bryant: *Medieval Archaeology*, XXI, 1977, figs. 41 & 44. Jugs of Saintonge polychrome were fired below 900°C – C. Platt & R. Coleman-Smith: *Excavations in medieval Southampton*, II, pp. 51-2.

67. A. J. Pollock & D. M. Waterman: *U.J.A.*, XXVI, 1963, appendix 2.

68. B. K. Davison: *U.J.A.*, XXIV-XXV, 1961-2, pp. 66-71.

69. D. M. Waterman: *U.J.A.*, XVII, 1954, pp. 123-35.

70. D. M. Waterman: *Medieval Archaeology*, III, pp. 157-61.

71. D. M. Waterman: *U.J.A.*, XV, 1952, pp. 109-15.

72. All these sites are unpublished: I am very grateful to the directors of them, T. G. Delaney, A. E. T. Harper, C. J. Lynn and C. Warhurst for allowing me to study the finds. The main finds from Armagh friary came from an area excavated by Mr Harper, not from the church, published by C. J. Lynn, *U.J.A.*, XXXVIII, 1975, pp. 61-80, which produced very little pottery.

73. D. M. Waterman: *U.J.A.*, XVII, 1954, pp. 122-3; *Medieval Archaeology*, III, 1959, p. 156.

74. C. J. Lynn: *U.J.A.*, XXXIX, 1976, p. 52.

75. *Calendar of Justiciary Rolls, Ireland*, II, p. 259.

76. J. T. Gilbert (ed.): *Annals of Ireland*, pp. 341, 345, 367.

77. E. Tresham (ed.): *Patent and Close Rolls, Ireland*, p. 38.

78. *Clyn's Annals*, 1343.

79. *Annals of Ireland*, (ed. J. T. Gilbert), p. 283.

80. *Patent and Close Rolls, Ireland*, (ed. E. Tresham), p. 112.

81. R. Newstead: *Liverpool Annals of Archaeology and Anthropology*, XXI, 1934, pp. 5-27; G. Webster & G. C. Dunning: *Medieval Archaeology*, IV, 1960.

82. H. Miles, in P. J. Davey (ed.): *Medieval pottery from excavations in the North-West*, pp. 60-61.

83. D. M. Waterman: *U.J.A.*, XV, 1952, fig. 3, no. 5.

84. T. E. McNeill: *U.J.A.*, XL, 1977, fig. 7, no. 1.

85. Jope et al: *Transactions of the Cumberland & Westmorland Archaeological and Antiquarian Society*, LV, 1956, pp. 59-107; R. Hogg et al: *Ibid.*, LXIV, 1964, pp. 14-62; Jope et al: *Proceedings of the Society of Antiquaries of Scotland*, XCI, 1957, pp. 117-38.

86. K. J. Barton: *Transactions of the Bristol and Gloucestershire Archaeological Society*, LXXXII, 1963, pp. 95-126.

87. M. Ponsford: *Ibid.*, XCI, 1972, pp. 1-9.

88. D. M. Waterman: *U.J.A.*, XVII, 1954, fig. 6, no.'s 1 & 2.

89. C. Platt and R. Coleman-Smith: *Excavations in medieval Southampton*, II, pp. 17-19.

90. C. W. Dickinson & D. M. Waterman: *U.J.A.*, XXII, 1959, fig. 6, no. 14.

91. C. J. Lynn: *Excavations*, 1973, p. 5.

92. T. E. McNeill: *Excavations*, 1974, pp. 8-9.

93. T. E. McNeill: *U.J.A.*, XL, 1977, fig. 8.

94. R. Nicholson: *Scottish Historical Review*, XLIII, 1963, pp. 30-40.

95. *C.D.S.*, I, no. 1364.
96. *Calendar of Patent Rolls, 1338-40*, p. 52; *Calendar of Close Rolls, 1339-41*, p. 396.
97. *Calendar of Patent Rolls, 1338-40*, p. 403.
98. *Patent and Close Rolls, Ireland*, (ed. E. Tresham), pp. 171, 178.
99. *C.D.S.*, III, no.'s 1273, 1639.
100. *Calendar of Close Rolls, 1339-41*, pp. 591-2.
101. *Ibid.*, 1374-7, p. 11.
102. *Ibid.*, 1307-13, p. 85.
103. *Calendar of Patent Rolls, 1317-1321*, p. 94.
104. *Patent and Close Rolls, Ireland*, (ed. E. Tresham), pp. 143, 193.
105. A. E. P. Collins, *U.J.A.*, XXXI, 1968, p. 56.
106. T. G. Delaney: *Excavations, 1972*, p. 4.
107. *Reports of the Commissioners respecting the Public Records of Ireland*, I, plate 2.

4

The Earls and the Administration
of their Earldom

THE people in the Earldom lived under the personal rule of the successive Earls, looking to them for justice and protection, in a Liberty only minimally affected by the royal government. The Earl's Court was limited by the usual four pleas of the crown, arson, rape, treasure trove and forestall (assault on the king's highway), and jurisdiction over church lands was also reserved to the King.[1] The Earl had no legislative independence, however, for any divergence of practice would be checked by bringing a writ of error before the royal courts: he was also bound to serve royal writs in his Liberty. The Earls, needless to say, sought to eliminate as far as possible any internal rivals to their control, who might be supported by royal authority. We have seen Hugh de Lacy expel the de Galloway family introduced by King John to Antrim, and replace them with men who held their land from him, not the Crown. The earlier quarrels between FitzWarin and de Mandeville reached the royal courts because of Richard de Burgh's minority, but the later lawsuit between FitzWarin and de Mandeville's sons resulted from an appeal to the King by Fitzwarin from the Earl's court. The de Mandevilles claimed they need not plead because of the Liberty and won the judgement that FitzWarin should take his case back properly to the Earl's court, and only if he did not get justice there should he come back to the royal court. Richard clearly favoured the de Mandevilles, and we can perhaps explain this by FitzWarin's claim to hold *in capite* from the King, repeated by his son Alan in 1305-1308, in a case between him and William de Mandeville over lands at Drumrothan and Neubyggynge.[2] Alan was able to appeal from the Liberty to the royal court because he held the land through inheritance from his great grandfather William de Serland,[3] who was granted it by King John, and so held in chief and not from the Earl. It must have irritated Richard de Burgh to have men in his Earldom claiming not to hold their land from him. Again, when Walter de Burgh harassed the Prior of Down,[4] this was probably a forerunner of the cases in 1306, when Richard de Burgh was accused in the royal court by the Prior of trying to usurp the Cross lands, force the bishops and abbots to his courts and seize the temporalities during vacancies, and in 1312 when he tried to seize the temporalities of the bishops of Down and Connor.[5] Richard seems to have been instigating a royal claim to issue writs of election for the Prior of Down, in the hope of being granted these rights, but the bishops and the Prior successfully maintained their responsibility to the King and the Bishop respectively. This line did not work elsewhere: Richard issued a licence to elect a new Prior of Muckamore in 1285 and was requested one by Movilla in 1297.[6] Richard de Burgh was clearly trying to enforce his control over all landowners in spite of their claims to be tenants in chief.

To administer his Earldom, the Earl relied on the advice and help of officials with specific delegated duties. At the beginning of the story we find John de Courcy, from the evidence of his charter witnesses, having a classic twelfth century baronial household.[7] He has a steward (Richard fitz Robert, called both *dapifer* and *senescallus*), a constable, and a chamberlain as well as a forester and at least one clerk, John, 'who wrote the charter' of Jordan de Courcy to Nendrum.[8] We know very little about the households of either Hugh de Lacy or Walter de Burgh, but with Walter's son Richard we can see the principal officers again. The role of the chamberlain has been divided, apparently, between a treasurer and a chancellor.[9] The most important man seems to have been the steward, always known now as the seneschal. This is the title given to the Earl's deputy in Ulster, when the Earldom is in the King's hands through a minority or confiscation, in the Pipe Roll of 1211-12 onwards. He was not only a deputy in the Earl's absence: Thomas de Mandeville was seneschal in 1282 when Richard de Burgh was trying to cope with Thomas' feud with William FitzWarin.[10] At the same time Thomas was involved on the Earl's behalf in the war between Domnall O Donnell and Aedh Buidhe O Neill.[11] His military duties continued on behalf of the Earl, although we do not know who was seneschal of Ulster during the period, for it was Thomas who led the Ulster contingent to Scotland in 1301.[12] It is tempting therefore to equate his role with that of the Earl's Marshal who held the rolls of his soldiers then in Dublin, in 1305.[13] If so, perhaps the seneschal had absorbed the office of John de Courcy's constable. The seneschal was also responsible for executing royal writs in the Liberty.[14] In the lordship of Kilkenny during the later thirteenth century, the main duty of the seneschal for the non-resident lords of Clare was to hold the county court of the Liberty.[15] In Ulster under Richard de Burgh the main court of the Earldom, from which appeals might reach the Justiciar in Dublin, was held in Carrickfergus, and the Rolls refer to cases heard there. When they do, the cases are recorded as held before the Earl's seneschal and bailiffs, in 1299, but thereafter (1305-8) as held before Nigel le Brun and the other justices of the Earl.[16]

Below this central administrative body lay the local units of bailiwicks of 1226 or the counties of 1333.[17] There are five of these in both lists: the bailiwicks of Ards and Blathewic were united by 1333 but the county of Twescard added to the Earldom. Presumably in 1226 the official who was responsible for these units was called a bailiff; afterwards both 'sheriff' and 'seneschal' are used equally. His main duty must have been to hold the county court, assisted by the main tenants of the county who we see in the 1333 Inquisition owing suit of the county court. This would have been perhaps the normal criminal court, with appeals possible to Carrickfergus: minor tenurial disputes would be dealt with at the fortnight courts for the manors, perhaps supervised by the county sheriff. The manors must have had bailiffs to collect rents and pass them on to the Earl's treasurer. These officials have varied backgrounds. The household officers who witnessed John de Courcy's charters obviously owed everything to him and his service, whether he granted them land or not: in the first generation of conquest we cannot talk of old landed families. This loyalty resulted in their disappearance, for all their names, except William the Forester's, appear on the list of hostages given for de Courcy in 1205.[18]

If he had given them land, it was confiscated by Hugh de Lacy or King John: they lost their hopes with de Courcy, unlike other families who came with him. Some of Richard de Burgh's officials came from a professional, clerical background. Neither his chancellor (John de Langston)[19] nor his treasurer (William de Aure)[20] have names which appear among the principal landholders of the Earldom in 1333. Nigel le Brun, who is described as Richard de Burgh's Justice in 1305 and 1308, appears as his legal representative during the same period[21] and was appointed a banneret in his army in Scotland in 1303,[22] coming to the Earl's service after training in the royal administration. He may have met Richard at his knighting by Edward I at Rhuddlan in 1283, but he was a royal servant in 1290 and had been seneschal of Kildare for some time by July 1297:[23] he left the de Burghs' service to be the royal escheator in Ireland, and a justice.[24] This professional element contrasts with the holding of the offices of seneschal of Ulster and sheriffs of counties by various de Mandevilles and by William FitzWarin, another prominent landowner.

The seneschal and sheriffs, as the chief general administrators in the Earldom, were better drawn from the chief tenants of the Earl: the others were not. The reason for this probably lay in the side of their duties other than the administering of justice. The Earldom was a frontier barony and so needed a constant machinery of defence. Part of this was provided by the local levies of each locality. In 1260 Brian O Neill was defeated at Down by the 'commonalty of the city and county of Down' under the command of the mayor and a local knight.[25] Aedh O Neill and O Cahan, allied to the de Mandevilles, raided Carrickfergus in 1273, but were beaten by the seneschal and Hugh Byset, whose family owned the Glens and land near Templepatrick.[26] The knights' fees of the Earldom may well have been more than a matter of social prestige for the tenants and an opportunity for scutage for the Earl under these circumstances. Castle guard appears to have been alive in 1332 from the precision with which it is recorded that Walter de Slymberg owed suit of court at Carrickfergus and maintenance of an armed man in time of war in Pollard's tower in the castle.[27] The constables of castles, either the county sheriff or other individuals responsible to the seneschal of the Earldom, must have played a real part here in the defence. The Earldom was considered to have been weakened by detaching frontier castles from central control in 1273.[28] The nature of war in Ulster must have been dominated by its border position — as pointed out in Chapter Two, nearly everywhere in the Earldom was within ten miles of its frontier. The local tenantry could no doubt be rallied to meet a major threat but it would take them time to concentrate. It would always have been sound policy to have a force of soldiers ready to counter quick raids in wartime. We see them being used in the 1211-12 Pipe Roll, where we hear of 40 men at Antrim, 30 at Dromore and ten at Maycove.[29] They were paid in cows, and wounded men at Antrim were given ten as a cure and to compensate them for losing their mantles; we can be nearly sure they were Irish. They were stationed on the borders of the Earldom at strategic points to guard these districts (in the case of Antrim against Ui Tuirtre to the north). In the Minister's accounts of Elizabeth de Burgh's manors of Antrim we see a continuation of the same policy. In 1354 Walter de Say of Coleraine was given his expenses for taking 40 horsemen to Antrim and back, while in 1353 and 1354 John de Camlyn is paid £2. 10. 0. for guarding Antrim (Appendix Three).

A map of the castles of Ulster (fig. 15) shows that mottes with baileys are concentrated on the borders of the Earldom or beyond. In the lands of South Antrim or North Down, the centre of the settlement, there are none, although there are many mottes without them. There are very few – only about 23% – of the total number of mottes which have baileys, in contrast to England where virtually all mottes have baileys.[30] It is most unlikely that Ulster farmers have been three times as keen as English ones to destroy them, especially as English mottes and baileys are more often urban and therefore financially more rewarding to destroy. Nor would the pattern of destruction be so selective within Ulster: although the bailey is vulnerable compared to the motte, this distribution along the Earldom's borders would seem to be real. The contrast with England is not just in the numbers of the baileys but in their size, for in Ulster they are quite small. Many were made by inserting a motte into a rath whose diameter was about 30 metres. Dromore counts as a large bailey in Ulster: its area is 900 sq. metres, while at Ballyroney where there are two baileys their combined area is less than twice that. An English motte and bailey castle functioned by having a hall, barns etc. in the bailey while the motte, with a tower on or in it, acted as a refuge like a keep. The Ulster baileys are too small for this role and too restricted in their distribution. Excavation has shed little light on the question of bailey use. At Castleskreen there was little built in it but nothing on the motte either;[31] at Clough and Dromore[32] the baileys were hopelessly disturbed, although the latter site must have contained the hall mentioned in the 1212 Pipe Roll[33] because it was not on the motte. At Duneight one or two slight buildings were put up when the pre-Norman fort was converted into a bailey,[34] but nothing like a hall. In 1212 Dundonald had a barn and equipment for three plough-teams,[35] yet the motte has no bailey. The only possible site for one is to the north-east, yet the motte ditch on that side is unbroken – had there been a bailey, now destroyed, its ditch should have joined the motte there.

The baileys attached to mottes in Ulster seem, from what evidence we have, to be found mainly in areas of military activity and to be singularly ill-fitted for an English type of function, as demesne centres. It is much easier to explain them as having a military purpose, to accommodate the soldiers guarding the borders in time of war. They do not need elaborate buildings in a large courtyard, especially if many are foot-soldiers, and this is what was found at Duneight. This is the purpose which also is likely for a few lesser stone castles in Ulster, those like Seafin, Co. Down (fig. 16). This castle is probably the castle of Maycove whose construction by the Justiciar of Ireland took place in 1252.[36] Brian O Neill attacked and destroyed it the next year,[37] but it was refortified in 1254.[38] It consists of the re-fortification of a former hilltop rath with a polygonal stone wall, enclosing a courtyard about 30 metres across, with a stone tower or keep attached.[39] It was built well outside the Earldom in a traditional site where the castle of Maycove was in use in 1211-12;[40] the earlier one has been plausibly identified with the nearby motte and bailey of Ballyroney.[41] It was always meant to serve, whether it was a motte and bailey or a stone castle, as a base for troops from the Earldom along the way between it and the Cenel Eoghain to the west. The other sites are at Doonbought, built over an Irish fort[42] (plate 8A), Court McMartin, Cross and possibly Connor (fig. 16). The last

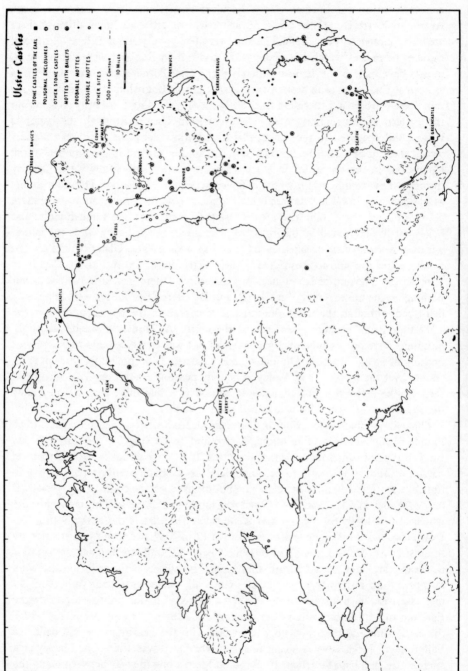

15 Map of castles in Ulster

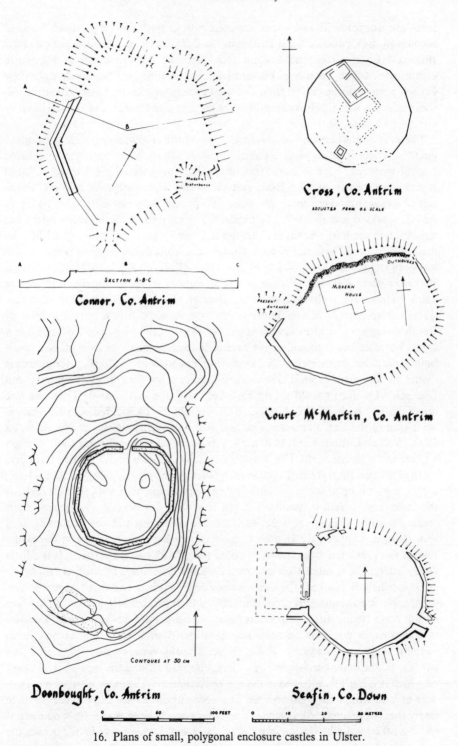

16. Plans of small, polygonal enclosure castles in Ulster.

three are unexcavated and Cross completely destroyed and only known from an account in the Ordnance Survey Memoir for Ballymoney parish. Occupation of the sites at least of Cross and Connor took place in the thirteenth or fourteenth centuries: at Cross a penny of Edward I minted in 1281 or 1282 was found, while French pottery of the period from Connor castle is now in the Ulster Museum. All these sites are small polygonal enclosures either on the borders of the Earldom or else, like Connor, outside it.

The provision of castles like this in Ulster and the employment of these troops to guard districts implies several points. First of all we must note the centralised control involved. The main tenants of the Earl may well have wanted to build strong stone castles on their lands or even mottes with baileys for soldiers. In the settled areas, however, there are none except the possible motte and bailey at Ardkeen, which was in the Earl's hands.[43] The only stone castle which might not have been in the Earl's hands and was not in a remote area is Dunluce (plate 8B). Its drum towers with base batter have always been considered Anglo-Norman and it has been suggested that it was built as a caput of his appanage by John de Burgh, Richard's son, who was given a group of manors in north Antrim probably in 1308.[44] However, in the minister's accounts of John's widow Elizabeth, Dunluce (Dundrif) appears as part of Dunseverick manor, while it is shown that John de Burgh was given Coleraine castle (Appendix Three). He had no need to build a new caput, but if he had it should surely have been called a manor of its own. Nor was it built earlier, for when Henry de Mandeville was allowed £112. 10. 0 for guarding castles in Twescard from 1258-62, these castles were Coleraine, Drumtarsy and Lochkel;[45] Dunluce should surely have been one if it had existed. There are two other castles, both in Co. Antrim, which might be considered as stone castles belonging to the Earl's tenants. The first is the very curious site at Portmuck, on Island Magee. Little remains of it: a short length of curtain wall along the cliff edge, a tower and a latrine shaft. The tower is a curious one, two barrel-vaulted chambers (with plank centring) abutted against each other on the ground floor, while the later, northern part is open at the end; in effect there is no northern wall, the side towards the courtyard. It had a chamber on the first floor, evidenced by a latrine shaft coming from it. There were walls leaving the tower to east and west at the southern end: there was apparently an arch to the west, perhaps the entrance to the castle. East of the tower lies what has been called since 1683 the 'sallyport'.[46] It is a little square turret, little more than one metre square internally, divided in two by an arch: one half is blocked, the other narrowed by corbels to a shaft about 30 cm. square. No man could sally from this shaft, which incidentally leads to a fifty-foot cliff: it was a latrine turret with shafts from courtyard and first-floor levels. The date is unknown: it was defaced according to Bagenal in 1568.[47] The second is on Rathlin Island, now known as Robert Bruce's castle, again on a clifftop site. It has two wards, the inner surrounded by an irregular wall around the near-stack of basalt on which it is built. It is linked to the rest of Rathlin and the outer ward by a narrow neck of land which has been bisected by a rock-cut ditch with sides so regular as to imply that they supported a bridge. The outer ward is large (some 40 × 60 metres) and cut off by a ditch. On the inner edge was a wall with a tower at either end, the southern one of which is partly preserved, showing a strong base batter. The plank centring to the larger tower, and the latrine tower at Portmuck, or the flanking towers with the base batter at Robert Bruce's are all atypical of fifteenth century castles in Ulster, which one would expect to be simple tower houses and bawns. But they may well date, as Dunluce appears to do, from the later fourteenth century, or from the early fifteenth. Certainly Robert Bruce's, with its command of the sea-routes to Scotland, would fit the needs of MacDonnells (who gained control in 1399) well: it seems an odd place for the main Byset castle in the days of the Earldom. They owned Rathlin, certainly, but it was not the centre of their power. Again Island Magee has no candidate to make it an important centre: none of the men we know of who owned land there was from an important family. The Earl seems not to have allowed his main vassals to build stone castles: if he had, they should be in places such as the Six Mile Water valley, not Rathlin. Dunluce is well sited but apparently later; if it is rejected, the other sites are less convincing.

Secondly, there is the question of dates implied in this story. While Ballyroney was probably considered obsolete in the 1250's by the Justiciar and therefore replaced by a stone castle, this was recent. The defences of Twescard county, not occupied until the 1230's or 1240's, were organised around motte castles, but none appears to have been built in connection with the advance in north Co. Londonderry at the end of the century. Apparently mottes became militarily obsolete in Ulster only in the second, or even third, quarter of the thirteenth century. They still were recognised as castles long after: Dundonald was described as such in 1333,[48] and the Antrim castle of Elizabeth de Clare's minister's accounts (Appendix Three) was probably the motte which is still there.

Thirdly, there is the overall strategy as portrayed here, to be compared with the interpretation of the motte distribution of western Co. Down as 'military works designed to hold a frontier'.[49] This interpretation assumes that mottes necessarily imply an Anglo-Norman presence, and that they could not have been built by Irishmen, a view which is open to doubt as discussed in Chapter Six. But it would also make impossible demands on the military organisation of the Earldom. The garrisons of 1212 were, as noted above, 10-40 men, yet the west Co. Down mottes are nearly ten miles of hilly country apart. To prevent Irish raiders passing between them would have needed many more men on patrol and in reserve and much better communications. It would have needed a regular army, not a feudal levy with small bands of footmen hired for the occasion by the week. The bases proposed here, around Antrim town, or at the entry to Lecale, for example, are much closer (about two miles apart) and much nearer the larger castles of Dundrum or Antrim.

The Earls always made use of Irishmen to fight their wars. John de Courcy depended on Irish help from his initial conquest, as we noted above. The soldiers of the 1212 Pipe Roll, as we can see from their mantles and payment in cows, were largely Irish. The King also summoned Irish kings to English wars: many from Ulster were summoned in 1244.[50] In 1260-61, Brian O Neill and the men of Ui Tuirtre still owed £100 and £200 respectively for aid to the King in the Gascon war of 1253-54,[51] while there were more sommonses in 1314.[52] These summonses were sometimes answered, as in 1297 when Cu-Uladh O Hanlon and Aenghus

MacMathgamhna were killed when coming back from Flanders,[53] or in 1303 when the Annals of Ulster record that both Gall and Gael went to Scotland with the Earl of Ulster. The position is formally summarised in the Inquisition of 1333, where the number of men whose service each Irish king owed to the Earl of Ulster is listed.[54] The major northern king not on the list is O Donnell. The number of men called satellites totals 345, also, somewhat naively, equated in money terms as £355.

This list is presumably both a formalisation of earlier, less precise agreements and the basis of the force of soldiers known as the Bonnacht of Ulster, an actual near-standing army. As such it survived the end of the organised Earldom to become a bone of contention between the later Mortimer Earls and the O Neills, who absorbed it into their own mercenary galloglas forces, in the fifteenth century.[55] This force was not unique in Ireland in the late thirteenth century. Maurice FitzThomas, Earl of Desmond, had a force of Irish mercenaries whom he billeted on the south-west in the 1320's.[56] In Connacht Aedh O Connor was killed in 1310 by one Seonac McQuillan, a mercenary in his pay, but who in this case was paid more for his treachery by Aedh's rival for the kingship.[57] Seonac McQuillan then joined William de Burgh, the Earl of Ulster's cousin, and was billeted on Sil Murray, which Richard de Burgh had tried to seize earlier, but Seonac himself was killed in the next year.[58] The name of McQuillan is connected with the Bonnacht of Ulster from this time onwards along with that of de Mandeville, although not, as Curtis thought,[59] because they were the same people. In 1387 Thomas de Mandeville obtained a confirmation of a charter originally granted to his grandfather Henry, by Richard de Burgh in 1323, and confirmed in between by Lionel Duke of Clarence, then Earl by right of his wife, for Henry's son Richard, in 1346.[60] This granted to Henry de Mandeville 'the intendance of the satellites of our bonnaght of Ulster', responsible to him as they were before to William McQuillan (McHulyn). This service was not always in de Mandeville control, for in November 1331, after the arrest of Henry de Mandeville for complicity in the Earl of Desmond's rebellion, one Stephen McHoulyn bound himself in £200 to the Earl of Ulster for the 'constablerie de bonnaght'.[61] It seems clear, therefore, that Richard de Burgh formalised and placed on a regular footing the general commitment to service that Irish chiefs owed as part of their admission of the general sovereignty of the Earl of Ulster and the King of England, and created from it a regular force to be billeted on his lands. This was not the first use of such troops, as we can see from the 1211-12 Pipe Roll and the castles of the border with their provision for small garrisons, but an extension of the idea in accordance with Irish conditions. That this force was both real and valuable is shown by its later history in disputes between English and Irish.

At the head of this force and the administration of justice was of course the Earl, the main formal link between the Earldom and the English crown. John de Courcy was obviously in close touch with English ways as a man of the first generation of the conquest. Hugh de Lacy had an Irish step-mother but was clearly at home outside Ireland. Apart from this exile when he fought in southern France, he had cousins and an elder brother who held land on the Welsh marches. He interfered himself in political affairs in the Isle of Man and Galloway as well as taking part in campaigns with his fellow magnates in the rest of Ireland. The de Burgh earls were of course also lords of Connacht and as such automatically among the most important men in Ireland. Richard de Burgh probably spent much of his minority at the court of Edward I and came over to Ireland in 1280 high in favour there: he returned to be knighted at Ruddlan in 1283.[62] He took a full part in the Scottish campaigns of Edward I, leading a contingent in 1296,[63] although his contract to go to Flanders the next year was cancelled by the King.[64] He was given an important command in the 1303 campaign,[65] was present at the negotiations in the following winter[66] and was in command of the Irish troops in 1314.[67] He married his family to members of the English and Scottish nobility (Appendix Two): one daughter, Elizabeth, to Robert Bruce, another, Matilda, to the Earl of Gloucester whose sister Elizabeth married Richard de Burgh's son John. John's son was William, the last Earl to be resident. He was brought up in England and married Matilda, daughter of Henry, Earl of Lancaster.[68] (Appendix One).

These English links can be seen in the castles these men lived in. We have already seen that Carrickfergus provided John de Courcy with a splendid chamber in the keep (plate 2A) and hall in the courtyard below (figs. 3 and 4). During the thirteenth century the designers of English castles spent more effort than previously on making them comfortable to live in as well as defensible. In this they were helped by the shift away from keeps as being militarily obsolete, which allowed them the whole courtyard to devote to domestic accommodation. The hall remained the centre of the castle, as it was bound to, for it symbolised all the social and administrative purpose of a castle. It was in the hall that a lord would meet his men and administer justice, discuss local business or simply enjoy himself. Attached to the hall or near it were the kitchen and service rooms on the one hand, the lord's chapel and chamber on the other, the chamber marked out by its signs of comfort and privacy such as a fireplace and small latrine. During the thirteenth century the chamber was developed and in the grander castles divided into two – the great and the private or privy chambers – to give the lord a suite of lodgings, the one for informal business and eating and the other for sleeping, while other suites were also built for his wife or a principal guest. The castles and houses of Henry III, from the 1230's on, show this trend first, as is to be expected from a man notorious for his appreciation of good building and love of comfort.[69] We can see it at such places as Westminster or Clarendon, where he rebuilt the private accommodation with great and privy chambers for himself and Queen Eleanor but left alone the halls he inherited from his predecessors.[70] These examples have the chambers built in a sprawling, unplanned complex, but towards the end of the century at major castles such as Ludlow or Chepstow the chambers are gathered into blocks at one end of the hall, to give separate suites of rooms on different floors.[71] The whole way these castles were lived in with the public, ceremonial hall as the hub for a series of chambers for the lord and his guests is portrayed in the fourteenth century poem 'Gawain and the Green Knight'. In the second section, especially stanzas XXXV-VI, Gawain is welcomed at Sir Bertilak's castle. He is taken by the servants from the gate to the hall, where Sir Bertilak's squires and knights are gathered. There Sir Bertilak greets him, having come from his chamber to meet this distinguished guest

properly, in a formal way. Gawain is then taken off to his chamber, away from both
Sir Bertilak's and the hall. Thereafter there are public events only, like feasts in the
hall: the private action happens in the chambers.

Previously we looked at Greencastle, Co. Down, as an example of Hugh de Lacy's
solutions to military problems (fig. 7). The point was made that it was constructed
by him and that it was a castle whose defence was based on its curtain walls and
towers, not on a keep. The building usually known as the keep[72] was a large first-
floor hall standing in the middle of the courtyard, entered at the west end and with
its dais at the east, marked by the fireplace, the window arrangements and small
latrine. South-west of this was a complex tower at the corner of the courtyard with a
number of rooms not interconnecting, which was different from the simpler
northern towers. The aim seems to have been partly to have a large tower at this
point of approach from the ferry to Carlingford, but also to provide a series of
private chambers for members of Hugh de Lacy's household. At the north-east
tower there was a different building. Here, after the secondary works already
outlined, there was a private chamber on the ground and first floors and a great
chamber, marked by the added stairs, latrine and lobby on the first floor. North and
west of the hall, reached from the smaller of its two doors, were probably the
kitchen and service buildings. It is a coherent set of buildings providing a full range
of thirteenth century living accommodation for Hugh de Lacy in the hall, great and
private chambers, and for his retainers in the other private chambers.

In the 1240's Henry III converted the castle at Ludgershall in Wiltshire into a
comfortable hunting lodge attached to the forest of Chute.[73] The castle had two
ringworks, of which only the northern one concerns us here as far as the results of
the excavation carried out in 1964-72 can tell. Unfortunately less than half of this
has been excavated, but the general plan seems clear. In the centre Henry rebuilt
the hall, probably as a ground-floor building, apparently with a dais at the east end.
North of this, over the former defensive inner bank, he built a new great chamber at
first-floor level, with a service room at the east and attached to a private chamber in
a pre-existing tower to the west (fig. 7). This latter was marked by a fine south-
facing window, a fireplace and a small latrine. The great chamber had a large
fireplace, part of which was found in the rubble of the sixteenth century
destruction, and was served by a large latrine off the lobby between it and the
private chamber. No kitchen refuse was found in the area around the east end of the
hall or the chambers: presumably the kitchens were at the other side of the
courtyard. The hall is dated to 1244-46 by documentary evidence because its
dimensions, given that the south buttress is a mid-wall one, correspond to those of
the hall which Henry ordered in the first year, and which was finished by the
second,[74] while the chamber was linked to it stratigraphically.

Greencastle, Co. Down and Ludgershall are thus very close in time, and the
parallels between them are striking. The same units of hall and greater and lesser
chambers are not only present but are in very similar relative positions. There are of
course differences, mainly in the hall, narrower (because unaisled?) and on the first
floor at Greencastle, but the principles which govern the design are the same. Hugh
de Lacy wanted a hall for public business, a great chamber for day-to-day living,

and a private chamber to sleep in. He also had to provide for members of his household or principal guests in the angle towers, the whole grouped irregularly around the courtyard whose shape was dictated by defensive needs.

Richard de Burgh built Greencastle on the Donegal shores of Lough Foyle in 1305, as we have noted above, to further his plans for penetrating the area. The site (fig. 17) is on a rock platform but this was too small to accommodate the castle as it was planned. As a result the gatehouse is below it and so has its first floor at the level of the main courtyard: the gate-passage leads only to a small lower courtyard from which steps lead up to the main one. The castle is oval in plan, with the gatehouse at one end and a large polygonal tower dominating the other at the north-east. There are three possible sites for the great hall of the castle where consideration of its domestic use must start. Waterman, in his account of the castle,[75] on which all other accounts, like this one, must be based, suggests that it was along the north wall next to the gatehouse, but the position is cramped between the curtain wall and the lower, entrance courtyard. Its south wall changes both in width and direction halfway along, suggesting two rooms and not a single hall. The second possibility is on the south side of the castle, where a large block of latrines would indicate a public building of some sort, although it might be for a block of lodgings. The site would have been a difficult one, for rock outcrops along this part and would make levels awkward.

The best site is along the north wall next to the large north-east tower. There are six windows here, three on the ground floor with undifferentiated dressings, and three on the first floor with sandstone ones; there were probably at least two more in a broken section of wall. These windows clearly mark an important room, for the windows, although not very wide, would seem to be something of a threat to the castle's safety along the main flank open to attack: it is unlikely that the garrison could have been assumed to be large enough to have a bowman at each window. The first floor was obviously marked out by its sandstone as the more important, but this raises a structural problem. There is still an offset for the floor to the west of the easternmost of the three windows, but not between it and where some toothing marks the line of the west wall of the tower, now missing. The offset itself might have been omitted, because a mural stair rises from the window embrasure, causing the builder to decide not to risk thinning the wall. There are no joist-holes or chase, however, so it would appear that the first floor here either stopped or at least the joists changed direction. There seems to have been a wooden, spere truss against the wall here, presumably dividing the first-floor room to the west from a passage leading to the staircase. This last presumably led to the wall walk, or the second floor of the north-east tower, or both.

The north-east tower is a large, polygonal structure cut off from the courtyard by a wall, now destroyed but clearly marked by a line of toothing in the north curtain wall. This wall presumably contained the stair to the first floor, which apparently did not communicate directly with the second floor or wall-walk. The position south of this north-east tower is interesting, with two parallel walls leading from it to a latrine tower, the outer wall curiously being the narrower. There is no latrine at courtyard level, but it looks as though there was a chamber at first-floor level with access to it, perhaps the only access to it. This arrangement is probably connected with a question raised by Waterman[76] of an earlier building represented now by a stray latrine chute in the circular foundation of the north-east tower. The thinner, outer wall south of the tower is not, in its lower courses, bonded into the tower and may therefore be an afterthought. The latrine chute itself is blocked nearly about three feet up, the blocking apparently being built in with the foundation. The whole can be explained as a small change of plan during the building, with a decision not to provide the first floor of the north-east tower with a latrine but to link it to the one to the south. The result was to provide at the first floor a suite of rooms, a great chamber in the tower with a private chamber and latrine off it.

The most impressive part of the castle now remaining is the great twin-towered gatehouse (plate 4A). The ground floor, like the rest, is much ruined, and is also choked with fallen masonry, so little can be said about it. There is little sign of a stair to the first floor and it seems to have been, at least in part, storage rooms or the like at the rear, and guardrooms to the front. The first floor is ruined, but enough remains for a legitimate attempt to reconstruct its arrangements (fig. 17). The basic design is of two polygonal chambers in the twin towers linked by two rooms behind. The larger of these is marked by a large fireplace in the wall which separates it from the south tower chamber. This fireplace extends across the line of the wall separating the south tower from the room over the entrance passage, so this rear chamber must have extended over the entrance passage as well. The line of the wall with the fireplace continued right across the gatehouse, as is shown by the toothing of its junction on the north wall. The rear chamber might have extended across the width of the gatehouse as well, but it is more likely that there were two rooms. If so, the position of the two doors and the sections of walling with no toothing on the north-east wall leave no other possible position for a dividing wall than along the line of the north wall of the gate-passage. The other assumption we can make is that the front half of the gatehouse would have been at least broadly symmetrical, and so we can postulate a wall between the chamber over the gate-passage and the one in the north tower. The part for which evidence is completely lacking is the south side. This involves the large latrine tower at the south of the smaller entrance courtyard which clearly was reached at first-floor, as well as at ground-floor level: not from the side of the large outer courtyard but from the gatehouse. If there were a stair and latrine turret attached to the south tower similar to that on the north, it might both cover and give access to the south tower cellar which appears a very curious feature.[77]

The visual appearance of the castle with polygonal towers outlined by polychrome masonry has been rightly compared with the great Edwardian castle at Caernarvon.[78] The overall planning can also be likened to Caernarvon, with the gatehouse at one end and the large polygonal tower at the other. In detail there is a close parallel between the layout of the accommodation of the gatehouse at Greencastle and that of another Edwardian castle gatehouse, Harlech. The reconstruction thus proposed (fig. 17) gives us five chambers, labelled A-E on the plan. The system on which each is organised is the same. There is a lobby at the entrance (A) which leads to a great chamber (B) marked by the large fireplace, and

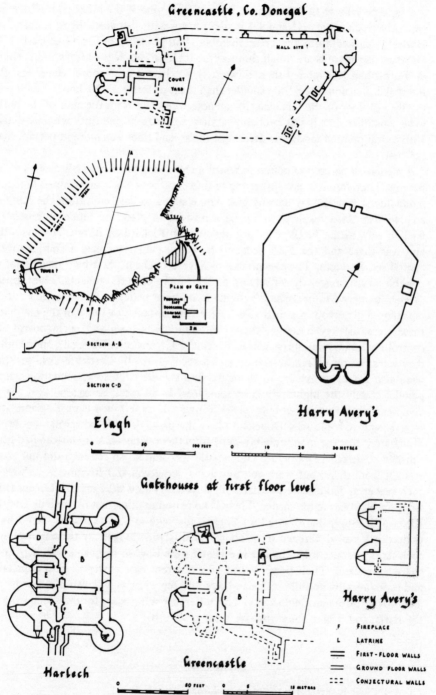

17. Plans of Greencastle, Co. Donegal (after Waterman); Elagh castle, Co. Londonderry; Harry Avery's castle, Co. Tyrone (after Jope).

access, especially at Greencastle, to the double latrine at the other end. There are two private chambers (C and D) in the towers with, between them, a chapel at Harlech, reached from the great chamber, but probably not at Greencastle. At Greencastle the walls are much thinner (the Irish had no siege engines and Richard de Burgh had less money than Edward I), so there are no mural chambers: the internal dimensions are a little smaller than those of Harlech. We know even less of the second floor of the Greencastle gatehouse, reached from the stair of the north tower chamber, but it was probably similar: to judge by the finer window detail, with trefoil pointed sandstone dressings, the second floor was more important than the first.

A mediaeval baron was bound to resent anyone who threatened his control of his barony. Therefore it is not surprising to find successive Earls determined to harass landholders, whether lay or religious, who claimed to hold land from the King or anyone else. As a result it would be a mistake to place too much emphasis on friction such as the FitzWarins' arguments with Richard de Burgh. However, the aim was there and the Earls seem to have been able to create a comparatively centralised Earldom. They seem able to have brought in their own men as far as possible to administer it, not relying on their more powerful tenants. They appear to have managed to organise a systematic military policy and enforce it on their tenantry. This involved a dual role for their major stone castles. On the one hand these were the key bases on their communications lines and springboards for controlling new conquests (as with Coleraine or Greencastle, Donegal); on the other they were centres of administration and justice, especially Carrickfergus, but they were also places to live in. In them we find standards of accommodation which parallel closely the highest English standards. In all cases, as was pointed out in Chapter Three, this probably involved bringing an expert over from England. It is clearest with Greencastle, Donegal, where the parallels with Edwardian castles in Wales show that the man probably came from there. The work at Harlech had been finished some ten years before Greencastle was started, so the man did not come straight from there: but work continued at Caernarvon and Beaumaris, as well as such castles as Kildrummy, either built directly by Edward I or, like Greencastle, along similar lines to his castles. There is no reason to think that if Hugh de Lacy or Richard de Burgh had invited an English magnate to visit them, he would have noticed any real difference from houses in England. Judged by their houses and their family connections, the Earls of Ulster were English magnates who happened to live in Ireland. Their power rested on a different base however, both politically and economically, and life in Ireland was different, just as a Welsh marcher baron was different from an English one. This difference was greater for their tenants than the Earls, and it is to them that we must now turn.

NOTES

1. A. J. Otway-Ruthven: *A history of medieval Ireland*, pp. 181-7.
2. *Calendar of Justiciary Rolls, Ireland*, II, pp. 11, 63; III, pp. 50, 56; cf. *43rd Report of the Deputy Keeper*, *P.R.I.*, p. 21.

3. Constable of Carrickfergus castle in 1216-23; see above, in Chapter One.

4. *C.D.I.,* II, no. 860.

5. *Calendar of Justiciary Rolls, Ireland,* II, p. 195; *Calendar of Close Rolls, 1307-13,* p. 546.

6. British Library *Add. mss. 6041,* items 14 & 55.

7. F. M. Stenton: *The first century of English feudalism,* chapter 2.

8. W. Dugdale: *Monasticon Anglicanum,* VI (2), pp. 1124-5; W. Reeves: *Ecclesiastical Antiquities,* pp. 191-2.

9. British Library *Add. mss. 6041,* item 57; *C.D.I.,* II, no. 1918.

10. *C.D.I.,* II, no. 1918.

11. *Annals of Ulster,* 1281; *C.D.I.,* II, no. 2049.

12. J. F. Lydon: *Irish Sword,* V, pp. 212-3.

13. *Calendar of Justiciary Rolls, Ireland,* II, p. 33.

14. *Ibid.,* p. 216.

15. M. Altschul: *A baronial family in medieval England,* p. 286.

16. *Calendar of Justiciary Rolls, Ireland,* I, p. 214; II, pp. 11, 56; III, pp. 50, 56.

17. *C.D.I.,* I, no. 1468; G. H. Orpen: *J.R.S.A.I.,* XLIII-XLV, 1913-15.

18. *C.D.I.,* I, no. 259.

19. *Ibid.,* II, no. 1918.

20. British Library *Add. mss. 6041,* item 57: he is rewarded with a carucate of land by de Burgh.

21. *Calendar of Justicary Rolls, Ireland,* II, pp. 63, 135; III, p. 56.

22. *Ibid.,* II, pp. 33-4.

23. *C.D.I.,* III, no. 665; *Calendar of Justiciary Rolls, Ireland,* I, p. 132; cf. R. A. Stalley: *Journal of the British Archaeological Association,* CXXXI, 1978, p. 39.

24. *39th Report of the Deputy Keeper, P.R.I.,* p. 28; *Calendar of Justiciary Rolls, Ireland,* III, pp. 40, 41, 60.

25. *C.D.I.,* II, no.'s 661, 668.

26. *Ibid.,* no. 952.

27. Armagh Public Library, ms. G.II.13 f 9; A. J. Otway-Ruthven: *J.R.S.A.I.,* LXXXIX, 1959, p. 7.

28. *C.D.I.,* II, no. 950.

29. O. Davies & D. B. Quinn: *U.J.A.,* IV, 1941, pp. 61-3.

30. D. F. Renn: *Norman Castles in Britain.*

31. C. W. Dickinson & D. M. Waterman: *U.J.A.,* XXII, 1959, pp. 67-82.

32. D. M. Waterman: *U.J.A.,* XVII, 1954, pp. 103-68.

33. O. Davies & D. B. Quinn: *U.J.A.,* IV, 1941, p. 57.

34. D. M. Waterman: *U.J.A.,* XXVI, 1963, pp. 55-78.

35. O. Davies & D. B. Quinn: *U.J.A.,* IV, 1941, p. 57.

36. *C.D.I.,* II, no.'s 32, 54; *Annals of Ulster,* 1252.

37. *Annals of Ulster,* 1253.

38. *Analecta Hibernica,* II, pp. 262ff.

39. D. M. Waterman: *U.J.A.,* XVIII, 1955, pp. 83-104.

40. O. Davies & D. B. Quinn: *U.J.A.,* IV, p. 57.

41. H. C. Lawlor: *U.J.A.,* I, 1938, pp. 84-9.

42. T. E. McNeill: *U.J.A.,* XL, 1977, pp. 63-84.

43. *C.D.I.,* I, no. 1264; *36th Report of the Deputy Keeper P.R.I.,* p. 54.

44. G. H. Orpen: *Ireland under the Normans,* IV, p. 149.

45. E. Curtis: *Proceedings of the Royal Irish Academy,* XXXIX (C), 1929, p. 10.

46. G. Hill: *The MacDonnells of Antrim,* p. 280.

47. H. F. Hore: *U.J.A.,* (1st series), II, 1854, p. 157.

48. G. H. Orpen: *J.R.S.A.I.,* XLIV, 1914, p. 63.

49. *A.S.C.D.,* p. 105.

50. *C.D.I.,* I, no. 2716.

51. *National Manuscripts of Ireland* (ed. J. T. Gilbert), plate 73.

52. *Liber Munerum publicorum Hiberniae,* (ed. R. Lascelles), I (IV), p. 5.

53. *Annals of Loch Cé,* 1298.

54. G. H. Orpen: *J.R.S.A.I.*, XLV, 1915, p. 141.
55. E. Curtis: *Hermathena*, XXI, 1931, pp. 87-105.
56. A. J. Otway-Ruthven: *A history of medieval Ireland*, p. 249.
57. *Annals of Ulster*, 1310.
58. *Ibid.*, 1311.
59. E. Curtis: *Proceedings of the Royal Irish Academy*, XLIV (C), 1938, pp. 99-113.
60. *Calendar of Patent Rolls, 1385-89*, p. 309.
61. British Library *Add. mss. 6041*, item 100.
62. G. H. Orpen: *Ireland under the Normans*, IV, p. 139.
63. J. F. Lydon: *Irish Sword*, V, 1962, 184-90.
64. G. H. Orpen: *Ireland under the Normans*, IV, p. 144.
65. H. Johnstone: *Edward of Carnarvon*, p. 89.
66. *Ibid.*, p. 92.
67. *Liber munerum publicorum Hiberniae*, (ed. R. Lascelles), I (IV), p. 5.
68. *Clyn's Annals*, 1328.
69. H. M. Colvin et al: *A history of the King's Works*, I, pp.99ff.
70. *Ibid.*, I, pp. 494-504; II, pp. 910-18.
71. P. A. Faulkner: *Archaeological Journal*, CXV 1958, pp. 176-8.
72. *A.S.C.D.*, pp. 211-19.
73. P. V. Addyman: *Medieval Archaeology*, XII, 1968, fig. 47; XVI, 1972, pp. 183-4.
74. *Calendar of Liberate Rolls, 1240-45*, pp. 234, 307; *1245-51*, p. 32.
75. D. M. Waterman: *U.J.A.*, XXI, 1958, pp. 74-88: the plans in fig. 17 are based on this.
76. *Ibid.*, p. 86.
77. *Ibid.*, p. 81.
78. *Ibid.*, p. 85.

5

The Earls' Tenants

WE can distinguish several grades of tenants in the Earldom, as we would expect, according to the tenure by which they held their land. At the top of the pyramid were the holders by knight service, and then those who held by suit of the county court or of the fortnightly manorial court. Next there were the farmers who paid rent for lands and the burgesses who held also mainly by rent. At the bottom were the cottiers (few are known) and the betaghs: no gavillers[1] are recorded in Ulster. The knight service, as we saw in Chapter Four, may well have involved real military service as well as scutage payments and prestige. By the time of the Anglo-Norman conquest of Ireland the concept of a standard knight's fee in each lordship was beginning to be accepted.[2] It can perhaps be seen in Ulster, in the 1333 Inquisition. In the Six Mile Water there are single fees at Ballynure (Twywys), Ballylinny (Lyn), Ballywalter (Waltirton) and Ballyrobert (Robertiston).[3] These lie regularly about two miles apart in a line along the strip of land between the Six Mile Water and the hills, two miles to the south: perhaps two square miles was considered a reasonable knight's fee in Ulster. King John appealed in his writ of 1204 for John de Courcy's arrest to the barons of Ulster (*baronibus Ultoniae*):[4] those men who were the most important of the Earl's tenants. Like their twelfth century equivalents in England they were not a formally constituted body, but nonetheless most contemporaries would probably have been able to name at least some of the families concerned.[5] We can try to see them from the men who witnessed charters of the successive Earls, and from other lists, such as hostages for John de Courcy in 1205,[6] those summoned to Parliament in 1310,[7] or the holders of knights' fees in 1333.[8] Many people on these lists are simply mentioned once and not again: incidental appearances of lesser men or else men whose name was not carried by sons and grandsons. At the other end of the scale four families stand out as pre-eminent in the Earldom: Savages, de Logans, Bysets and de Mandevilles.

Two of these leading families are associated with John de Courcy, the Savages and the de Logans. One William Savage witnessed a de Courcy charter[9] and provided his son Robert as a hostage for him in 1205. A Robert Savage, presumably the same, was granted lands by Hugh de Lacy in Dalrod (probably Dalriada, i.e. in Twescard).[10] These lands were probably those which were the subject of the Inquisition held in 1276[11] after Henry's death, for he was Robert's son and received them from Walter de Burgh as such.[12] Valued at £63. 10. 4 in 1276 (although the escheator actually accounted for only £50. 7. 8¼ for the two years before February 1277),[13] they were presumably near Bushmills (Portkaman), where the Inquisition was held. Richard Savage, called to Parliament in 1310, held $1\frac{1}{16}$ knight's fee at Ballylough (Loghton),[14] two miles from there. No Savages appear to witness an Earl's charter other than de Courcy's, yet they are clearly of considerable importance, and presumably in some favour with Hugh de Lacy to be granted their large Twescard estate. After the murder of the Earl in 1333, Robert Savage became the chief man in Ulster: the only one to sit on two 1333 Inquisition juries,[15] seneschal of Ulster in 1334[16] and in 1347 granted estates in the Six Mile Water valley for his services.[17] The de Logans seem to have retained the confidence of the successive Earls rather more than the Savages. Walter de Logan witnessed a charter for John de Courcy[18] and was captured at Carrickfergus defending it for Hugh de Lacy in 1210.[19] Robert de Logan witnessed charters of Richard de Burgh and his court in the 1280's.[20] The next generation is represented by John de Logan; son of Alan, summoned to Parliament with Adam de Logan in 1310 he was presumably the man who distinguished himself fighting Edward Bruce in 1316:[21] a Henry de Logan was pardoned in 1319, however, along with Robert and John Savage, for joining Bruce.[22] Their centre appears to have been along the upper parts of the Six Mile Water valley. In 1333 William de Logan held a knight's fee at Ballylinny (Lyn) and another at the nearby but unidentified Balyhaghan, while Ralph held one at Ballywalter (Waltirton).[23] In the 1306 Taxation Ballywalter was called Walter de Logan's town,[24] while nearby was Hugh de Logan's town (Templepatrick).[25] John de Logan was involved in the Earl's murder in 1333 and burned Carnmoney in the troubles after it.[26] Their later history is very obscure, but it is curious to note that there are still Logans common in that part of Co. Antrim.

We have already noted how Hugh de Lacy brought the family of the Bysets into the Glens of Antrim in the 1230's or 1240's. The Inquisitions of 1278[27] involved two John Bysets, father and son, but it was a Hugh Byset who seems to have been the most active member of the family: capturing cows for O Flynn, King of Ui Tuirtre in 1259,[28] with William FitzWarin beating off the O Neill/de Mandeville raid on Carrickfergus in 1273,[29] and witnessing charters at Richard de Burgh's court.[30] It is is unlikely that this was the same Hugh Byset who was summoned with John, William and Hubert Byset to Parliament in 1310 and whose lands were confiscated for adherence to Bruce in 1319.[31] The Bruce invasion proved a crisis for the family, with their lands particularly vulnerable to Scottish depredations and their own Scottish links perhaps still alive. We do find Bysets acting against the Scots and Bruce: John, in 1307, commanded a fleet looking for Bruce in the Isles;[32] Hugh was given £20 in 1297[33] and £500 in 1300 for services in Scotland[34] and joined with John Logan in attacking Bruce successfully in 1316.[35] However, unlike other Ulster lords, Hugh Byset was not pardoned for (presumably later) joining Bruce, but his lands of Glenarm and Rathlin granted to John de Athy,[36] the Anglo-Norman admiral in Ireland and constable of Carrickfergus castle. As a result, the only Byset to appear in 1333 was Robert, juror for Carrickfergus county and holder of half a knight's fee at Craigarogan, near Templepatrick, Co. Antrim (Le Crag).[37] The Bysets recovered their lands after John de Athy's death, however, and they had passed by marriage to John MacDonnell by 1399.

The first de Mandeville we hear of in an Ulster context is Robert, who came over to Ireland with King John[38] and who witnessed a charter of Hugh de Lacy in about 1224.[39] The family flourished and, although it is not true that all the lawsuits we know of from Ulster involved a de Mandeville, a majority did. They also provided a number of key officials for Walter and Richard de Burgh in particular. Henry was

Sheriff of Twescard in 1259-62, appointed by the future King Edward and rendering the accounts there already discussed; it was his refusal to hand over Twescard to the Seneschal of Ulster, appointed after Walter de Burgh's death in 1271, which led to the troubles with William FitzWarin. He was killed in these soon after 1272 but his sons carried on the fight.[40] In the succeeding years there are three important men in the family, of whom one is William, Seneschal of Ulster in 1277,[41] Sheriff of Down and Blathewic in 1281,[42] witness of de Burgh charters[43] and probably a principal in lawsuits between 1305 and 1308.[44] Robert and Thomas de Mandeville, the latter Seneschal of Ulster by 1281,[45] were apparently Henry's sons, for they gave sureties against renewing war against FitzWarin, among whom was the same William de Mandeville.[46] Thomas was Richard's chief soldier, leading an expedition against Cenel Eoghain in 1283[47] and commanding the Earl's contingent of the army sent to Scotland in 1301:[48] he led a relief expedition to lift Bruce's siege of Carrickfergus in 1316 but died in the fighting in the town.[49] His prominence is reflected in his position at the top of the list of Ulster tenants in Parliament in 1310, and it carried with it other profitable offices: he was collector of Carrickfergus customs in 1313.[50] Henry de Mandeville[51] then becomes prominent; he was not summoned with Thomas to Parliament in 1310, presumably because of his age. He was made Constable of the Bonnacht in 1323, was Seneschal of Ulster, and was *custos pacis* in the bishopric of Down in 1327, and in 1331 when he was arrested for murder and complicity in the Earl of Desmond's rebellion.[52] These problems for the family were as nothing, however, compared to those which followed the murder of William de Burgh in 1333. According to Clyn,[53] although he was actually killed by Robert FitzMartin and Robert FitzRichard de Mandeville (with John de Logan), the murder was instigated by Richard de Mandeville and his wife, a view certainly believed by William de Burgh's widow, Matilda, in 1337, when she put a price of 100 marks on their heads.[54] It is not clear whether this Richard was the son of the arrested Henry, still in Dublin gaol in November 1333[55] (and therefore with a good alibi himself), but that would help to explain Richard's dislike of the Earl. In the history of the Bonnacht of Ulster, given when it was granted to Thomas de Mandeville in 1387, he is described as the son of Richard de Mandeville (granted the Bonnacht in 1346), who was the son of Henry, granted it in 1323 and, as assumed above, the Seneschal arrested in 1331.[56] It is difficult to devise a chronology to allow this Richard to be old enough to be the father of Robert FitzRichard, the murderer of 1333, and yet also of Thomas, granted the Bonnacht of Ulster in 1387: presumably Robert the murderer is the son of another Richard de Mandeville[57] The crisis of 1333 did however help Henry: in 1334 he was organising the defence of Greencastle, Co. Down, against the Irish.[58] A John de Mandeville helped to avenge the murdered Earl later in 1333.[59] The exact relationship of all these men seems now to be lost.

The lands of the family were scattered over the whole of the Earldom, according to the 1333 Inquisitions and other sources. In Twescard the ex-sheriff Henry de Mandeville's lands are mentioned in 1275-76,[60] while Richard held $1\frac{1}{2}$ knights' fees at an unspecified place probably in that county (to judge by its place in the order of the list) and $\frac{1}{20}$ of a fee at Dunluce: John FitzJohn held a fee at Dunaghy at the south of the county.[61] In Antrim county, Richard held a further fee at Ballykennedy: Robert FitzRichard, one of the murderers named by Clyn, held a fee at Donegore, while Thomas FitzHugh shared one with John Sandal at Ballynure.[62] In Carrickfergus county, a Lord de Mandeville (Richard?) held a fee at Ballyrobert, while Robert held six carucates in Belfast.[63] In Blathewic county, William de Mandeville gave an acre near Comber to St. John the Baptist, Downpatrick;[64] de Mandeville lands near Killyleagh (eight carucates) and at Castlebeg, Groomsport and Ballyphilip were confiscated in 1333.[65] In Down county, Henry de Mandeville's lands at Castleward had been confiscated.[66]

This group of pre-eminent families all have individually differing histories in Ulster. The Byset lands seem to have been mainly concentrated along the east coast of Co. Antrim, and the Logans in the Six Mile Water valley, although members of both families are found outside; for instance Henry and Thomas de Logan were tenants of Henry Savage in Twescard.[67] The Savage lands seem to have been centred on Twescard, but they acquired considerable lands in Antrim county in the 1340's.[68] The de Mandevilles, however, had considerable interests everywhere in the Earldom. The prominence of these last in the administration of Richard de Burgh is also exceptional. Logans are found witnessing charters of John de Courcy, Hugh de Lacy and Richard de Burgh, and are found in other important roles, such as being summoned to Parliament in 1310, but do not seem to have been chosen for official positions. The Bysets have a similar history, although, in spite of his original political association with them, they do not witness Hugh de Lacy's charters: their involvement in Scottish wars is ambiguous and they seem to be employed more by Edward I and II directly than by Richard de Burgh. The Savages are the most curious in this respect, for William witnessed a charter of John de Courcy and gave his son Robert as hostage in 1205, but none witness a charter of Hugh de Lacy although, like the Bysets, Robert Savage benefited from his conquest of Twescard, and they drop completely out of the de Burghs' favour. They were still powerful, as shown by Richard's summons to Parliament in 1310 and their assumption of power after 1333 and the de Mandeville eclipse, but were on bad terms with the new family of the Earls.

These families were pre-eminent but not sharply demarcated from others. There was John Talbot who held a whole knight's fee and came from a family whose members had witnessed a single charter of each of the Earls, but whose names never seem to occur in other records.[69] The Sandals seem to have belonged to a rising family who came to Ulster with the de Burghs. William de Sandal and his son Thomas were the recipients of six pieces of land mainly in Twescard in the years around 1300:[70] in one, William is described as a clerk. John Sandal shared a fee at Ballynure with Thomas FitzHugh de Mandeville.[71] Patrick Sandal held one quarter of a fee in 1333 at Ballyaghran, near Coleraine, which seems to be the same land as Elias Cendal unsuccessfully claimed from Hugh de Beumes in 1280-81:[72] he appears in the 1350's as Elizabeth de Burgh's bailiff of Antrim. The Sandals seem to have followed a path from the Earl's service to the land. Of the other tenants, almost all our information comes from the 1333 Inquisition, where we find three types of tenure often overlapping: by suit of the county court, the fortnight court, or by fee farm. The men who hold land by suit of county court alone have the biggest holdings, at least a carucate, and do not often owe any other kind of service, except in Antrim county where they owe 1/- or 2/- for the land as well. Those who hold by suit of the manorial fortnight court normally owe a money rent as well. They are a very mixed bunch. The suitors of the fortnight court at Doagh included Hubert Byset who held a carucate and also owed 3/4, John de Rydale who had a reasonable holding at Ballyeaston and owed by suit of court only, and John le Masoun who held ten acres and also owed 1/-.[73] We can tell very little about the farmers except that they were common. The size of the holding and individual bargains of tenure were clearly more important than these categories.

Unfortunately we can say next to nothing about the origins of these men before they came to Ulster, except for the Bysets who came from Galloway. It is below this level of society that the craftsmen and traders lived, whose work we saw in Chapter Three, men like John le Masoun with his ten acres at Doagh. As we saw then, these men seem to have come from north-west England, if they were masons or potters, unless like one group of the latter they came from other parts of Ireland.

All these tenants, and indeed, as we saw in Chapter Three, nearly everyone in the Earldom, depended for their livelihood on the produce of the land. The lands they are recorded as holding, their manorial centres and indeed the parish churches all lie in the lower parts of the country below the 500-foot contour line. There is other evidence of exploitation of the uplands: pollen cores from Beaghmore 600 feet up in Co. Tyrone[74] and a series of high north Antrim sites, notably Altnahinch Burn,[75] c. 800 feet above sea level, show forest clearance associated with cereal production broadly datable (by Carbon 14 methods) to the Anglo-Norman period. These are probably to be explained as the result of summer grazing on the hill pastures when some spring corn was often sown. These indications apart, we must examine the mechanisms which were used to solve the basic economic problem as we saw it solved in Chapter Three: how to organise the mixed lowland agriculture of Ulster and market the produce.

All through our accounts the basic unit for this task is the manor, as it was all over feudal Europe. It is therefore at the manors that we must look. Most of our information on these is derived, because of the nature of our sources, from the lands of the Earls. Here, where we might expect centralised manors of the English demesne farming, such as probably existed in south-east Ireland,[76] the manors are more dispersed settlements. In 1333 the Earl's manor of Dundonald apparently included his lands at Holywood.[77] This had once been a settlement held by burgage tenure: it also lies some five miles away on the other side of the Craigantlet hills. As noted above, John de Rydale was a free tenant of the Earl in the manor of Doagh in 1333, holding lands at Ballyeaston (Austynestoun) by suit of the fortnight court at Doagh.[78] Doagh is again some five miles away, but we also know more about John de Rydale's holding because he died in the next year. An inquisition held as a result[79] found that John de Rydale received some £8 per year from rents and issues, profits of his court and mill (the largest item) and four shillings from his tenants' work services. The church of Ballyeaston was valued more highly than that of Doagh in 1306.[80] Neither Holywood nor Ballyeaston in 1333 belonged to the manors of Dundonald or Doagh in an economic or settlement sense. These manors were fiscal centres, places where tenants went to pay rent or deal with minor crime and administration: they were not villages. The situation can be seen in 1282[81] when de Mandevilles burned William FitzWarin's manor of Croscarnadry with five of its 'circumjacentes villae'. There is, of course, no means of knowing whether or not these vills were themselves any more or less nucleated than the manorial 'centres'.

The demesne land, where it is mentioned at all, appears in almost all accounts as parcelled up into rent-paying parcels of lands usually named. The distinction appears to be one of tenure, by rent alone and therefore probably without security, as opposed to holding by suit of court. In Henry Savage's large manor in Twescard, according to the Inquisition held after his death in 1276, there were 18 carucates of demesne, which was worth £55-3-4 from the issues of its rents, mills and other issues: there was no income from villeinage (i.e. work services). There were also free tenants paying £8-7-0 and tenants by suit of court.[82] Some of these rentals could be remarkably stable. In 1259-62 Henry de Mandeville accounted for £2 received from the 'villa' in Twescard called La Père.[83] This is almost certainly the Stantone, a free tenancy in Coleraine county, worth £2 in 1327 and 1333,[84] and the Stanton, in the manor of Bushmills, rendering £2 per annum between 1353 and 1359.[85] Over a century this value has not changed: it cannot be anything but a rent. This raises the same question as Henry Savage's manor does. If most of the lands we find recorded are rented, down to quite small parcels like the 80 acres of demesne, also at Stanton, worth one mark between 1353 and 1359, how was this rent paid? It is possible that we have a system of small farms marketing their own produce for money which then goes to pay the rent, but this would be to propose a remarkable market economy. Not only is it unlikely but it would need a very different coinage than the one we find. An alternative is suggested by the account of one of Henry de Mandeville's frauds of the 1260's and 1270's. The jury at the Inquisition into his behaviour in Twescard before 1272 complained that 'he had false measures to receive rents in corn from the farmers'.[86] The system employed to grow the corn in Ulster which kept the mills profitable was not the direct demesne farming of Midlands England and the settled manorial system, but one of leasing out parcels of land on a basis of rent-paying in kind.

That it was an organisation as outlined here that formed the basis of rural settlement in the Earldom receives support from the remains of the mottes found in it. It is clear from the numbers of mottes surviving (fig. 15) that they were a normal feature of the landscape in the Earldom. They were built in Ulster by men who were the heirs of at least a century of practice in England and who must have had a fair empirical knowledge of earth construction as part of their normal military education. We can best see this facility at work at the small motte at Dunsilly, two miles north of Antrim town. Here a motte was about to be destroyed for farm improvement in 1974, and so it seemed best to destroy it archaeologically first, by cutting it in half, to find out how it was constructed.[87] It had been built on a former house platform set against the bank of a rath, disused and grass-grown by this time, at a point where the rath bank overlooked a low but steep drop to the Dunsilly

Burn. It was by no means a crude dump construction but one whose aim was to have a stable mound after a very short period for settlement. The side of the house platform facing the drop was reinforced with a double layer of large field stones, while the rest was levelled with a layer of clay. The ditch was then excavated and the spoil from it piled on the inner edge to the same height as the rath bank: it was distinguishable from the rest of the mound material because the ditch had cut through occupation layers of the former rath. The result was a ring around the intended motte perimeter, mostly composed of unconsolidated ditch spoil but partly made of the old rath bank, grassgrown and stable. The motte was then brought to its full height at the side away from the rath bank, by tipping the soil against this stable bank. Finally the last material was tipped, working in from this first high point to cover the rath bank. As a result the edges were all at an angle of rest, while the major tip lines all rested against the one consolidated piece of earthwork in the construction, and the whole rested on a firm base. The bulk of the material did not come from the ditch (it was less than two metres deep): it was probably derived from quarrying the bank down to the stream to steepen the approach on that side. The results were clearly a success: the profile of the motte on the undamaged north side was still very steep in 1974, while the section (admittedly not precisely vertical) through the motte stood through the wet winter of 1974-75, with very little collapse, because it was, by a stroke of luck, aligned along the tip lines. The motte must have been usable within a very short time of construction: curiously, it never was. What must be emphasised here is that there is no reason at all to consider this motte an important one: the expertise displayed here must have been normal. We can perhaps see a similar construction uncompleted at Piper's Fort, in Co. Down,[88] where the builders may have intended to fill in the hollow and make a small motte.

Of the approximately 120 probable mottes in Ulster,[89] seven have been excavated. This proportion is lessened by the discovery that the top of the motte on Coney Island, Co. Armagh, was too disturbed to tell us anything.[90] The motte at Castleskreen, Co. Down, appeared never to have been used,[91] while the motte top at Dunsilly was covered with a spread of stones, on which a small fire had been lit but that was all. Some 90% of the area of the top was excavated and the site was not eroded, for over it had grown a soil which was used as the base for a nineteenth century summer house: we can be sure that it was not used after its erection. The excavations at Ballyroney, Co. Down, were limited to a trench six feet wide across the top, less than an eighth of the area:[92] Dromore likewise was only partially excavated.[93] Clough and Lismahon mottes were fully excavated.[94] The results of excavations, therefore, apply in effect to a sample of less than 5%. The earliest 'phase' at two sites, Clough and Dromore, consisted of a central hollow and its filling, while at Ballyroney two levels of occupation were separated by a layer of soil thicker in the centre which might be the same thing. If these sites had been built like Dunsilly, with a ring bank filled in, these hollows might be no more than the result of initial settlement of the mound material. Dromore, Lismahon and Clough all produced similar evidence of defences. The perimeter was defended by a palisade, reinforced at Clough and Lismahon by pits in which archers could stand

and fire without having to expose themselves over the palisade top. At Lismahon there was a timber tower marked by its large post-holes: at Dromore there seems to have been a slighter one, while at Clough a later stone tower may well have succeeded a timber one of the earlier phases.

The two completely excavated mottes, Clough and Lismahon, produced quite similar results about the residential aspects of the sites: in both cases there was more than one period involved. At Lismahon the first period saw the erection of two buildings within the defences of tower, palisade and archer's pit. One was a rectangular, rather hut-like house beside the tower, the other was a smaller, subsidiary one, interpreted as an iron-workshop or smithy. Both the tower and the workshop survived into the second period, but the house was demolished and in its place, over the filled-in archery pit, was a true hall building. This was divided by a double screen on either side of the door in the long wall into a service chamber on the left and the main body of the hall, with its hearth towards the far end, to the right. At the end of the hall away from the door was a further partition marking off a small private chamber from which the tower was reached. The plan of the hall as published,[95] which includes posts 20 and 24, implies that it was internally divided into two aisles: these two posts however might well have belonged to the earlier house, leaving the hall to be a clear room approximately 20 feet square. The workshop's iron-smelting pit was filled when it was rebuilt, but it was still used for some activity involving fire;[96] it may well have become a kitchen. The results from Clough were comparable although more complex. Here the hall was built after an initial primarily defensive phase with mortared stone walls rather than the timber and sod walls of Lismahon hall; it had clasping buttresses, and one door (the one on the side of access to the hall from the bailey) had neatly dressed jambs with stopped chamfers. It was, however, (to judge from the burnt straw derived from its destruction) thatched. The doors, because of the hall's position, were not opposite each other: the main one was about one third of the way along the south wall, the other approximately midway. There was no clear evidence of internal partitions, unlike Lismahon. In the destruction debris was much burnt wattle and daub, which the excavator interpreted[97] as the upper parts of the wall filling. Some may have been from partitions, for it would seem unlikely that there were none. This hall, as the excavator pointed out, seems to have been very little used before its destruction by fire: it lacked a proper floor and a hearth.

The possibility that the arrangements at Lismahon and Clough were typical for Ulster mottes receives support from field survey.[98] Here there are few details which may be noted and all are, of course, liable to distortions unknown until excavation. Two of these details are the height of the mound and its breadth across the top, from which we can see their proportions. It must be a rough and ready exercise; erosion by nature or man, collapse of revetments or the later raising of the mounds could all affect any individual site: some sites may not be mottes at all. It is the only way, however, that we can compare the mottes of Ulster with those built elsewhere. The sites in the table below[99] have been divided into five groups by the proportion of the height to the diameter of the top: in group A, it is 1:1; group B, 1:2; group C, 1:3; group D, 1:4; and group E, 1:5 or more. The figures are percentages of the total. In England apparently few are in group A but quite a number in B or C.[100]

Region	Total	A	B	C	D	E
N.E. Wales	43	25	27	29	4	15
S.W. Wales	39	10	51	26	7	5
Scotland	49	4	12	24	14	44
Ulster	116	1	18	28	22	31

The proportion of sites in group C is very similar, but otherwise there is a division between the two Welsh groups on the one hand, most of which are narrower for their height than 1:3, and the Scottish and Ulster mottes which are broader. Ulster mottes are perhaps not much lower than others; following Continental surveys, Cathcart King was able to use 10 metres' height to define the largest mottes in England.[101] In Ulster, the highest three (Donegore, Co. Antrim; Dromore, Co. Down and Managh Beg, Co. Londonderry) are respectively 11 +, 12.2 and 9-15 metres high, only just coming within the limit. A proven motte, such as Lismahon, varies in height over the surrounding land from 6 metres to as little as 3.3. The mean size for mottes in Ulster is that of the site at Duncrue, Co. Antrim, whose height is 4.3 metres and the diameter of whose top is 14.6 metres: most in England are about 5 metres high.[102] Ulster mottes are generally broader and lower in proportion, however; the reason probably lies in the halls of Clough and Lismahon. If these were normal, the mottes had to be broad to provide space, not for a tower as in England or elsewhere, but for a hall. If, then, they are so broad they will tend to be lower, partly because of the earth-moving involved in producing such a platform at a height, but also for convenience. It is one thing to have a refuge tower you hope to use but rarely perched at the top of a steep climb; it is another to have your home up there and have to climb it daily.

In Chapter Four, we noted the comparative rarity and selective distribution of baileys in Ulster, which was explained as being the result of baileys being used for troops. As outlined above, the normal landlord's house, the hall, would be safe on its motte, but it would be alone in being so. If he had a barn or a byre, these would apparently be left not even protected by a bailey bank and ditch. The oddity of this is heightened by the rarity of the moated sites, which seem to be the normal manorial settlement in the more intensely Anglo-Norman south-east of Ireland. These sites are not very strong militarily but they do at least surround a fair-sized courtyard with a ditch so that theft from the buildings within is made much more difficult. In Ulster these sites are very rare. One cannot simply include all the square or squarish enclosures in the land, for most are more likely to be raths, whose plan can vary from the circular to the square. Some are seventeenth century bawn enclosures: there could be a link between the raised interior angles of such a site as Ballycarrickmeddy, Co. Antrim,[103] and artillery forts with two angle bastions.[104] Perhaps the best, or even the only, candidate for such a site is the now destroyed earthwork at Ekenhead, Belfast.[105] Yet Ulster, as we saw in Chapter Two, is all march country very liable to raids, and it seems incredible that manorial buildings would have been less well protected here than in other parts of Britain or Ireland.

G

If we put the documentary and archaeological evidence together, we can produce a conjectural picture of the way of life of the tenants of the Earl with whom we started this chapter. Unfortunately it is impossible to be sure of the owners and builders of the mottes we can list now, but they seem to include the upper tenants at least. As we saw in Chapter Four, the Earls appear not to have allowed their tenants to build stone castles, while as important a castle as Antrim seems always to have been a motte. How low in the social scale one could have found a man with a motte is quite unknown, but Lismahon was probably owned either by the bailiff of Christ Church, Dublin,[106] or the Earl's tenant who held two carucates there by suit of the county court at Down in 1333.[107] The men who owned them seem to have been living in a hall, fortified by being placed on the motte, and so at least riot- or raid-proof, but not the centre of a centralised farm. They exploited their land, as did the Earls, by leasing it out on a basis of crop-sharing or rent in kind. The actual farming seems to have been done in smaller units, smaller certainly than the manors, and probably even than the carucates and other parcels we find composing them. The main item of centralisation in the farming pattern must have been the mills which the lord of each small estate seems to have had, to judge from John de Rydale at Ballyeaston and the mills which rendered or are mentioned by Elizabeth de Burgh's ministers in the 1350's, at vills within the manors. These vills are the places that mattered in day-to-day life rather than the larger, purely fiscal unit of the manors. The documents stress the manors because the clerks were trained to draw up accounts like that, not because they were the key things.

We can trace this system back to the 1211-12 Pipe Roll. The expenditure and income recorded there is connected usually with large castles, but apparently one section applies to Dundonald manor;[108] expenditure on a mill at Villa Owaveran which follows it. This name applies to a place which appears in the 1333 Inquisitions as $5\frac{1}{2}$ carucates of demesne;[109] before 1218 it had been held by John de Courcy's constable, Roger of Chester.[110] It is to be identified with Ballyoran, which was a parish in 1307,[111] and is about $1\frac{1}{2}$ miles from Dundonald. This is a separate vill, not part of a centralised manor. Again, in 1212 Roger Pipard accounted for '1042 coombs of flour for the fourteenth year, from the fixed rents of the small manors (minutis maneriis) of Ulster',[112] surely the same as the 'circumjacentes villae' burnt in 1272.

The system goes back apparently, therefore, to the time of the Anglo-Norman conquest. When he took over land, John de Courcy (or Hugh de Lacy) established a manorial centre for his own administration, but then divided the land among his followers to hold by various tenures in vills which were fiscally and administratively dependent on the manor, which might itself be some miles away, but no more. These tenants lived, on a motte if they could, off fixed renders from the men who actually farmed the land. The corn went to the mill to be ground from many different farms, therefore, and the flour would either be sold there or taken to the lord of the vill's motte, possibly in small amounts as the rent fell due. He therefore had no need of large barns by his motte. The whole process seems very deliberate: the vills and manors, like the counties in which they lay, appear to have served their purposes well, for they lasted long. The holders of the vills do not seem to have rushed up their mottes in a hurry. If you visit all the mottes of Ulster, there gradually grows on you a fair respect for their builder's eye for country. They are almost always sited to combine defence and domesticity effectively. They defer to the needs of the first by being on a hill or ridge or at the edge of a scarp. The approach is usually not precipitous on all sides, however, and a normal means of access is clear: it will be easy to walk up but hard to run and usually well in sight from the motte for at least two or three hundred yards. Very rarely indeed is there an alternative site nearby: they almost always pick the best available. These vills seem to fit the landscape well and the system of rents fits the social system of the Irish that they found. These fixed renders cannot in fact be new at all but based on what the Irish lords took as food renders from the farmers when the Anglo-Normans arrived. If this was the way that the Anglo-Norman conquest worked in Ulster, intensifying the Irish agricultural productivity (see Chapter Three) but not changing its structure, it would explain why no-one has found, after thirty years of mediaeval archaeology in Ulster, deserted mediaeval village remains even at known centres now deserted like Kilclief or Greencastle, Co. Down, or any sign of ridge and furrow in the fields. It would explain how Dundonald manor could still be functioning in 1333, when its buildings had been burned by the Scots at least fifteen years before.[113]

This Irish base can be seen in the continuity of the divisions of the land from before John de Courcy's time to our own. If we look at the land grant of that time to the Bishop[114] and Abbey[115] of Down and to Christ Church, Dublin,[116] we find that the charters simply give lists of names. The names are of places, translated by the clerks into Latin as 'villae', which need no further definition: there is no delineation of boundaries as in Anglo-Saxon charters, for example. About one half of these vills can be identified with modern townlands in the area of Lecale and the south Ards. When marked on a map of the townlands (fig. 18), they seem in fact to group into larger blocks of land, the estates of the churches concerned. Some of the modern townlands are now divided (e.g. Upper and Lower Ballybranagh or Ballyclander), while the four vills of Christ Church have become three townlands.[117] It would therefore be too extreme to use this evidence to state that the modern townlands existed in the 1170's: some at least are known to have been decided on during the first Ordnance Survey of the 1830's.[118] What we can see, however, is that behind the vills of the Church in Lecale, the vills of the Earl's tenants and the modern townlands probably lies a common unit: the block of land which a group of Irish of the pre-Norman period farmed.

The real element of continuity, the fate of the Irish who lived in and around the Earldom, we must leave for the next chapter while we look at the evidence of life in towns in Ulster. This immediately raises the somewhat tiresome question of what a town is. It is not a village, for it has a market and it has permanent institutions to distinguish it from a seasonal fair. In Ireland we must beware of equating these institutions alone with a town in any social or economic sense: what Glasscock calls[119] the 'rural borough' was simply an administrative device to tempt English settlers to new Irish villages by the offer of burgage tenure and freedom. The problem of distinguishing villages from towns is made more difficult by the absence

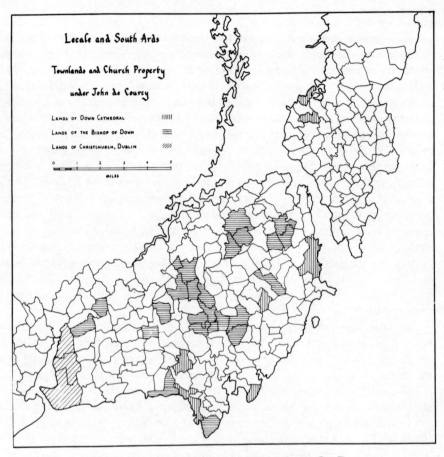

18. Townlands and church estates in south-east Co. Down.

of any reference to markets or charters granting the right to hold them in any of the boroughs listed. Thomas FitzLucian was granted the right to hold a weekly market at the otherwise unknown vill of Molendinis in the Ards in 1260.[120] The nearest we get are references to tolls, tout court, in the 1350's at Coleraine, Portrush and Antrim, perhaps market tolls. The question of size is another one which is clearly important. It has often been assumed since Orpen[121] and Bateson[122] that the customs of Breteuil, which were certainly prevalent and granted to the largest Irish towns, were universally applicable in Ireland. If so, the population could always be calculated on the basis of one burgage per shilling of rent.[123] It seems clear that this did not apply in the towns of the Earldom. The figures of money received from boroughs are all highly conventional. In 1326 and 1333[124] the valuations of boroughs were as follows in ascending order:

	1326	1333	
Newtownards (Blathewic)...	3/4	3/4	
Carnmoney (Coule)........	10/-	0	
Belfast (LeForde)........	£1- 0-0	0	
Holywood	£1- 6-8	13/4	
Greencastle	£2- 0-0	0	
Larne (Dunmalys)........	£8- 0-0	£2- 0-0	(includes 800 acres let)
Carrickfergus	£2-16-8	£2-16-8	

The figure for Newtownards is shown to be conventional and not related to population by the agreement of 1297 between the Abbot of Movilla and Richard de Burgh. [125] Here they agree to commute the farm of the town and its mills, which had been 40 crannocks of oats, to six marks per annum. Another deal had clearly been done between then and 1326. The burgesses of Antrim are recorded as paying only two pence per burgage in 1358-59, [126] probably as a result of a recent agreement, for the figure has changed since 1353.

In spite of these provisos we can, and must, try to sort out, from the fifteen places in Ulster which are called boroughs, the ones which may have been towns in a modern social or economic sense. That some never graduated is clear. The Bishop of Down was granted the right by John de Courcy to make boroughs at Kilclief and Maghera, Co. Down. [127] In the escheator's account of 1305, Kilclief had burgesses paying rent but Maghera does not figure. [128] Richard de Burgh gave Limavady (Roo) to James Stewart, including its castle and borough, in 1296. [129] In 1333 the fortnight court, lands and mills appear, but no burgages. [130] These presumably never came to anything: both were marginal settlements. Seven we can class along with Glasscock's rural boroughs, settlements which were stable and institutionally boroughs but part of the agricultural, not the marketing, side of the economy. In 1293 Richard de Burgh granted his brother the town mill and five carucates of land at Carnmoney (Coule); the community of the place made an agreement with de Burgh in 1300. [131] In 1333 Càrnmoney was back in the Earl's hands but valued very low, as seen above: its main value must always have been in those five carucates of land. In the 1333 Inquisition the burgesses of Dunmalys owed rent for 800 acres of land as well as their burgages, [132] so they must have been a very agricultural community. At the same time, Holywood's burgesses held 80 acres [133] and the boroughs of Belfast and Greencastle were clearly very much overshadowed in value by the agricultural lands of the manors attached to them. [134] At Kilclief in 1305 the burgage rents were included in the renders of the mills, court and fifteen carucates and ten acres of land. [135] The men of Bushmills (Portkamen) are called burgesses in 1272, [136] but in the 1350's Elizabeth de Burgh's ministers [137] account only for agricultural renders, principally from the nine carucates of the tenements.

Three places seem to be more than rural boroughs, yet it is difficult to be sure of their status. Newtownards was the centre of a county from the early days but is very little referred to in documents. If the Abbot of Movilla was in control (see above), this may be the reason, for the Earl would then be less interested. The Dominicans chose it as one of their friary sites, with Coleraine, when they came to Ulster in 1244, and the house flourished enough to be the site of general chapters. [138] Portrush is curious, for it would not really be thought of any consequence but for the evidence of Elizabeth de Burgh's ministers. As at Bushmills, its men are called burgesses in 1272,[139] but this is all the other evidence; it was worth a reasonable amount in the 1260's.[140] In the 1350's[141] we hear of a mayor who rendered the accounts of 1354 and 1358-59, and tolls produce 2/- per annum through the years. It was a fishing port − a prise of fish also is a regular item − and these tolls may be harbour dues for the boats, but it was probably a trading port as well. Men from Portrush traded to the Western Isles in 1338 and 1357.[142] The evidence for Antrim is again confined to the one source,[143] although the castle was important early and it was the seat of a county. In 1358-59, however, there were 80 burgesses paying rent (in earlier years there were fewer because of war) and again tolls appear in 1354 and 1358-59. There could be no ferry or even bridge tolls at Antrim, for the Six Mile Water can be easily forded there, so these may be market tolls. There are grounds for postulating a pottery industry near Antrim. In the 1350's we seem to have a fair-sized town by Irish standards here which is inland and not a port, the only one in Ulster (fig. 9).

Coleraine was clearly an urban centre. Its early history as a military base for the conquest of Twescard we noted in Chapter One: it went on to become the centre of the county's administration. The burgages and the Earl's demesne were worth £11-10-4 in the 1259-62 de Mandeville accounts,[144] and only 3/4 less in 1350's.[145] Then the burgages (the *assisis villae*) are £4-0-0 per annum, while there are tolls paid either on the port or market and also on the Bann bridge. The town's commercial activity is witnessed by the ship, the *Grace Deu* of Coleraine, trading to Gascony in 1317, in spite of the Bruce wars.[146] The port was presumably the exporting point for the fisheries of the Bann, at Coleraine itself and at Lyn (the Cutts two miles upstream), which we saw in Chapter Three to be a considerable source of income. Another cause of its prosperity must have been the bridge over the Bann, erected in 1248.[147] It may have been broken down in 1315,[148] but there was a bridge in existence in 1381 when it was repaired.[149] We learn that it had towers at both ends, an Ulster example of a fortified bridge, like a little Pont Valentré at Cahors.

Downpatrick offers a contrast to the rest in that it was largely a religious centre. Its origin lay back in the days before John de Courcy, both with religious houses and probably also as the capital of the Kingdom of Dal Fiatach: curiously, it never seems to have had a castle of the Earls, probably because of its 'neutralisation' as an ecclesiastical centre (Chapter One). Its religious houses and topography have already been fully discussed elsewhere.[150] The main problem is that the only fixed point we know is the cathedral inside the former hill-fort; all the other places are unidentified. The problem can be seen in a grant of land by John de Courcy whose boundaries run 'from the walls on the right of St. George's to the curia of St. Columba; from St. Columba's along the road to the Cross of St. Monninna; and from there to the walls'.[151] This might well define a block of land beside the present line of English Street leading to the cathedral ('the road'), but there is no evidence. If a later de Courcy grant of 1202-05 is to be believed, some parts at least were very densely built up, for he grants three burgages there, of which two are described as stretching from the street to the river and being 120 feet long and 8 feet wide.[152] This last must be a mistake, however, although the picture of long, narrow plots perhaps from English Street again down to the Quoile marshes is a reasonable one. The town was defended, however; that is clear, although 'muri' (walls) could easily have referred to a bank and ditch. The defences were either in need of extending or, more likely, repair in 1260, for after their good service at the Battle of Down, the mayor and citizens were granted relief from the £5 they owed the King each year, in order to enclose the town.[153] The main wealth of the town, with its mayor and defences, was derived from the churches and monasteries listed by Reeves.[154] Apart from the cathedral and Benedictine abbey which served it, there was a house of regular canons, dating from pre-Norman times; two canons' houses founded by John de Courcy; a Franciscan friary, founded by Hugh de Lacy; and a nunnery of unknown date. It had a commercial side, however. There was the pottery near the cathedral hill, hardly a unique kiln. Although Strangford was named in a list of 1275-82 of the Ulster customs ports as the only one in Lecale,[155] in 1376 Robert Savage was appointed Collector of the Customs at Coleraine, Carrickfergus and Downpatrick.[156]

Carrickfergus was clearly the most important place in the Earldom. We saw in the last chapter its role as the caput of the Earl's administration, and its castle figures largely from the early years of John de Courcy. Unlike Downpatrick, it was not a place dominated by religious houses: there was the Premonstratensian house founded by de Courcy, a Franciscan friary founded by Hugh de Lacy, and a small hospital of unknown date. Its parish church, however, was the largest by far in Ulster that we know of, and almost certainly served as a pro-cathedral for Connor diocese. It had, of course, a mayor who reported on de Mandeville/FitzWarin troubles, lining himself up on FitzWarin's side.[157] Its trading role can be seen in the establishment of an exchange for foreign merchants there in 1251.[158] A Carrickfergus man was a member of the Dublin gild of merchants in 1256-57.[159] When the Ulster customs are farmed they are referred to as the Customs of Carrickfergus.[160] In 1308 Thomas le Mercer of Carrickfergus was joint-owner, with a Drogheda man and two Gascons, of a ship wrecked at Beaumaris on her way from Gascony with a cargo of wine.[161] Evidence of its internal trading or manufacturing role is confined to the pottery industry probably located there (Chapter Three), the two mills of 1406 and before,[162] and some ironworking remains found in Market Place in 1972. It has received the most systematic archaeological examination, in the years since 1972, of any town in Ulster. The excavations have shown a continuity of property boundaries from mediaeval times to the present in both the modern Market Place and High Street:[163] the former has the characteristic triangular mediaeval plan. The plots are aligned on these streets which form the core of the present town and so its inner street plan goes back at least to the mediaeval period. Unfortunately the sealed groups which would date these remains closer have not so far come to light. Again without any considerable remains of the mediaeval buildings preserved for the excavators, as with the lack of dated deposits, few results can be given here. As yet we can say little about the burgess housing, either in detail, or as to whether there was any social segregation: beyond the inner core, we cannot even say how far the occupation extended. We are still in no position to compare town conditions in Carrickfergus with those of English towns, or the life in Carrickfergus between the thirteenth and fifteenth centuries.

NOTES

1. A. J. Otway-Ruthven: *J.R.S.A.I.*, LXXXI, 1951, pp. 11-12.
2. A. J. Otway-Ruthven: *J.R.S.A.I.*, LXXXIX, 1959, p. 10.
3. G. H. Orpen: *J.R.S.A.I.*, XLV, 1915, p. 139.
4. *C.D.I.*, I, no. 225.
5. F. M. Stenton: *The first century of English feudalism*, Chapter 3.
6. *C.D.I.*, I, no. 259.
7. M. V. Clarke, in *Fourteenth century studies* (ed. L. Sutherland & M. McKisack), pp. 31-2.
8. G. H. Orpen: *J.R.S.A.I.*, XLV, 1915, pp. 139-40.
9. W. Dugdale: *Monasticon Anglicanum*, VI(2), p. 1124.
10. British Library *Add. mss. 6041*, item 19.
11. *C.D.I.*, II, no. 1328.
12. British Library *Add. mss., 6041*, item 20.
13. *36th Report of the Deputy Keeper, P.R.I.*, p. 32.
14. G. H. Orpen: *J.R.S.A.I.*, XLV, 1915, p. 139.
15. *Ibid.*, XLIII, 1913, pp. 136, 141.
16. *Patent and Close Rolls, Ireland* (ed. E. Tresham), p. 38B.
17. *Calendar of Patent Rolls, 1345-48*, p. 298.
18. W. Dugdale: *Monasticon Anglicanum*, VI(2), p. 1124.
19. *C.D.I.*, I, no. 476.
20. *Calendar of Patent Rolls, 1334-38*, pp. 304-5.
21. *Annals of Ireland* (ed. J. T. Gilbert), II, p. 298.
22. *Calendar of Patent Rolls, 1317-21*, p.313.
23. G. H. Orpen: *J.R.S.A.I.*, XLV, 1915, p. 139.
24. W. Reeves: *Ecclesiastical Antiquities*, p. 64.
25. *Ibid.*, p. 66.
26. G. H. Orpen: *J.R.S.A.I.*, XLIII, 1913, p. 137.
27. *C.D.I.*, II, No. 1500.
28. *De L'Isle and Dudley mss.*, I, pp. 31-2.
29. *C.D.I.*, II, no. 952.
30. *Calendar of Patent Rolls, 1334-38*, pp. 304-5.
31. *Ibid.*, *1317-21*, pp. 211, 313.
32. *C.D.I.*, V, no.'s 610, 627.
33. *Analecta Hibernica*, II, p. 235.
34. *Calendar of Justiciary Rolls, Ireland*, I, p. 305.
35. *Annals of Ireland* (ed. J. T. Gilbert), II, p. 298.
36. *Calendar of Patent Rolls, 1317-21*, pp. 271, 313.
37. G. H. Orpen: *J.R.S.A.I.*, XLIII, 1913, p. 136; XLV, 1915, p. 139.
38. *C.D.I.*, I, No. 406.
39. *20th Report of the Deputy Keeper, P.R.I.*, No. 35: in view of Hugh de Lacy's position in 1224, this charter might well be several years later than that date.
40. *C.D.I.*, II, No.'s 929, 1918.
41. *De L'Isle and Dudley mss.*, p. 32.
42. *C.D.I.*, II, No. 1918.
43. *Calendar of Patent Rolls, 1334-38*, pp. 304-5.
44. *Calendar of Justiciary Rolls, Ireland*, II, pp. 11, 63; III, pp. 50, 56.

45. *C.D.I.*, II, No. 1918.

46. *C.D.I.*, II, No. 1918.

47. *C.D.I.*, II, No. 2049.

48. J. F. Lydon: *Irish Sword*, V, 1962, pp. 212-3.

49. *Annals of Ireland* (ed. J. T. Gilbert), II, p. 350.

50. *39th Report of the Deputy Keeper, P.R.I.*, p. 47.

51. By this time, there were clearly many de Mandevilles in Ulster, but here I have assumed that all these Henry de Mandevilles are the same person, referred to in: *Calendar of Patent Rolls, 1385-89*, p. 308: *Patent and Close Rolls, Ireland* (ed. E. Tresham), p. 33; *Calendar of Close Rolls, 1330-33*, p. 410.

52. A. J. Otway-Ruthven: *A history of medieval Ireland*, pp. 249-50.

53. *Annals*, 1333.

54. *Calendar of Close Rolls, 1337-39*, p. 170.

55. *Ibid.*, 1333-37, p. 187.

56. *Calendar of Patent Rolls, 1385-89*, p. 308.

57. A Richard de Mandeville was *custos pacis* of the bishoprics of Connor and Derry in 1327: *Patent and Close Rolls, Ireland* (ed. E. Tresham), p. 33.

58. *Ibid.*, p. 38.

59. *Clyn's Annals*, 1333. A John de Mandeville was Sheriff of Down and Newtownards in 1327: *Patent and Close Rolls, Ireland* (ed. E. Tresham), p. 33.

60. *36th Report of the Deputy Keeper, P.R.I.*, p. 32.

61. G. H. Orpen: *J.R.S.A.I.*, XLV, 1915, pp. 139, 140.

62. *Ibid.*

63. *Ibid.*, XLIII, 1913, p. 139.

64. *Calendar of Patent Rolls, 1334-38*, p. 305.

65. G. H. Orpen: *J.R.S.A.I.*, XLIV, 1914; p. 66.

66. *Ibid.*, p. 64.

67. *C.D.I.*, I, No. 1368.

68. *Calendar of Patent Rolls, 1345-48*, p. 298; Appendix Three.

69. G. H. Orpen: *J.R.S.A.I.*, XLV, 1915, p. 140; *Calendar of Patent Rolls*, 1334-8, pp. 304, 305; *20th Report of the Deputy Keeper, P.R.I.*, No. 35.

70. British Library *Add. mss. 6041*.

71. G. H. Orpen: *J.R.S.A.I.*, XLV, 1915, p. 140.

72. *Ibid.*, p. 139; *C.D.I.*, II, No. 1782.

73. G. H. Orpen: *J.R.S.A.I.*, XLIII, 1913, p. 142.

74. J. R. Pilcher: *U.J.A.*, XXXII, 1969, pp. 73-91.

75. A. Goddard: *Studies in vegetational changes* (unpublished Ph.D. thesis, Queen's University, Belfast).

76. A. J. Otway-Ruthven: *J.R.S.A.I.*, LXXXI, 1951, pp. 1-13.

77. G. H. Orpen: *J.R.S.A.I.*, XLIV, 1914, p. 64.

78. *Ibid.*, XLIII, 1913, p. 142.

79. *44th Report of the Deputy Keeper, P.R.I.*, p. 56.

80. W. Reeves: *Ecclesiastical Antiquities*, pp. 66, 68.

81. *C.D.I.*, II, No. 1918.

82. *C.D.I.*, II, No. 1328.

83. *National Manuscripts of Ireland* (ed. J. T. Gilbert), II, plate 73; E. Curtis: *Proceedings of the Royal Irish Academy*, XXXIX(C), 1929, p. 10.

84. G. H. Orpen: *J.R.S.A.I.*, XLV, 1915, p. 129.

85. Appendix Three.

86. *C.D.I.*, II, No. 929.

87. T. E. McNeill: *Excavations 1974*, pp. 4-5; *Ibid.*, 1975-6, pp. 5-6. To this list should be added a probable motte at Tullygowan, Co. Antrim (D 073006) and a possible one at Forttown, Co. Antrim (C 928 289).

88. D. M. Waterman: *U.J.A.*, XXII, 1959, pp. 83-7.

89. T. E. McNeill: *U.J.A.*, XXXVIII, 1975, pp. 49-56.

90. P. V. Addyman: *U.J.A.*, XXVIII, 1965, pp. 78-101.

91. C. W. Dickinson & D. M. Waterman: *U.J.A.*, XXII, 1959, pp. 67-82.

92. D. M. Waterman: *U.J.A.*, XVIII, 1955, pp. 83-104.

93. *Ibid.*, XVII, 1954, pp. 164-8.

94. *Ibid.*, pp. 103-63; D. M. Waterman: *Medieval Archaeology*, III, 1959, pp. 139-76.

95. *Ibid.*, p. 148, fig. 57.

96. *Ibid.*, p. 155.

97. D. M. Waterman: *U.J.A.*, XVII, 1954, p. 120.

98. T. E. McNeill: *U.J.A.*, XXXVIII, 1975, pp. 49-56.

99. The sources for this table (apart from those of Ulster) are as follows: N.E. Wales, Royal Commission on Ancient Monuments: *Caernarvon, Denbigh, Flint, Montgomery, Radnor;* S.W. Wales, Royal Commission on Ancient Monuments: *Carmarthen, Pembroke;* Scotland, Royal Commission on Ancient Monuments: *Dumfries, Kirkcudbright, Wigtown.* Compare also the mottes of Upper Clydesdale (five or seven mottes, one with a bailey, and low and broad in proportion) – C. Tabraham: *Transactions of the Dumfries & Galloway Natural History and Antiquarian Society*, 3rd series, LIII, 1977-8, pp. 114-28.

100. D. Cathcart King: *Château Gaillard*, V, 1970, pp. 101-10.

101. *Ibid.*

102. *Ibid.*, p. 101.

103. *A.S.C.D.*, p. 169.

104. E. M. Jope: *U.J.A.*, XXIII, 1960, fig. 16.

105. E. M. Jope & W. A. Seaby: *U.J.A.*, XXII, 1959, pp. 112-5.

106. W. Reeves: *Ecclesiastical Antiquities*, p. 210.

107. G. H. Orpen: *J.R.S.A.I.*, XLIV, 1914, p. 61.

108. O. Davies & D. B. Quinn: *U.J.A.*, IV, 1941, p. 57.

109. G. H. Orpen: *J.R.S.A.I.*, XLIV, 1914, p. 64.

110. *C.D.I.*, I, No. 833.

111. W. Reeves: *Ecclesiastical Antiquities*, p. 20.

112. O. Davies & D. B. Quinn: *U.J.A.*, IV, 1941, p. 61.

113. G. H. Orpen: *J.R.S.A.I.*, XLIV, 1914, p. 63.

114. *Calendar of Patent Rolls, 1340-43*, p. 509.

115. W. Dugdale: *Monasticon Anglicanum*, VI(2), p. 1124.

116. W. Reeves: *Ecclesiastical Antiquities*, p. 210.

117. *Ibid.*, pp. 211-2.

118. This is stated, for example, in the Ordnance Survey *Memoir of Templecorran parish.*

119. R. E. Glasscock: *Irish Geographical Studies* (ed. N. Stephens & R. E. Glasscock), pp. 162-77.

120. *C.D.I.*, I, No. 665.

121. *Ireland under the Normans*, II, pp. 315-6.

122. *English Historical Review*, XV, 1900; XVI, 1901.

123. This calculation is for example followed by B. Graham: *The development of the Irish town* (ed. R. A. Butlin), pp. 43-7.

124. G. H. Orpen: *J.R.S.A.I.*, XLIII, 1913, XLIV, 1914.

125. British Library *Add. mss. 6041*, item 95.

126. Appendix Three.

127. *Calendar of Patent Rolls, 1340-43*, p. 509.

128. W. Reeves: *Ecclesiastical Antiquities*, pp. 167-8.

129. *C.D.I.*, IV, No. 338.

130. G. H. Orpen: *J.R.S.A.I.*, XLV, 1915, p. 127.

131. British Library *Add. mss. 6041*, items 33, 34.

132. G. H. Orpen: *J.R.S.A.I.*, XLIII, 1913, p. 140.

133. *Ibid.*, XLIV, 1914, p. 60.

134. *Ibid.*, XLIII, 1913, p. 139; XLIV, 1914, p. 64.

135. W. Reeves: *Ecclesiastical Antiquities*, p. 167.

136. *C.D.I.*, I, No. 929.

137. Appendix Three.

138. A. Gwynn & R. N. Hadcock: *Medieval religious houses, Ireland,* p. 228.

139. *C.D.I.,* I, No. 929.

140. *National Manuscripts of Ireland,* (ed. J. T. Gilbert), II, plate 73; E. Curtis: *Proceedings of the Royal Irish Academy,* XXXIX(C), 1929, p. 10.

141. Appendix Three.

142. *C.D.S.,* III, No.'s 1273, 1639.

143. Appendix Three.

144. *National Manuscripts of Ireland,* (ed. J. T. Gilbert), II, plate 73; E. Curtis: *Proceedings of the Royal Irish Academy,* XXXIX(C), 1929, p. 10.

145. Appendix Three.

146. *Calendar of Patent Rolls, 1317-21,* p. 94.

147. *Annals of Ulster,* 1248.

148. G. H. Orpen: *Ireland under the Normans,* IV, pp. 168-70.

149. *Patent and Close Rolls, Ireland* (ed. Tresham), pp. 115, 118.

150. W. Reeves: *Ecclesiastical Antiquities,* p. 229; *A.S.C.D.,* pp. 272-4.

151. W. Dugdale: *Monasticon Anglicanum,* VI(2), pp. 1124-5.

152. *Calendar of Patent Rolls, 1340-43,* p. 509.

153. *C.D.I.,* II, No. 661.

154. *Ecclesiastical Antiquities,* pp. 229-32.

155. *C.D.I.,* I, No. 1902.

156. *Patent and Close Rolls, Ireland,* (ed. E. Tresham), p. 91B.

157. *C.D.I.,* II, No. 952.

158. *C.D.I.,* I, No. 3201.

159. *39th Report of the Deputy Keeper, P.R.I.,* p. 38.

160. *Historical and municipal documents of Ireland* (ed. J. T. Gilbert), p. 136.

161. *Calendar of Close Rolls, 1307-13,* p. 85.

162. *Patent and Close Rolls, Ireland,* (ed. E. Tresham), p. 91B.

163. T. G. Delaney, *Excavations 1972,* p. 4; *Excavations 1974,* pp. 7-8.

6

The Earldom and the Irish

NONE of what we have discussed so far took place in a vacuum. From John de Courcy's first attack, the Earls and their tenants were faced continually with the question of their relations with the Irish who lived on the land they had conquered or would like to. Clearly the political leaders of the Irish were ejected, for example the MacDunleavys of Dal Fiatach or the O Loingsighs of Dal nAraide: the former eventually settled in Cenel Connaill, while the latter seem to have been completely suppressed. These men suffered from the invasion but, as we have seen in the last chapter, the basis of the agricultural system was Irish. The men who paid the food renders in the vills of the Earl and his tenants were hardly English peasants taking part in ethnographic reconstructions but must have been the descendants of the Irish who had worked the land before on similar terms. When the King granted two carucates from his demesne in the Ards to the Bishop of Down in 1225, he ordered that only the land should be handed over: the Justiciar was to re-settle the Irish living there on some other part of his demesne.[1] These men were the betaghs who must have been the basic workforce everywhere. The classic statement of their conditions comes from the manor of Lisronagh in Co. Tipperary in 1333.[2] Here the betaghs owed rent for seven different tracts of land, as well as work services, money for the use of handmills rather than the lord's mill, etc. Similar conditions can be seen in Ulster with segregation of the betaghs' lands from the Earl's demesne. In the 1350's there was attached to Elizabeth de Burgh's borough of Antrim the settlement of Irish Antrim, where the betaghs had just over two or three carucates for rent (the amount varies in different years) and work services commuted for money; they had separate brewers who paid a prise probably on harsher terms than the burgesses.[3] The work services were clearly light, and seem to have normally been commuted by the end of the thirteenth century as elsewhere in Ireland.[4] The betaghs' works were included with the other sources of income at Carrickfergus Manor in 1274-75 and Ballyeaston in 1333-35, where they are called works and harvest services.[5] The tenants of the Bishop of Down, however, owed no work services between 5th March and 1st July 1305, but only in the autumn: not being levied in the spring, they can hardly have been an important feature of the Bishop's farming.[6] The real exaction levied from the betaghs of the vills in Ulster was rent, as it had been before the Anglo-Normans came.

Irishmen continued to live within the Earldom at a higher social level than the betaghs', at least occasionally. In 1260, Sir Roger de Altaribus requested that he be granted the land in Twescard which had belonged to an Irishman who had been killed (this was in the aftermath of the Battle of Down) and which therefore was in the King's hands: he valued it at £2-0-0 per annum.[7] He was apparently granted it, the land in Coleraine county which had belonged to O Hageran, to hold in fee farm as had the previous tenant.[8] The 'villa O'Hatheran' rendered £2-0-0 per annum in de Mandeville's accounts between November 1261 and April 1262, when it was granted, not to Sir Roger, but Robert de Beumes.[9] De Beumes certainly had the land later, for a Hugh de Beumes won his case to have it in 1280-81 on the basis of a charter from Henry III and Lord Edward to his brother: there were then over five carucates in the holding.[10] Its eventual fate, however, is less important here than the fact that here was a relatively large holding in the hands of an Irishman on English tenure. His widow, too, was given a dowry, for de Mandeville claimed it in his expenses in the next year's account.[11] Stephen Makhoulyn, presumably one of the mercenary family of McQuillan, is called a clerk in 1353 and is found collecting rent from another Irishman, Maknanus, in Antrim and paying protection money for Elizabeth de Burgh.[12]

These instances raise the question of the relationship between the two nations in the Earldom: is there nationalistic tension apparent between them? We do not know how or why O Hagheran was killed, although his widow seems to have been treated well: if he had no heirs, then his lands would have been granted as they were. Apart from the questions of the Earl's policy, we find examples of political co-operation between Anglo-Norman and Irish lords. In 1259-60 Hugh Byset helped O Flynn, king of Ui Tuirtre, to recover cattle captured by O Cahan.[13] In the de Mandeville/FitzWarin troubles both sides had Irish help. Most of the kings of the Irish clans of the North claimed to have helped FitzWarin against O Neill and O Cahan, including O Flynn of Tuirtre, O Neill of Inishowen and MacDunleavy of Ulster.[14] On the other hand the de Mandevilles instigated men of Ui Tuirtre to kill English travelling through their country, and in 1272 we find O Flynns and O Cahans with other Irish happily burning FitzWarin's lands in 1282.[15] Thomas de Mandeville, fighting in Cenel Eoghain lands in 1283, can be called the partly Gaelic name of MacMartin in the Irish annals.[16] But these are all from occasions when a man would have been a fool to turn down help; when nationalistic prejudice would have cost even more than it normally does.

Nationalism could flourish more, perhaps, away from the hard decisions of a real world. The political and social organisation of the Earldom certainly affected the Church's arrangements. One aim was to draw up the administrative boundaries so that an official would, as far as possible, deal with men of only the one nation. The first example of this was the detaching of the diocese of Dromore, unmentioned in the synod of Rath Bresail in 1101 or of Kells-Mellifont in 1152: it had happened by 1197, probably in 1191 or 1192.[17] This was done, as noted in Chapter One, to provide for those parts of the diocese of Down not conquered by John de Courcy. In contrast the diocese of Connor was not divided; instead the deanery of Turtrye (Ui Tuirtre) was created for the Irish within it, as seen in Chapter Two. This produced a complication, for the Cathedral lay in theory at Connor in the Irish area. As a result, unlike the situation in Down, there are no references to an organised dean or chapter for Connor. The archdeacon and clergy elected the bishop in 1263 and 1321, in both cases at Carrickfergus.[18] In the 1306 Taxation only an archdeacon is mentioned, while it was the abbot of the nearby Augustinian house of Kells who had the advowson of the vicarage and rectorial tithes of Connor parish.[19] This is why St. Nicholas' Church in Carrickfergus was so large; especially perhaps it explains the enlargement of its chancel. Presumably John de Courcy had hoped to have the see moved from Connor to the caput of his principality but never managed it. Both Down and Connor had an overwhelmingly English episcopate: Down totally so and Connor, which had the first English bishop in Ireland, with only two Irish bishops Henry MacOireachty (1295-97) and James O Kerney (1324-51), as listed by Reeves.[20] On the other hand, the bishops of Clogher, Derry, Dromore and Raphoe were always Irishmen.

The deanery divisions, which reflect the conquest of Twescard but not the Anglo-Norman penetration into north Co. Londonderry, probably date from the mid-thirteenth century. They also correspond closely to the counties of the Earldom with Blathewic and Ards divided. The parish system seems also to have hardened by then. As elsewhere in Ireland, this was dominated by the sub-infeudation of the Anglo-Norman lordship.[21] The lands settled and well divided among tenants in the counties of Antrim, Carrickfergus, Blathewic and Down have many small parishes, the result of tenants of the earl each wanting to have a parish church on his holding (fig. 10). The exception, Twescard with its comparatively few but large parishes, was settled later and kept much more in the Earl's hands: his large manors alone form the parish framework. There is not 100% correspondence, however, between the fifty or so manorial centres (knight's fees, boroughs, county or fortnight courts) and the parishes of 1306. Five only have chapels, not full parishes; they include the knight's fee at Ballyrobert and the Earl's borough and castle of Belfast.[22] Seven have not even a chapel. Two are of lesser importance, half fees at Kirkistown and Ballycraigy in Twescard county. The other five are more interesting, however: two full fees, at Dunover and Rowreagh in the Ards; the large de Mandeville manor of Killyleagh; the Earl's manor at Dunseverick; and, most surprisingly, his borough and castle at Greencastle (whose ruined church is thought to be late mediaeval in date).[23] All must have lain in parishes already organised when these centres were created. It is probably significant that they lie either in the diocese of Down, where parochial development may date back to the first Malachi, or else in Twescard county, settled later.

The secular church thus showed that it could accommodate itself flexibly to the situation of a divided Ulster. The result was to formalise and perhaps harden the divisions in the long term in the interests of short-term peace. There were disputes between bishops and the secular authorities, of course, but it is difficult to see them as nationalistic. The de Burgh Earls harassed the Church, as we saw in Chapter Four, but this was because of land tenures. Likewise, the King's escheator claimed the temporalities of the dioceses of Dromore during vacancy in 1283, and by extension Clogher, Derry, Kilmore and Raphoe, against the claims of the Archbishop of Armagh.[24] The Archbishop was Irish, Nicholas Mac Maol Iosa, and he defended himself by claiming them as his customary rights, while the escheator claimed that his predecessors had not collected the revenues only because the bishoprics were Irish. The judgement went against Nicholas but this was not a blow at Irish practice, *per se*, but part of Edward I's insistence on all his royal rights. Likewise Nicholas has been seen as a champion of Irish claims, and was so at the time, but it is easier to see him as champion of the rights of his see, as any mediaeval prelate was bound to be.[25]

It was in the monastic orders' affairs that we can find national rivalry. John de Courcy had sought English mother-houses for his Cistercian foundations of Inch and Grey abbeys: Macosquin (whose founder is unknown) also had a foreign mother-house. The two Irish foundations which belonged to the Filiatio Mellifontis, Newry and Assaroe, were outside the Earldom. As a result the Conspiracy of Mellifont had little impact in Ulster: although the abbots of Newry and Assaroe were among the leaders, deposed in 1227, Newry was one of the three where Irish abbots were permitted in the final settlement.[26] Again the conflict was avoided by a geographical division. The friars came first to the Anglo-Norman areas, being slower to found Irish houses: they were still an urban order in the mid-thirteenth century. The Franciscans again formalised the division, putting their houses of Carrickfergus and Down into the Custody of Dundalk, while Armagh and Cavan, with the Connacht houses, were in the Custody of Nenagh.[27] The result of this sort of division, especially in closed societies like monasteries, is that jealousies and rumours arise. On a national scale, after the Conspiracy of Mellifont it centred around the Franciscan friars, especially in the later thirteenth century, with fighting at the provincial chapter in 1291 and the friars' involvement with Bruce.[28] In Ulster it was monastic. In 1293, the Bishop of Down, himself an Englishman, was accused, with Nicholas Mac Maol Iosa, of not permitting English clerks to be admitted to the Augustinian priory of Saul in Co. Down.[29] He disavowed any ordinance that had been made and revoked it if it existed. The house was an old one with venerable Patrician traditions, and had shortly before been built up by Archbishop Nicholas who had disinterred the bodies of Patrick, Columba and Brigit there.[30] This must have been seen as a direct blow to the prestige of Downpatrick, where John de Courcy had found the same saints' bodies in 1186. The story is clearly a tangled one. During the Bruce war, Domnall O Neill issued to the Pope his famous Remonstrance against the Anglo-Normans in Ireland.[31] One of its complaints was that it was preached at two Cistercian abbeys that killing an Irishman was no sin: one of the two thus singled out was Inch. Again this is not impartial testimony: it is in a long line of political propaganda. It would clearly be wrong to say that Irishmen and Anglo-Normans lived in universal joy in this period, but they clearly were not automatically sworn enemies. Our evidence of tension comes from where one would expect it, where institutionalised division led to rivalries. We must not allow it to colour our whole view.

When John de Courcy invaded the north of Ireland it was divided into three power blocks, the Cenel Connaill, Cenel Eoghain and Ulaid. The first was hardly affected by the Earldom of Ulster; the Anglo-Norman lordship nearest to it was that of Connacht. It is convenient, however, to discuss the political relations between the Earldom and the Irish around it in terms of the other two blocks. Of the Ulaid, two elements survived John de Courcy's attack. The one, Ui Echach Cobo, which occupied the approximate area of the diocese of Dromore, was already split into MacCartans and Magennises before de Courcy's time. This division continued with the MacCartans to the south. They let 18 carucates near Dundrum in '1333, and in 1282 William FitzWarin escaped to Dublin because his friendship with MacCartan allowed him to go by the Newry pass uncontrolled by the Earldom.[32] In Ui Echach the Anglo-Normans built the castles of Dromore and Magh Cobha, but actual settlement was absent. We know rather more of the other kingdom in this position, the Ui Tuirtre of Co. Antrim and south Co. Londonderry. We saw in Chapter One how they chose to join de Courcy against the Cenel Eoghain, contributing their control of the north shores of Lough Neagh and the ford of Toome. Hugh de Lacy conquered the lands of the Fir Li (Twescard county) from them but they held on to their mid-Antrim lands until after 1333. This is clear from the deanery of Turtrye in 1306, the route through Turtrye taken by men going from Doagh overland, via Collin mountain to Twescard,[33] and the absence of references to any settlements in the Main valley.

The attitudes of this kingdom to the Earldom varied with time and circumstances. In 1212 they were at war and men guarded the district of Antrim against them.[34] Men of Ui Tuirtre joined de Mandevilles in attacking FitzWarin in 1282, although O Flynn of Ui Tuirtre had joined FitzWarin against O Neill, O Cahan and de Mandeville in 1272.[35] It is the Irish allies of de Mandeville in 1272 that probably caused this attitude. In 1260 M. O Flynn of Ui Tuirtre made an agreement with Hugh Byset over cows which Byset had recovered from O Cahan for O Flynn.[36] As with other Irish kings, O Flynns of Ui Tuirtre were summoned to join the King of England in his wars: to Scotland in 1244, 1314 and 1315.[37] They did not always respond: in 1260-61 the men of Turtrye still owed £200-0-0 for the Gascon aid of 1253-54.[38] In the 1333 Inquisition Ui Tuirtre owed the Earl the service of 30 satellites, along with the other Irish kings in the north.[39] These last items indicate a formal lordship of the Earl and the English kings, but its formality was probably much in evidence: these summonses also went to the O Neills. There is no reason to doubt that in all practical matters the Earls would have considered Ui Tuirtre as outside their Earldom.

The land of west and central Co. Down occupied by Ui Echach Cobo is dominated by drumlins, so that communications are difficult and the soil is often heavy. It was capable of supporting a reasonable population under Irish agriculture, as witness the numbers of raths in the region,[40] but to the Anglo-Normans it may well have appeared unattractive to settle and hard to conquer. Not so the lands of Ui Tuirtre in mid-Antrim, which are in many places naturally fertile and well-drained by Ulster standards. Especially after the conquest of Twescard, Anglo-Normans occupied country to the north and south of Ui Tuirtre with no natural barriers to their expansion into these lands during the later thirteenth century when their capacity to take over new lands is shown by their penetration into north Co. Londonderry. The survival of Ui Tuirtre, therefore, requires explanation.

One factor which may have helped them is their ownership of lands in south Co. Londonderry which offered a line of retreat from an Anglo-Norman raid. It did not of course stop settlement unless as a base for counter-attacks, while it was itself an area under attack by O Cahans and O Neills. The only way to make an area strong in the face of Anglo-Norman attack would have been to use their own method against Irish attacks and build castles. In this area of mid-Antrim there are a number of mottes, including the fine example of a motte and bailey at Harryville outside Ballymena (fig. 15). It is often claimed that only the Anglo-Normans built mottes in

Ireland:[41] it is a theory which satisfies the demands of both Irish and English national pride. It is inherently unlikely, however. A motte, even if carefully constructed, is hardly a difficult thing to erect: the Irish had built fortifications in earth before 1169. It is sometimes suggested that mottes away from areas of Anglo-Norman settlement were built as bases during raids, that they were 'campaign-mottes'. Mottes would be useless on a campaign, however. They would take a long time to build and would offer protection to only a small number of men: they are hardly well designed for keeping valuable horses in safety. What an army needs is a ring-work, where an open central area is protected by a bank and ditch so that all the men, horses and baggage can be accommodated. The long perimeter is no problem, for there is an army to defend it: a motte is designed to be defended by a few people. That the Anglo-Normans built ring-works on campaign is shown by the castle of Mount Sandal (fig. 2), the Kil Santain erected by John de Courcy as a base from which to raid north Co. Londonderry.[42] This is a ring-work, much stronger with its deep ditch than a normal Irish rath. It has two platforms[43] on the bank on the side facing the line of approach, possibly the site of towers with an entry contrived between them with a flying wooden bridge over the bank and ditch as it has been reconstructed recently.

Evidence that the men of Ui Tuirtre built castles comes from the site of Doonbought.[44] This is on a spur overlooking the junction of the valleys of the rivers Main and Cloughwater (plate 8A) and so commanding the line of the boundary between Twescard county to the north and Ui Tuirtre to the south. Here a polygonal castle like that at Seafin was built over an earlier fort (fig. 16). There was little if any interval of time between the two periods, for the courtyard material of the later castle was dumped straight into the empty slots cut in the natural soil for the timber buildings of the first period before they had a chance to become silted up. This dumped material contained thirteenth century pottery of several types, which, combined with the type of polygonal enclosure of mortared stone, makes a thirteenth century date for the earlier fort probable. This fort, however, is not easy to parallel. Its overall plan, an inner enclosure on the top of an artifically steepened knoll of rock, with two courtyards north and south of it along the spur, looks modelled on a motte and bailey. It is hard to see an Anglo-Norman putting up the central enclosure, however, defended by a drystone wall of large boulders and resembling most nearly a cashel: the southern outer fortification apears to have been a drystone wall also. If the Ui Tuirtre were to put up a castle in the mid-thirteenth century it could well look like this – a hybrid cashel with two baileys – and it is in a position which makes considerable strategic sense. M. O Flynn who made the pact with Hugh Byset in 1260, already referred to, drew it up at Connor, where there is another polygonal mortared stone castle near the church (fig. 16). It is unexcavated, although thirteenth-fourteenth century French pottery from it is in the Ulster Museum; it may well have belonged to the Bishop of Connor, but may have been the home of the King of Ui Tuirtre. With a fort like Doonbought on the Twescard frontier, a stone castle at Connor and a dozen mottes scattered over their lands, it would hardly be surprising if the Anglo-Normans decided that Ui Tuirtre were a less attractive proposition to attack than the O Cahans.

H

The Cenel Eoghain were the main threat to the security of the Earldom throughout its life, just as they had been for the Ulaid before them. There were two ways of countering this threat, apart from the fortification and patrolling of a frontier which would have been hopelessly beyond mediaeval resources. The first was direct attack, a policy followed by John de Courcy in his series of raids into the lands west of the Bann between 1185 and 1200 (see Chapter One). The Justiciar John de Gray also favoured attack in 1212 when the Earldom was in the King's hands. He was, of course, able to mobilise the resources of the whole of Anglo-Norman Ireland in the campaign, which combined attacks by the de Galloways along the north coast, by men from Connacht to the Erne, and a main expedition under himself from Meath to Clones.[45] The attacks failed, and before he could avenge the capture of Clones and Caol Uisce on the Erne, the Justiciar was called away to deal with Munster troubles. When the Earldom was again in the King's hands, successive Justiciars revived the same policy of aggression. In 1248 John FitzGeoffrey established a foothold over the Bann opposite Coleraine, but it was the next, Maurice FitzGerald, who rebuilt Magh Cobha Castle in 1252 and rebuilt it in 1254, while leading raids to Armagh in 1252 and 1253. The effort culminated in Brian O Neill's attempt to rally other Irish support and then his invasion of the Earldom leading to his death at the hands of the local levies at Down in 1260. The Justiciar did probably lead a revenge expedition (the armies of Keneleun, Greencastle, etc. appear in the Pipe Roll of 45 Henry III).[46]

The most all these raids achieved was the toe-hold at Drumtarsy castle and the levying of hostages which usually failed to inhibit O Neill ambitions. There could be no steady pressure from the Justiciar, and without it direct attacks on Cenel Eoghain simply invited counter-measures.

The policy of Hugh de Lacy and the de Burgh Earls was based on exploiting the internal politics of Cenel Eoghain instead of attacking them. Notoriously the Irish kings had problems with rivals and successors: in the period 879-1607, 39% of the known members of Cenel Eoghain died at the hands of kinsmen or in internecine war:[47] a simplified genealogical tree of the O Neills is to be found in Appendix Two. The Earldom was rarely faced with an unopposed king of Cenel Eoghain. The man whom John de Gray attacked in 1212, Aedh O Neill, was the son of the man of the same name who had broken into the MacLochlainn line of succession to the kingship in 1176 (he lasted just the year). This younger Aedh was not secure: he was first king in 1196 but was deposed briefly in 1201 by Conchobar MacLochlainn, returning with the help of Cenel Connaill. Hugh de Lacy was on good terms with Aedh O Neill, who protected him on his return to Ireland from exile in 1222-23 (see Chapter Two); Aedh probably welcomed his support. In 1230 Aedh died and the kingship was disputed between his son Domnall and Domnall MacLochlainn; Domnall O Neill had Cenel Connaill support in 1230 which made him king until 1234, and in 1238 Hugh de Lacy supported him in a second attempt on the kingship, which lasted only a year until his death at Domnall MacLochlainn's hands in 1239. The whole position was changed, however, at the battle of Cameirghe when Domnall O Neill's cousin Brian, with Cenel Connaill help, broke the power of the MacLochlainn line for ever. So many were killed that the descendants of Aedh O Neill, king in 1177, were never challenged for the kingship.

Hugh de Lacy died in 1243, so he probably never faced the consequences of his friend's relation's success. We have seen how the Justiciars in the 1250's met Brian O Neill's power with a direct attack leading to the battle of Down in 1260. Walter and Richard de Burgh, however, reverted to the policy of supporting one line consistently for the kingship of Cenel Eoghain. This was the line of Aedh Buidhe O Neill, Brian 'Battle of Down's' cousin and son of the Domnall O Neill who had been supported by Hugh de Lacy. After a short period of rivalry from his brother Niall Culanach, from 1261 to 1263, Aedh Buidhe was king until 1283. Walter de Burgh, Earl of Ulster from 1264, raided Cenel Connaill with him in 1267, with little result, and made a formal agreement with him in 1269 at Antrim,[48] which shows us what Walter de Burgh exacted as the price of his support. Aedh Buidhe was to give a tribute of 3,000 cows and hostages, and promised to treat his wife Eleanor, the Earl's cousin, well (an intriguing clause): if he failed to carry these conditions out, Walter could deprive him of his kingship. This support continued after Walter's death: in 1281 Thomas de Mandeville helped Aedh Buidhe in the battle of Disert-da-Crich where they killed Domnall O Donnell.[49]

Richard de Burgh continued his father's policy, supporting Aedh Buidhe's kin against Domnall, Brian 'Battle of Down's' son, who was a very able and persistent man. Richard de Burgh intervened against him in 1286, 1290 and 1291 on behalf of Aedh Buidhe's brother Niall Culanach (king from 1261 to 1263). In 1294 Richard was captured during his quarrel with Maurice FitzGerald, and during the confusion Domnall returned to kill Niall. In 1296 de Burgh became involved in Edward I's Scottish wars: he was in no position to open new fronts in Cenel Eoghain. In 1314 he seems to have tried to establish Niall, Domnall's brother, as a rival king of Cenel Eoghain. Two English documents of 1314 and 1315[50] include both men in lists of Irish kings, but Niall is called King of Cenel Eoghain, in Irish terms a higher title than that accorded to Domnall, King of Tir Eoghain. The Annals of Ulster, Loch Cé, Connacht and the Four Masters all record Niall at his death in 1314 in glowing terms which go far beyond what one would expect for a king's brother, yet do not recognise him as King of Cenel Eoghain. His death ended the attempt, and in 1315 came the invasion of Edward Bruce, whose only steady ally was Domnall O Neill, who profited more than anyone from the invasion, which allowed him to revive his father's claims to be a national leader of the Irish in his 'Remonstrance'.[51]

Richard de Burgh made a final effort to install Aedh Buidhe's kin when he helped them in 1319 to depose Domnall briefly and kill his son Brian. Domnall died in 1325, and the succession was disputed between him and the Clann Aedha Buidhe, who killed another of his sons, Cu-Uladh, in that year. In 1333 both Henry, Aedh Buidhe's grandson, and Aedh Mor, Domnall's fourth son, appear as kings of Cenel Eoghain in the list of the Earl's satellites.[52]

The policy of division seems to have been very largely successful, certainly more so than the alternative of attacking the Cenel Eoghain. The Earls of Ulster seem to have aimed at ensuring that the king was either their ally (Aedh Buidhe) or else opposed by a man with as good a claim. Normally the Clann Aedha Buidhe (first called this in the Annals of Ulster in 1319) were there to provide the 'anglicising' party, after the demise of the MacLochlainns, who had driven all the O Neill line into this role. Presumably the death of Aedh Buidhe's son Brian in 1295 left no candidate old enough, so that Richard de Burgh turned to Domnall's brother in 1314. While the Cenel Eoghain are recorded as raiding the Earldom on each occasion when they had been directly attacked, under the divisive policy all the fighting was in their lands. The divisive policy was based on political realities: the Earldom did not have the resources needed to conquer and hold the lands of Cenel Eoghain, while the Justiciars, who could assemble the whole forces of Anglo-Norman Ireland, never had the chance to give the north their undivided attention over years. It was much better to wait for internal divisions to appear and then react quickly, for events could move rapidly. In 1290 and 1291 both Domnall O Neill and Richard de Burgh invaded Cenel Eoghain twice. During de Burgh's Earldom, the Anglo-Normans were able to infiltrate along the coast of Co. Londonderry (the O Cahans were O Neill's principal sub-kings) and expand into Inishowen from the base at Greencastle, founded in 1305: greater gains than a policy of direct attack could show. The exception was, of course, when Domnall O Neill was able to bring in foreign support himself in the shape of Edward Bruce – the exception which proves the rule. The ability of Hugh de Lacy and the de Burghs to exploit the O Neill divisions and neutralise Cenel Eoghain shows the relative success of delegating control of a frontier to a resident marcher lord, as against irregular intervention from Dublin.

If we look at the economic relationships which lay behind the political affairs we have been discussing, the best evidence to begin with is the coinage. The Irish of the twelfth century did not live in a money economy: coin-using was based on the former Viking towns alone. The complex European trading world to which Anglo-Norman Ulster was linked was based on the silver penny. The general pattern of the coinage in Ulster is not distinctive from that of the rest of Anglo-Norman Britain. Dolley has shown that under Edward I, who minted most coins in the period, the Irish mints produced coins for English not Irish needs;[53] the outflow of silver was balanced to a certain extent by an influx of English and Scottish coins. Before the later fourteenth and fifteenth centuries, in spite of the geographical proximity, Scottish coins do not appear in Ulster in larger numbers than in the rest of Ireland: this is a later phenomenon.[54]

There are no significant distinctions between Ulster and elsewhere in the denominations of coin found. Had the rents recorded as money been paid as such, and the lack of work services meant much paid labour on demesne farms, there should have been more half-pennies and farthings around in Ulster. From the table of the chronological incidence of hoards below (fig. 19), it can be noted that the Ulster hoards are rather later in date than those from the rest of the island. This impression is reinforced when it is remembered that there are very few hoards from the rich and settled south-east of Ireland.[55] It would appear that Ulster was rather slow in turning to a money economy. This need not be contradicted by the regular though infrequent occurrence of single coins of King John or John de Courcy on excavations, as at Ballyroney, Castlescreen, Clough, Lismahon, Carrickfergus or

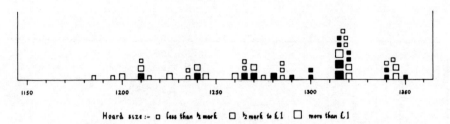

Hoard size :- □ less than ½ mark   □ ½ mark to £1   □ more than £1

19. The chronological distribution of coin-hoards in Ireland (open symbols) and Ulster (solid symbols), 1160-1360.

Muckamore. These are all mottes or sites closely associated with John de Courcy, places where money would have circulated before it was in general use.

As indicators of use, hoards are very much more useful, although they will not necessarily record the pattern of coin in circulation (higher denominations and finer coin will be selectively chosen). To possess a hoard, a man must either steal from someone who has accumulated coin, be given a lump sum, or else steadily put away over a period coins which he receives as part of his normal business. If he is not in a coin-using society and gets hold of a hoard by theft or gift, it will only be of use to him as bullion and he will soon melt it into a silver object, or ingots. The presence of hoards of coins in an area indicates, therefore, that it is likely that the people in that area used coin in their daily lives. In Ulster the coin hoards found from the thirteenth and earlier fourteenth centuries do not come from the lands west of the Bann, except for three from Counties Cavan and Monaghan (which relate to Anglo-Norman Oriel) and one from Macosquin in Co. Londonderry some five miles from Coleraine (fig. 20). The hoards are not, however, confined to the area of the Earldom: out of sixteen hoards (other than the Cavan and Monaghan ones), ten come from inside the Earldom. Three are from its borders, including Macosquin as such at the date it was buried (c.1265), while three come from the lands of Ui Echach Cobo. Single finds are very hard to evaluate; many are now lost and have to be identified by often poor descriptions, while many come from stray losses from modern collections. The apparently more reliable ones have been put on the map. They do seem to have travelled into west Ulster Irish hands somewhat more, but mostly to Co. Londondery where six have been found. Half are from the period between 1272 and 1350 when there was an Anglo-Norman presence along the coast, while two (one of Henry III and one of John) come from Maghera and Dungiven with their Augustinian abbeys of the twelfth century. Again a coin comes from Devenish abbey. The coastal finds from Donegal come from an area which has produced stray finds of Iron Age and Roman times as well.[56] The conclusions from this map seem to be that while the men of Cenel Eoghain and Cenel Connaill, in the widest sense, did not use coin, the men of Ui Echach Cobo and Ui Tuirtre apparently did. They seem to have carried their political links with the Earldom over into economic life.

We can use the distribution of pottery as an indicator of the extent and nature of trade between English and Irish within the Earldom and without. There are three classes involved, the glazed jugs and cooking pots of English type (discussed in

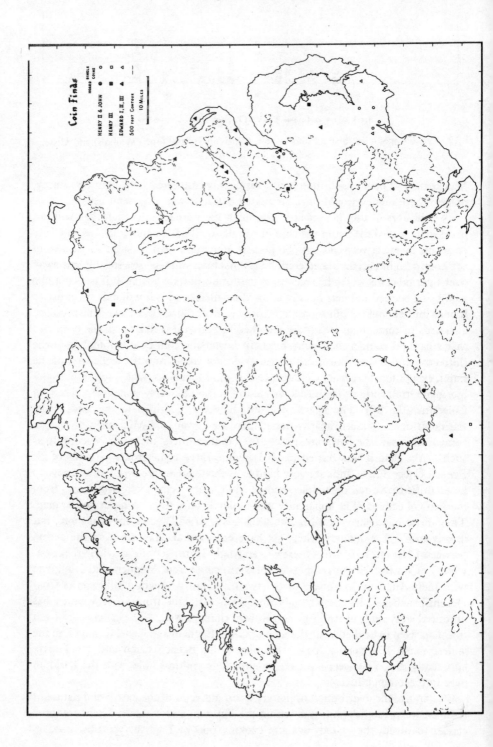

Chapter Three) and Irish cooking pots (fig. 21). The jugs seem to have been marketed all over the north of Ireland. The distribution is weighted to the east, but this is probably to be attributed to the distribution of excavations carried out: there are few sites of this date investigated west of the Bann. Again it is not to be wondered at that glazed jug sherds were found at the Franciscan friary at Armagh with all its anglicised connections, but they were also found at such secular sites as Island McHugh and Coney Island, Lough Neagh. The latter was probably owned by the Archbishop of Armagh but it was hardly lived on by him. Island McHugh was a crannog of the O Neills but its occupation date when the jug arrived may have been later than our period. However, there seems little doubt that the Cenel Eoghain would have been using, if only rarely, jugs purchased from the Earldom. A sherd of Mediterranean polychrome ware from the friary at Armagh reminds us of the probable origin of this trade in the wine that was coming from the south of France. How the Irish paid for these things is unclear, but presumably from the evidence noted above it was in kind, very probably cattle.

The distribution of cooking pots made in the English style at Downpatrick or elsewhere contrasts in particular with the widespread distribution of jugs. The cooking pots do not seem to have reached the Anglo-Norman areas of Co. Antrim beyond the immediate hinterland of Carrickfergus. The reason presumably lies in questions of marketing, as we have seen in Chapter Three. While there was no native industry producing anything which could compete with an Anglo-Norman glazed jug, there was one producing cooking pots. These were not as good as the English products, being softer and more fragile, but they might well have been cheaper, coil-built and fired in simple bonfires. They would have been made locally while the English-style pots would have had to be transported, increasing costs (and breakages): unless there was a reasonably well-concentrated market for English cooking pots they may not have been easily saleable.

The Irish cooking pots which filled this market were based in the pre-Norman souterrain ware tradition,[57] and the first problem of this relationship to be answered is when the production of souterrain ware ended and when and where the so-called everted rim cooking pottery started. This last is very similar to souterrain ware in the preparation of the clay, its manufacture without a wheel, and its firing to a low temperature in a smoky fire to give a rather soft blackish-brown fabric. The distinction between the two lies only in the shape of everted rim pots: instead of the straight-sided bucket shape we have more globular vessels with distinct necks or rims, either more or less sharply everted, or else nearly upright but always with a shoulder. As one goes west in geography and probably forward in time, to the fifteenth-sixteenth centuries, it merges with the rougher 'crannog ware', which has more and larger pieces of grit (some can only be called stones) in the fabric and is more decorated with stab and slash marks as well as handles.[58] Souterrain ware has been found at several rath sites in Co. Down, such as Ballyfounder[59] or Ballynarry,[60] in upper levels along with Anglo-Norman glazed wares. These sites seem to produce the ware in too large quantities to be simply rubbish survivals from the pre-Norman layers beneath, but it is impossible to prove such a statement. The earliest everted rim ware yet found is the pots from Dundrum Castle excavations,[61] which were found in a layer laid down later than the building of the inner curtain but before the building of the keep. As stated above, in Chapter One, there is reason to believe that the keep was built by 1211, and if so the everted rim pottery at this site can hardly have been made after 1200, i.e. it dates from the first generation after John de Courcy's invasion. Again it was found in proportionately larger quantities on the motte at Ballyroney, and at Duneight, both sites referred to from 1211-12 or before,[62] and the earlier phases at Clough.[63]

At the site of Doonbought, in the material dumped over the earlier of the two periods (the possible Irish castle discussed above), both these wares occur together.[64] The context is apparently mid-thirteenth century, and with the Irish wares were found quantities of Anglo-Norman glazed pottery. Some of the souterrain ware sherds were large, too large to have remained unbroken as rubbish survivals from an earlier time. As one might expect, the body sherds, where the identifying shoulder was absent, could not be attributed to one ware rather than the other: as was noted above, only the shape distinguishes them apart. It seems clear that in the Earldom and its vicinity souterrain ware lasted on into the thirteenth century, while the everted rim wares began to be made around 1200 if not before. In view of the similarity between the methods of production of the two, it would be perverse not to conclude that the makers of souterrain ware did not simply change the shapes of their pots to produce the new ware. It has been noted that everted rim ware is not found in Anglo-Norman period contexts at sites such as Greencastle, Co. Down, Muckamore Abbey, Co. Antrim,[65] or earlier layers at Carrickfergus. To argue from this that the ware is later would, however, be to ignore the social context of these deposits. It is not going to be at Anglo-Norman monasteries or the Earl of Ulster's castle and chief town that the Irish potters are going to find their markets, but in fringe sites like Doonbought, Ballyroney or Duneight, and on the mottes of the Earl's tenants.

They must have changed the style of their pots in response to Anglo-Norman cooking pots of the late twelfth century. The examples which seem closest to the everted rim pots come from the area of the Bristol Channel. As seen in examples from the Pithay in Bristol or from Ham Green just outside the city,[66] the shapes match very well, as does the size that is rather smaller than many English cooking pots. They are even plainer than the usual examples from Ulster, but examples are found of two of the more common motifs in Ulster, impressions on the back of the rim and combing horizontal lines along the outer surface of the neck. This last feature is prominent in some of the pottery excavated at Penmaen, especially the pots of the excavator's 'ware A'.[67] These pots were usually fired in a reducing atmosphere, to give dark-coloured fabrics in contrast to the usual oxidised, red or buff English cooking pots, a feature which made them closer to the souterrain ware tradition. Pottery found in Ulster, the rather anomalous small cooking pots from Clough,[68] can be paralleled with a similar small pot from the Pithay, Bristol, so it is not difficult to imagine that the Irish saw these pots too. This is the area from which the Anglo-Normans mounted their invasion of Ireland.

Inducing a small group of craftsmen to change the appearance of their products can hardly be called a profound impact on the economy of the Irish except in that it may represent other crafts we know little of. However, a distribution map of everted rim pottery shows that there was more to it than that (fig. 21). The souterrain ware market was overwhelmingly confined to the north of Ireland east of the Bann. The new style, however, is found everywhere north of a line from Dundalk to Sligo.[69] Wherever anyone excavates a site, whether of this date or not, or even visits sites with exposed surfaces such as crannogs, at least a sherd of it is found. This is not to claim a major new industry sprang up in the north of Ireland, for there is no reason to assume any greater equipment or capital with these men than with the makers of souterrain ware. However, Irish society was immensely resistant to change, as we can see in the stable boundary of the souterrain ware market: elsewhere they did not use pottery at all for centuries while the Irish of Counties Down and Antrim did. In this context even as much of a shift as to buy pottery from a group of men travelling by and probably unknown in the area was a significant change in life.

The key site by which we may hazard a guess as to when this change might have happened is that of Coney Island, off the Co. Armagh shore in Lough Neagh. It was excavated extensively in 1962-64, although parts could not be finished, and a full interim report was published.[70] It was a very long-occupied site in whose history only three phases distinguished by the excavator (E, F and G) concern us here. They are primarily identified by the occurrence in the layers which were thus assigned to them of, respectively, souterrain ware, glazed jugs and everted rim ware, which would imply a fourteenth century date at the earliest for phase G. The phasing can be challenged, however. The only clear break to be seen in the published section is above phase G, when a turf-line some six inches deep grew over the site before the occupation in the sixteenth century, in phase H. The body sherds of the souterrain ware and the everted rim ware could not be told apart and there was apparently only one layer in which souterrain ware sherds (i.e. rims) were found without any everted rim sherds.[71] Nor is the souterrain ware typical of that of the rest of Ulster, in its form or its location, miles to the west of the nearest find-spot. The nearest parallels to the small cups or bowls Addyman found were the small bowls found at Doonbought,[72] where a similar mixture was found. The differentiation of the intervening phase F is based on finding the few glazed sherds in the motte ditch, in silting layers below those containing everted rim sherds. The division of the phases E and G, however, was based on the stratigraphy of an industrial site south of the motte: no glazed sherds came from this area. The distinctions were based therefore on grounds which can be explained away. It is easier to follow the stratigraphy of the southern area and put together phases E and G, and to explain the apparent distinctiveness of phase F on social grounds: the workers at the industrial site did not bring jugs down there, but only their cups and cooking pots. The motte was destroyed at some time and only then did the everted rim sherds find their way into the motte ditch. All this would mean that at Coney Island there was a site using a form of souterrain ware with glazed jugs and everted rim cooking pots at some time – a longish time – before the sixteenth century. It would fit well in time with the Archbishop of Armagh's obtaining a grant of the island from Walter de Burgh in 1265-66.[73] It was not Walter's to give, but he had just been made Earl and perhaps the Archbishop's own title was recent and therefore vulnerable.

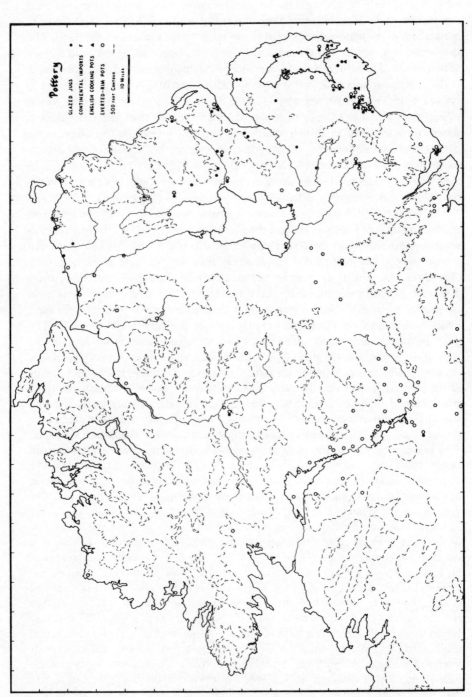

21. Map of pottery finds in Ulster.

This everted rim pottery industry could, then, be summarised as follows. It started when the Irish potters copied Anglo-Norman cooking pottery forms at the end of twelfth century and gradually, over the next two generations, replaced souterrain ware shapes. From their old markets the potters moved into Cenel Eoghain as well, perhaps by the end of the thirteenth century. There is no evidence as to the speed of the spread of the new custom over the rest of the north of Ireland, except that its widespread occurrence on crannogs implies that it was common everywhere by 1500, or before. The ware, like its predecessor, proved remarkably conservative. A pot of the middle or later sixteenth century from Dungiven[74] or a less closely datable sixteenth century sherd from Bonamargy could not be distinguished from sherds 300 years older.[75]

The site of Coney Island was interesting for another reason. The period outlined above was dominated by a motte, but in the industrial area to the south were two large furnaces for iron-smelting. They were large and well built and clearly meant for production on a considerable scale. In Chapter Three we noted that the Anglo-Normans seem to have changed the pattern of iron production in Ulster. Instead of the traces of iron-working and smelting occurring on a small scale on many rath sites, it was now more centralised and put on a full industrial base, at least in some cases urban. Here is the Archbishop of Armagh, an Irishman himself although closely in touch with the Anglo-Norman world, establishing a site in Irish areas to exploit the Lough Neagh bog ores. It is unknown whether this was widespread: the Church as an economic innovator need not have been imitated by Irish lords but the possibility is there.

If we turn to social effects, much hinges on the question of the implications for Irish society of the building of castles. We saw that there was a case for saying that the men of Ui Tuirtre used castles systematically to hold on to their mid-Antrim lands. As might be expected, the other area where motte building by Irish seems to have been a regular feature of life is in Co. Down. Here we know that Ballyroney and Dromore were Anglo-Norman outposts: judging by its inclusion in de Courcy's dower charter, Duneight was probably also built by Anglo-Normans. Others in the west of the county must be Irish: as we noted in Chapter Four the idea of a western screen of outposts will not stand up to analysis. In mid-Ulster there are a few mottes which are even less likely to have been the work of Anglo-Normans: they only went to these parts to raid, not to settle. They include the remarkable site of Managh Beg,[76] whose motte is the biggest in the north of Ireland and which has a large platform bailey attached. The whole is a little odd in its overall effect, however. It is built out of a gravel ridge and is overlooked by higher ground quite near; the top of the large motte is 36 × 17 metres across – too big for easy defence: it looks like work built to impress (which it certainly does) rather than from a true understanding of how a motte should work. It seems impossible to tell an Irish motte by looking at it, although Leask claims that 'the presence of concentric banks and ditches ... is almost conclusive proof of a non-Norman origin for the earthwork.'[77] This may hold elsewhere in Ireland, although the overall survey work to justify it has not been done there, but not in Ulster. Against Ballymaghery, Co. Down, with an outer bank and ditch which was Irish, one may put Red Hall, Co.

Antrim,[78] in the heart of the Earldom: like Red Hall, however, the outer banks of mottes in the richer lands are more vulnerable to later destruction.

The finest candidate for being an Irish castle built before the tower-houses of the fifteenth century is the one called Harry Avery's near Newtownstewart, Co. Tyrone, well described by Jope and Rees-Jones and Waterman,[79] but still not as well-known as it should be (plate 4B). Unfortunately the only dating evidence is its traditional association with Henry Aimreadh O Neill, who died in 1392:[80] there are neither documentary references nor datable masonry details surviving. In plan, however (fig. 17), it combines the two kinds of castle known in the Earldom from the thirteenth century, while at a later date one would expect a tower-house. It has a polygonal curtain wall enclosing the crest of a natural hill, some 40 metres across or less, like Seafin, to which is attached a fine twin-towered gatehouse or tower. The work of 1961 showed that it was the only way into the castle behind and that a bridge-pit enhanced its resemblance to an Anglo-Norman gatehouse, like Carrickfergus for example.[81] It was not a true gatehouse, however, for the entry does not lead to the courtyard but to the vaulted ground-floor room below a hall stretching across behind the two towers. To reach the courtyard one must climb a stair in one of the side walls to the first floor. At this level in the gatehouse was the hall with two private chambers in each tower, one at first- and one at second-floor level, served by latrines. It is a fascinating amalgam of Anglo-Norman living conditions, almost to be compared with those of the gatehouse at Greencastle, Co. Donegal, and the small border castles of the Earldom; being Irish, there is no provision for valuable war-horses in the castle. As Jope pointed out in 1950, it is not unique, but to be compared with the more ruined Elagh Castle in Co. Londonderry. Here the site is a rock platform defended by a stone wall, traces of which can be seen along the crest in the grass (fig. 17). There is one tower of the gatehouse left which has part of the portcullis slot with a door-check and draw-bar behind it surviving on one side. Like Harry Avery's castle, the ground floor is solid, but there was probably a chamber on the first floor. Its date is even less certain than that of Harry Avery's castle.

The implications of these castles affect the internal balance of the Irish kingdoms. During the later thirteenth century the Irish kings began to import the West Highland mercenaries known as galloglasses.[82] They are known of course mainly for their role in the external wars of the clans, in particular against the Anglo-Normans, but must have increased the king's power within his clan. When O Flynn talked of cattle raiding as 'contra pacem meam et contra pacem domini comitis' in 1260 in his agreement with Byset signed at Connor and dated by Henry III's regnal year, he was probably doing more than trying to capture some of the Earl of Ulster's reflected glory. If at Connor he was living in a castle, which could be a recognised centre for Ui Tuirtre, he was strengthening his power. A castle, whether a motte or a stone enclosure, defended by mercenaries would make a king far harder to defeat or even defy than a simple pre-Norman Irish rath. The sons of Henry Aimreadh O Neill (the Sliocht Henry) formed a distinct element in the politics of fifteenth century Ulster, partly because of their royal kinship, but possessing a centre for lordship must have helped. The O Neills were intensely conservative and took a long time to adopt the system of tanistry by which a king chose his successor before his death. As Hogan pointed out,[83] there are only some eight examples known among the O Neills before the seventeenth century, of which six are in the sixteenth century. It must be significant that the first king to formally appoint a tanist was Domnall who chose his son Brian who died in 1319 before his father. He was the arch-opponent of Richard de Burgh who supported Edward Bruce against the Anglo-Normans, yet it was he who shifted the O Neill centre from the traditional rath at Tullahogue to a castle at Dungannon. The idea was not totally new; as we saw with the English mount at Downpatrick, the Irish might have built stronger forts than raths before the Anglo-Normans came. These remained few and rare: it was during the Anglo-Norman period that Irish kings became accustomed to castles, which led to their widespread adoption of tower-houses in the fifteenth century.

NOTES

1. *C.D.I.*, I, No. 1264.
2. E. Curtis: *Proceedings of the Royal Irish Academy*, XLIII(C), 1935-7, pp. 41-73.
3. Appendix Three.
4. A. J. Otway-Ruthven: *J.R.S.A.I.*, LXXXI, 1951, p. 9.
5. *36th Report of the Deputy Keeper, P.R.I.*, p. 54; *45th Report*, p. 56.
6. W. Reeves: *Ecclesiastical Antiquities*, p. 167.
7. *C.D.I.*, II, No. 661.
8. *Ibid.*, No. 677.
9. E. Curtis: *Proceedings of the Royal Irish Academy*, XXXIX(C), 1929, pp. 10-11; *National manuscripts of Ireland* (ed. J. T. Gilbert), II, plate 73.
10. *C.D.I.*, II, No. 1782.
11. E. Curtis: *Proceedings of the Royal Irish Academy*, XXXIX(C), 1929, p. 11.
12. Appendix Three.
13. *De l'Isle and Dudley mss.*, I, p. 31.
14. *C.D.I.*, II, No. 953.
15. *Ibid.*, No.'s 929, 1918.
16. *Annals of Ulster*, 1283; *C.D.I.*, II, No. 2049.
17. W. Reeves: *Ecclesiastical Antiquities*, p. 307; A. Gwynn & R. N. Hadcock: *Medieval religious houses, Ireland*, pp. 69-70.
18. *C.D.I.*, II, No. 735; W. Reeves: *Ecclesiastical Antiquities*, p. 261.
19. *Ibid.*, pp. 98, 100, 261.
20. *Ibid.*, p. 257. A. Gwynn & R. N. Hadcock: *Medieval religious houses, Ireland*, p. 66, omits the first of these men.
21. A. J. Otway-Ruthven: *J.R.S.A.I.*, XCIV, 1964; K. Nicholls: *J.R.S.A.I.*, CI, 1971.
22. G. H. Orpen: *J.R.S.A.I.*, XLIII, 1913, p. 139; XLV, 1915, p. 140; W. Reeves: *Ecclesiastical Antiquities*, pp. 4, 6.
23. *A.S.C.D.*, p. 302.
24. *C.D.I.*, III, pp. 9-10. Here again Dromore is clearly treated as an Irish diocese.
25. A. Gwynn: 'Nicholas macMaol Iosa', in J. Ryan (ed.): *Feil Sgribhin Eoin Mhic Neill*, pp. 394-45.
26. J. A. Watt: *The church and the two nations in medieval Ireland*, chapter 4.
27. *Ibid.*, p. 179.
28. *Ibid.*, pp. 182-94.
29. *Calendar of Justiciary Rolls, Ireland*, I, pp. 102-3.

30. *Annals of Ulster*, 1293.

31. E. Curtis & R. B. McDowell: *Irish Historical Documents, 1172-1922*, pp. 38-46.

32. *C.D.I.*, II, No. 1918.

33. *Ibid.*, No. 929.

34. O. Davies & D. B. Quinn: *U.J.A.*, IV, 1941, p. 62.

35. *C.D.I.*, II, No.'s 929, 1918.

36. *De l'Isle and Dudley mss.*, I, p. 31. O Flynn is called 'rex Curcrie' (Cork) in this printed version: there was no king of Cork in 1260, nor would he have been an O Flynn. This must be an example of the easy confusion of 'C' and 'T', and should read 'rex Turtrie'.

37. *C.D.I.*, I, No. 2716; *Liber munerum publicorum Hiberniae*, (ed. R. Lascelles), I (IV), pp. 5-6.

38. *National manuscripts of Ireland* (ed. J. T. Gilbert), II, plate 73.

39. G. H. Orpen: *J.R.S.A.I.*, XLV, 1915, p. 141.

40. *A.S.C.D.*, fig. 72.1.

41. G. H. Orpen: *Ireland under the Normans*, II, p. 344; R. E. Glasscock: *Château Gaillard*, VII, 1974, pp. 95-110.

42. *Annals of Ulster*, 1197.

43. The northern of these two platforms is larger, apparently as a result of adding material derived from the shallow ditch which cuts across the inner area at its base. This might represent the start of an attempt to turn the site into a motte and bailey: if so it was not nearly finished, for the platform is still linked to the bank at either end.

44. T. E. McNeill: *U.J.A.*, XL, 1977, pp. 63-84.

45. G. H. Orpen: *Ireland under the Normans*, II, pp. 289-93.

46. *35th Report of the Deputy Keeper, P.R.I.*, pp. 39, 43, 45.

47. J. Hogan: *Proceedings of the Royal Irish Academy*, XL(C), 1932, pp. 186-254. This article, together with the *Annals of Ulster*, gives the factual basis for much of the argument which follows here.

48. *De l'Isle and Dudley mss.*, I, p. 31.

49. *C.D.I.*, II, No. 2079; *Annals of Ulster*, 1281.

50. *Liber munerum publicorum Hiberniae*, (ed. R. Lascelles), I(IV), pp. 5, 6.

51. E. Curtis & R. B. McDowell: *Irish historical documents 1172-1922*, p. 38.

52. G. H. Orpen: *J.R.S.A.I.*, XLV, 1915, p. 141.

53. R. H. M. Dolley: *Proceedings of the Royal Irish Academy*, LXVI(C), 1968, pp. 235-97.

54. R. H. M. Dolley: *Medieval Anglo-Irish coins*, pp. 52, 59.

55. *Ibid.*, p. 60; R. H. M. Dolley & W. A. Seaby: *Anglo-Irish coins, John-Edward III in the Ulster Museum, Belfast*.

56. D. B. Bateson: *Proceedings of the Royal Irish Academy*, LXXIII(C), 1973, pp. 43, 65.

57. M. Ryan: *Proceedings of the Royal Irish Academy*, LXXIII(C), 1973, pp. 619-45. While this article does give a good idea of the basic shapes of the ware, it discusses the context and dating, in particular the end of the tradition, very little.

58. W. G. Wood-Martin: *The lake dwellings of Ireland*, figs. 67-102.

59. D. M. Waterman: *U.J.A.*, XXI, 1958, pp. 39-61.

60. B. K. Davison: *U.J.A.*, XXIV-V, 1961-2, pp. 39-87.

61. D. M. Waterman: *U.J.A.*, XIV, 1951, fig. 4.4.

62. Ballyroney is identified, as in Chapter One, with Maycove or Magh Cobha castle; *Annals of Ulster*, 1182; O. Davies & D. B. Quinn: *U.J.A.*, IV, 1941, pp. 56, 60, 62. Duneight is identified with the Dunechti of de Courcy's dower charter; A. J. Otway-Ruthven: *U.J.A.*, XII, 1949, pp. 77-81.

63. D. M. Waterman: *U.J.A.*, XVII, 1954, fig. 7.5-6.

64. T. E. McNeill: *U.J.A.*, XL, 1977, pp. 71-76.

65. C. J. Lynn, in *Excavations 1971*, pp. 10-11; *Ibid.*, 1973, p. 5.

66. K. J. Barton: *Transactions of the Bristol and Gloucester Archaeological Society*, LXXXIII, 1963, pp. 95-126. Compare the pots in the British Museum reference collection, No.'s 1970 12/5 − 4, 5, 7, 13: 1926 P27, P32.

67. L. Alcock: *Antiquaries Journal*, XLVI, 1966, fig. 11.1-8. The twelfth century background in England to this tradition is discussed in this article.

68. D. M. Waterman: *U.J.A.*, XVII, 1954, fig. 7.

69. The sites producing everted rim/crannog ware marked on fig. 21 are listed in my unpublished Ph.D. thesis for Queen's University Belfast, appendix H. Since then (1973) the following sites should be added to the list:-

Co. Down	— Carnalbanagh	—	J152604
	Rathmullan	—	J477374
Co. Fermanagh	— Aghnahinch Lough	—	H423239
	Carrick Lough	—	H095540
	Corban Lough	—	H310375
	Digh Lough	—	H325332
	Drumnaveale Lough	—	H472196
	Inver Lough	—	H518311
	Killymackan Lough	—	H330207
	Liscreevin Lough	—	H202577
	Mill Lough (Cackinish)	—	H337214
	Mill Lough (Killyfole)	—	H465313
	Mullyduff Lough	—	H431255
	Raymond Lough	—	H286386
	Yvan Lough	—	H255421
	Lisdoo	—	H363333

The lough sites are the result of a survey of Co. Fermanagh crannogs conducted by Miss C. Foley of Historic Monuments Branch, Department of the Environment, N.I; Rathmullan, Co. Down was excavated by Mr. C. J. Lynn, and the other two sites by Mr. N. Brannon, both also of the Historic Monuments Branch. I am grateful to all three for their information.

70. P. V. Addyman: *U.J.A.*, XXVII, 1965, pp. 78-101.

71. *Ibid.*, p. 89.

72. T. E. McNeill: *U.J.A.*, XL, 1977, fig. 8.18-19.

73. British Library *Add. mss.* 6041, item 60.

74. Excavated by A. E. T. Harper in 1966.

75. E. M. Jope: *U.J.A.*, XIII, 1950, fig. 4.4.

76. T. E. McNeill: *U.J.A.*, XXXVIII, 1975, No. 118.

77. H. G. Leask: *Irish Castles*, p. 10.

78. T. E. McNeill: *U.J.A.*, XXXVIII, 1978, No.'s 61, 80.

79. E. M. Jope: *U.J.A.*, XIII, 1950, pp. 81-92; S. G. Rees-Jones & D. M. Waterman: *U.J.A.*, XXX, 1967, pp. 76-82.

80. *Annals of Ulster*, 1392.

81. S. G. Rees-Jones & D. M. Waterman: *U.J.A.*, XXX, 1967, pp. 79-81.

82. G. A. Hayes-McCoy: *Scots mercenary forces in Ireland*.

83. J. Hogan: *Proceedings of the Royal Irish Academy*, XL(C), 1932, p. 246.

7

The End of the Earldom

IN one sense the Earldom of Ulster never ended: the title continued to be handed down, from William de Burgh's daughter to her husband the Duke of Clarence, to Edmund Mortimer who married their daughter, and so to the Yorkist line of the English royal family (Appendix One). Henry VIII and Elizabeth I used their title to the Earldom as a factor in their policy in the north of Ireland. Conn Bachach O Neill was created Earl of Tyrone, not Earl of Ulster, in 1542. Likewise the English never lost control of Carrickfergus and the south-east of Co. Down, with Greencastle, at least in name. Likewise there was no great single battle which resulted in the loss of the English lands in Ulster to the Irish. What we must answer is the question of when the Clann Aedha Buidhe (Clannaboy or Clandeboy), O Neills with the MacQuillans and MacDonnells principally, took over the four northern counties of the five of the Earldom. As already pointed out, Down county was hardly affected by actual loss of land to the Irish, although it was involved of course in fighting. For example, Greencastle was attacked in 1334 and captured in 1343.[1] The key to the Anglo-Norman position lay in the counties of Antrim, Carrickfergus and Blathewic: linked to these was the land of Ui Tuirtre in mid-Antrim. The land was under the control of Robert Savage, Sheriff of Twescard in 1327, who seems to have been the main organiser of the 1333 Inquisition, for his name is the only one to appear on more than one jury list. He was Seneschal of Ulster in 1333 and 1343 and received lands in Antrim county to add to his Twescard estates.[2] During his time the area seems to have been held for the Anglo-Normans, and Savage was certainly seen in Dublin as the main opponent of Irish conquest. In the Laud manuscript Annals he is the subject of two stories: one of his hospitality to the English troops before a battle, and one of how he started to build castles on his lands but gave up when his son told him to put his trust in men instead, castles of bones not stones.[3] The latter story ends with the moral twist that after his death in 1360 his lands were overrun because there were no castles. That the lands of Antrim county were still in English hands up to his death is shown by Elizabeth de Burgh's ministers' accounts for Antrim town.[4] This lay in the position most exposed to Irish attack, yet the receipts for 1358-59 exceed those of 1353-54; in particular the rents of the burgages in the accounts show a rising trend of numbers let. Most were waste because of war from February to August 1353, when they yielded 3/4, but in the next two six-month periods they produced £1-4-3 and £1-5-0, while in 1358-59 there were eighty burgages let, although only at 2d per annum.

After 1360 the pressure seems to have increased on the English of Ulster, but it affected their Irish allies first. In 1333 the kingship of Cenel Eoghain was divided between the families of Aedh Buidhe, represented by Henry O Neill and of Brian Battle of Down, represented by Aedh, later known as Aedh Mor. They continued to divide the power until 1344, when the Lord Deputy Ralph d'Ufford (married to William de Burgh's widow) came to Ulster. Here he either instigated or sanctioned Aedh Mor's expulsion of Henry; if he did instigate the act it was contradicting a century of the Earl's policy to Cenel Eoghain.[5] Henry took with him his kin, the Clann Aedha Buidhe, whom he ruled as king until his death in 1347. They seem to have established themselves in south Co. Londonderry, which became their base in the later expansion to the east.[6] They had established themselves as a political unit by 1354 when they allied with the English of Co. Louth to defeat Aedh Mor O Neill.[7] From their position north of Lough Neagh, the nearest land for them to take was that of Ui Tuirtre, and so we find evidence of conflict between them: in 1359 Muirchetach O Flynn, heir of Ui Tuirtre, was killed in treachery by Aedh Buidhe's grandson, Henry O Neill's brother Aedh, while in 1368 Thomas, Muirchetach's father and the last man to be called king of Ui Tuirtre, died.[8]

We may conclude from this that by about 1370 Clann Aedha Buidhe was in control of the south Londonderry and mid-Antrim lands of Ui Tuirtre and so in direct contact with the south Antrim lands of the Earldom. This conquest coincided with a time of further division in Cenel Eoghain: after Aedh Mor's death in 1364, when his sons Domnall (supported by Clann Aedha Buidhe) and Niall Mor fought over the kingship. In 1370, however, Domnall submitted to Niall and ended the internal dissension.

The resulting period saw the surviving English areas of the Earldom under increasing pressure. In 1370 Sir James de la Hyde, Seneschal of Ulster for Mortimer, now Earl of March and of Ulster by right of his marriage to Clarence and Elizabeth de Burgh's daughter, was killed by Magennis.[9] In 1374 and 1375 Niall Mor O Neill attacked the English, in the latter year defeating them at Downpatrick, while Magenis captured Greencastle.[10] Niall O Neill raided south Co. Antrim in 1383, a raid also marked by warfare between Savages and Bysets: in 1384 he burned Carrickfergus town.[11] In 1389, however, Niall's son was captured by the English, and in 1395 both father and son submitted to Richard II at Drogheda.[12] The two O Neills were the main Irish chiefs from the north to submit, either because others like the Clann Aedha Buidhe accepted their lordship (*pace* Curtis,[13] this seems unlikely) or because their position in Ulster was too strong. Perhaps Niall O Neill hoped by this submission not only to regain his hostages from 1389 but also to assert his authority over the others attacking the Earldom. One such was John MacDonnell of the Isles who submitted to Richard as constable of the Irish of Ulster and captain of his nation, as a galloglas leader, but by 1399 he had married Marjory Byset, heiress of the Glens, presumably with the consent of Edmund Savage, then Seneschal of Ulster, who was given her wardship in 1389-90.[14]

The first quarter of the fifteenth century probably saw the completion of the conquest of the central part of the Earldom. In 1387 Thomas de Mandeville had considered it worthwhile to seek the granting of the Bonnacht of Ulster, while three years later, to counter the devastation of the lands of Ulster, Carrickfergus castle, although repaired in 1381,[15] was ordered to be put into a state of defence again.[16] A dispute of the priory of St. Andrew in the Ards as an alien priory dragged on in

J

royal courts from 1365 to 1392.[17] The organisation of the settlement seems to have been working, although under heavy pressure up to the respite of 1391-95. In 1403 Carrickfergus had been destroyed again and the mayor was petitioning for relief of the annual £5 farm of the customs.[18] In 1405 Edmund Savage, Seneschal since 1388, was made so for life and granted all the King's lands in Ulster because they were so wasted by the Irish and Scots.[19] In 1423 the lieutenant, Ormonde, attempted to help the English of Ulster.[20] In 1425 the garrison of Carrickfergus killed Brian O Neill, King of Clann Aedha Buidhe, for which they were forced to pay a yearly fine to his successors.[21] In 1427-28 Carrickfergus was being attacked by Scots, and the constable complained that he had only 10 marks of income.[22] Earlier in that year the northern chiefs submitted to Mortimer, Lieutenant in Ireland from 1423 to his death in 1425: the list included the two contenders for the Cenel Eoghain kingship, Domnail and Eoghan, O Donnell, Brian O Neill of Clann Aedha Buidhe and McQuillan 'alone, by himself'.[23]

The McQuillans were at this time following the example of John MacDonnell in the 1390's, and changing from galloglas captains of their 'Route', in part at least based on the old Bonnacht of Ulster (see Chapter Four), into territorial chiefs of specific lands. In a far-flung series of campaigns in 1433 we find McQuillans and Savages in alliance together being attacked by Eoghan O Neill of Cenel Eoghain: McQuillan lands appear to have been in Dufferin, the area west of Strangford Lough, while the Savages controlled the Ards.[24] In 1469 the constable described Carrickfergus as surrounded by Scots and Irish.[25] The Savages retained the Ards until Tudor times, and the McQuillans retained a similar interest in Dufferin. A hangover from the collapse of the Earldom in mid-Antrim was the presence of O Flynns in the 'Turtars' in the Ards in the sixteenth century:[26] they must have joined the Savages in the Six Mile Water about 1370 and then followed them to the Ards.

The question of the McQuillans of the Route leads to a consideration of the Anglo-Norman position in Twescard. There is little reason to doubt that the parts west of the Bann, Irish rents in Inishowen or the settlements at Limavady or at Camus, which are described in 1333 as waste because of war with the Irish, were never recovered. On the other hand Elizabeth de Burgh's manors east of the Bann were clearly stable and productive in the 1350's, with few signs of serious trouble. The mills at Coleraine, Ardbegan and Tiperdornan were brought back into commission during the period, which more than compensated for the damage done by Henry Savage at Portrush in 1359.[27] Sir Robert Savage was buried in the Dominican friary of Coleraine in 1360, while in 1376 its inhabitants captured Cu-Mighe O Cahan, sent him to Carrickfergus and defeated a revenge attack by his sons.[28] In 1381 the Dublin government ordered the repair of Coleraine bridge and Drumtarsy castle on the opposite bank, damaged by the Irish.[29] Traders from Portrush received safe conducts for voyages to the Western Isles of Scotland in 1338 and 1357.[30] There seems little sign of Irish pressure on Twescard until the mid-fifteenth century. We find O Cahans and McQuillans fighting in 1442, the first indication of McQuillan interest in Twescard, and allied in 1454.[31] In 1472 there was renewed fighting during which Clann Aedha Buidhe and Godfrey O Cahan

attacked McQuillan. They are described as invading 'The Route', after which Conn
O Neill and Rughraidhe McQuillan made peace and Rughraidhe met O Cahan after
crossing the Bann in a small boat, whereupon O Cahan killed McQuillan.[32] In
contrast with the entry in the Annals of Ulster for 1470, when Magennis attacked
McQuillan, and the 'Rout' was located in Lecale, by 1472 the 'Route' can be
applied to north Co. Antrim. How the McQuillans came to gain power in the area is
unknown. It was clearly in spite of O Cahan's efforts (and we find O Cahans on the
north Antrim coast at Dunseverick in the sixteenth century): one possibility might
be that when the Savages were under pressure to quit south Antrim in the earlier
fifteenth century, they made over their Twescard interests to McQuillan. The two
were certainly allies in 1433, just before McQuillan interests seem to arise in
Twescard.

The actual process of the loss of the Earldom's lands to the various Irish tribes is
thus clearly complex and long-drawn-out. While some peripheral lands were lost
immediately after the Earl's murder in 1333, the situation was quickly stabilised
until after the death of Sir Robert Savage in 1360. Clann Aedha Buidhe had
attacked Ui Tuirtre, and then the pressure mounted against the English lands of
south Antrim in the next twenty-five years. After a brief respite in the 1390's the
Savages were driven into the Ards by the 1430's, leaving Clann Aedha Buidhe in
control of south Antrim. In those years and the next thirty the McQuillans
established themselves in Dufferin and Twescard.

This chronology runs counter to the normal explanation of the end of the
Earldom which tends to attribute it to the consequences of the Bruce invasion and
the murder of the Earl. Clearly both caused considerable upheavals and damage,
especially when combined with the short descent by Robert Bruce on Ulster in
1327.[33] The damage recorded by the chroniclers as done by the Scots is notorious,
and the dislocation is well illustrated by the chronological table of coin hoards in
Chapter Six. Curiously, however, the Inquisitions of 1333 use values of 1326, only
eight years after Edward Bruce's death, as a yardstick of value some six times higher
than that given for 1333. This 'old extent' records lands of approximately £650
value, not counting the Irish satellites valued at £355. This compares well with
William FitzWarin's receipts between April 1273 and January 1275 of just over
£830 or approximately £500 per annum,[34] and the Dunheved and de Mandeville
accounts of 1260-61 when Twescard produced c.£230 per annum and the rest was
farmed for £200.[35]

Either the damage done by Bruce was repaired very quickly or we must distrust
the 'old extent' values of the 1333 Inquisition as applying to real 1326 conditions. It
is the differential between the old and new extents of 1333 that constitutes the main
case for widespread damage following the Earl's murder: the direct record of
damage there appears confined to Coule and Belfast.[36] Rather than attributing the
discrepancy between the two values to the events of 1333, we should perhaps
consider it to be the result of damage done in the eighteen years before. It is, of
course, possible as well that the jurors of 1333 undervalued the rents that could be
levied on their lands. Leaving this on one side, however, the record of damage is
severe: the counties suffered on average a drop in value of 65%, with Blathewic the

least at c.42%, and Twescard the greatest at 85%. Yet the damage clearly could be repaired, as seen in the later history of Twescard with the records of Elizabeth de Burgh's ministers and the Anglo-Norman resistance until the end of the century.

If we therefore abandon the events of the first third of the century as being the prime cause of the Irish taking control of the Earldom, we must look for explanation deeper into the structure of the Anglo-Norman society and economy that they replaced. We have seen how the Earldom made little use of natural frontiers or regions: it was conquered piecemeal according to Irish political units and their relative strength or weakness. The Earldom of Ulster was always march land, vulnerable to Irish attack and depending on a rather fragile mixture of local military superiority and exploitation of basic Irish divisions and institutional weaknesses. On the one hand, the strength of the Earldom depended on settling the land densely with men who would fight for it, on the other, this fragility and lack of fellow-settlers discouraged men from taking up offers of land. This reluctance was obviously stronger among the lower classes; the lower down the social structure that a man was, the smaller the rewards for his effort might be. The result, as we saw in Chapter Five, was a society based not on English nucleated manorial settlement at all but one which had taken over a basically Irish agricultural organisation. In Ulster the Anglo-Normans were not lords of demesnes and villages living off the sale of corn grown by their villeins, but a resident rentier class. They lived off rents levied in kind from their tenants, perhaps at the mills which occupy a key position in the accounts: there is no reason to assume that the actual producers of the corn were anything but Irishmen. The Anglo-Norman lords exploited the land efficiently, as we can see from the records of the economy, by using their commercial contacts to change the old subsistence aims of the Irish chiefs into a marketing structure, but the actual system they seem to have left intact. Nor does it look as though they expanded the production so much by working the peasantry harder, for the work services levied remained light, but more probably by taking in more land, and riding the crest of population expansion that was affecting all Europe in the twelfth and thirteenth centuries. There is no reason to doubt that this could affect Ireland as well, and the Irish: the Irish chiefs would have seen it as more men to control, but the Anglo-Normans as more peasants to grow corn. The result of this system was that land remained in Irish hands, only being Anglo-Norman in the upper classes. This struck the writer of a memorandum on the state of Ulster in 1327, as a result of Bruce's descent on the country in that year.[37] According to him, the land was out of control as a result of Richard de Burgh's old age and not one-tenth was settled: more men from Wales or England should be brought in. Yet we have seen the 1333 Inquisitions look back to this time as a prosperous one: the account depends on the viewpoint of the writer. The Earldom was effective as long as it could go on without being seriously attacked by the Irish, but in that case it was very vulnerable with its thin resources of manpower. A similar analysis must lie behind the Dublin annalist's story of Robert Savage and his son Henry with his castles of bones not stones: the annalist points the moral of the overrunning of the Savage lands after 1360.

This society was held together, administratively and militarily, by the successive Earls. Each one seems to have made a point of keeping his control over his Earldom as tight as possible. The Earls were able to go a long way towards eliminating tenants in chief of the King, the supreme example being the de Galloways in Antrim expelled by Hugh de Lacy. The result was a lifestyle for the Earls in many ways comparable to that of fellow barons in England. Their income, such as we know of it, seems comparable to that of English earls.[38] The castles they lived in were as comfortable as any in the British Isles for the period and were consistently so throughout the life of the Earldom. The young Richard or William de Burgh, after an upbringing at the English court, would not have felt out of place riding into a castle like Carrickfergus or the two Greencastles. It would have been in their political problems and administrative routine that they would have seen the results of their being border Irish earls. An English barony of the later thirteenth century was largely orientated towards the financial control of demesne farms, with resulting complex audits and apparatus. As a result the chief officials with whom the baron would have daily dealt would have been a wardrober or receiver-general and estates or household stewards.[39] In south-eastern Ireland, as in the Liberty of Kilkenny, had the Clares been resident they would have found a simpler council structure centred around a single seneschal or steward whose main pre-occupation would seem to have been the administration of justice in the Liberty.[40] In Ulster, the Earl was faced by a continuous series of problems in politics and war, given the exposed nature of the Earldom, and its complex relations with Irish kings. As a result the Earl was the head of a barony which was administered much more like an English one of the twelfth century: a single seneschal and a constable, or a man uniting both offices as the chief official, with justices, treasurer and chancellor professional administrators but of less social prestige. The Earl controlled formidable military power with his castles to quarter Irish mercenaries on the borders, by 1300 a semi-permanent force, the Bonnacht, and was able to field a great mass of men as he showed in 1296 in Scotland.

The result of the combination of a powerful earl and a local gentry thinly spread on the ground was a power vacuum in 1333. It did not, as we have seen, produce anything like a sudden collapse of the Earldom. What it did produce was a situation inherently unstable. The Earls had shown in their handling of the Irish that local control of policies was essential. When they were handled by the Justiciar from Dublin, the result seems always to have been war, often enough inside the Earldom. Justiciars were not present continuously to impress their lordship on the Irish, or to intervene to exploit or stimulate succession struggles in Cenel Eoghain in particular. Instead they were tempted into making frontal attacks or raids which would have required much greater resources than the Earldom possessed to be turned into solid gains and which only provoked counter-attacks. Unfortunately for the Earldom, William de Burgh's heir, Clarence, also died leaving only a daughter, but when he had come to Ireland, it was as King's lieutenant, with more urgent duties than looking after Ulster. The same problem arose with Mortimer in the 1390's. The position in Ulster devolved in 1333 to Sir Robert Savage until his death in 1360, but this too was no lasting solution. The problem here was twofold. On the one hand, the Savages like the other families had been prevented from building up their own power anywhere in Ulster. We have seen how the Earls inhibited other men from building mottes with baileys or stone castles. On the other hand, there were other families who would not take kindly to Savages ruling them. The de Mandevilles had occupied a much higher position in the de Burghs' councils, while we find Bysets and Savages fighting each other in 1383.[41] There was no single pre-eminent family to take control in Ulster as the cadet de Burghs did in Connacht.

The last point to make on the subject of the Earldom's apparent collapse is that we can exaggerate the gulf between the Irish who were to take over and the Anglo-Norman Earldom they seized. We have seen the Irish aspects of the agricultural system of the Earldom, but we must not forget the Anglicising influences which we saw affecting the Irish chiefs (Chapter Six). They had come to terms with Anglo-Norman political organisation in some aspects, especially in the case of Ui Tuirtre, with galloglasses and castles. Some Irish had apparently been drawn into the money economy of the Earldom, while all seem to have had some commercial contacts – to judge by the pottery – with the Anglo-Normans. As a result they could have been able to take over much of the economic structure of the Earldom without difficulty. It would have involved only replacing the local Anglo-Norman rentier gentry with their Irish-based agriculture, while continuing to exact the same renders from their villae, to sell through the merchants of the ports as before. This need not even have involved violence or automatic enmity. The de Mandevilles brought in Irishmen to help them against FitzWarin, and in Chapter Six we saw how there was at least as much evidence of the two nations co-operating as there was of hostility between them. The Clann Aedha Buidhe were the section of Cenel Eoghain in closest contact with the Earldom. Culturally, too, the Anglo-Normans of Ulster were not unacquainted with the Gaelic world. Hugh de Lacy's stepmother was Irish, while Walter de Burgh's cousin married Aedh Buidhe O Neill. Richard de Burgh was a patron of Irish poets and an elegy was composed on his death in 1326.[42] When Sir Robert Savage's son John died in 1374, the Annals of Ulster lament, 'orphaned is learning after him'. That the change could be peaceful is shown by John MacDonnell of the Isles gaining control of the Glens of Antrim by marriage to Margery Byset: something similar may have happened with MacQuillans. In short we may be over-estimating or at least misunderstanding the 'Gaelic Revival' if we look for it to be signalled by battles recorded in the Annals or elsewhere and think in terms of invasions and war.

The society of later fifteenth century Ireland and its organisation is usually considered a new phenomenon arising from the Anglo-Norman collapse of the fourteenth century. The measures described by Frame[43] show the Dublin government re-organising itself in accordance with the changed situation. The over-riding problem for it was the security threat posed by the Leinster Irish based on the Wicklow hills. To meet it the government organised wards of soldiers to guard districts, usually based on local castles on the frontiers, and tried to follow a steady policy of enforcing personal lordship over the individual Irish leaders. This was not a new solution; we can see it had been in existence on the borders of the Anglo-Norman colony in Ulster since the times of John de Courcy, or at least Hugh de

Lacy. During this late mediaeval period the lords of the south-east of Ireland, Ormonds or FitzGeralds and the rest, increasingly based their power on Irish exactions and ideas of lordship. Again, we have seen this to have existed in Ulster from the beginning when the Anglo-Normans compromised with the Irish system of agriculture and linked it to their own market economy, while that typically fifteenth century phenomenon, the mercenary band billeted on the country, can be seen linked with the castle of ward in the Bonnacht of Ulster. As we have seen in the Earldom of Ulster and as Lydon points out,[44] this situation, although superficially unstable with raids and violence, was not fundamentally chaotic. The building projects of the Earls of Ulster and the establishment of towns there in the thirteenth century were reflected in the friaries and castles of the fifteenth century. At a lower level of society, the Earl's tenants living in halls made raid-proof by being perched on mottes are found again in the lesser lords of fifteenth and sixteenth century Ireland living in the many tower-houses of the time. The accommodation of the tower-houses, when contrasted with the demesne farming castles of the local gentry in England, is essentially comparable to the mottes like Clough or Lismahon. They provide a hall and one or two chambers over a vaulted store-room: both are defensible by a small number of men. In neither case are the barns and other equipment of demesne farming present: their wealth is provided by renders in kind from their tenants. In short, the way of life which was typical of the later mediaeval period in Ireland may not have been a new development of the fourteenth century. Its origins are to be found in the compromises of life in the frontier lordships like the Earldom of Ulster: other areas such as Connacht or in particular Kerry under the FitzGerald lords of Desmond would probably show the same features. The history of the later lordship of Ireland may not have been so much a story of the evolution of new answers to life in Ireland but the application of the frontier baronies' ways to the more English south and east.

There are general implications in this survey for the general study of the history of mediaeval Ireland. By concentrating on writing accounts of the whole of Ireland, usually largely based on royal documentation, historians have given a picture of Ireland which is perhaps too uniform and organised. This has resulted in a tendency to blur the details of the events and society in any one area. This tends to produce an account which inevitably leans more heavily on the better documented areas and implies that the same situation prevailed everywhere. The other problem is that a general account will tend to accept the Dublin governmental view of affairs and will tacitly assume that the wishes of that government reflect the view of all Anglo-Normans in Ireland; that there was a colonial situation in Ireland. The keystone of this comes in accepting a crucial division of the people of the island into the English or Anglo-Norman and the Irish, and from this follows the assumption that the two groups were normally or even automatically hostile. This is indeed probably true, and certainly the violence resulting from the divisions dictated much of life for many people. Yet when we look at a border earldom, the contrast between it and other Anglo-Norman lordships was clearly considerable. At the fringes of the English settlement the lack of actual numbers of settlers forced the Earls and their tenants to work on an Irish basis for their economy and much of their social system.

Even the boundaries of the earldom, on close analysis, are to be seen in Irish terms. On the other side of the fence, we can see that Irish reactions to the incomers differed. Twelfth century Irish society was by no means static and so this variability is not to be wondered at. We have seen how there was a difference between the Irish of eastern Ulster and the others, in particular Cenel Eoghain. The former, the Ui Tuirtre and Ui Echach Cobo, were often allied to the Earldom politically and seem to have seen the Anglo-Normans as preferable to their old enemies to the west. The clearest illustration of this is the complaint of O Flynn that O Cahans had raided cattle 'contra pacem meam et contra pacem domini comitis', in a document dated by Henry III's regnal year. These Irish seem to have employed coin, and so been linked economically to the Earldom. They were apparently able to use castles too in a widespread and effective manner, in the case of Ui Tuirtre, to hold off any Anglo-Norman conquest. The Cenel Eoghain were not devoid of outside influences, however, as shown by sporadic castles in their area, while the evidence from pottery shows them importing objects, and indeed a small industry from the economic system of the Anglo-Normans. It is significant that the evidence of real nationalistic conflict comes from the area most sheltered from real conflict: the Church, in a more settled part of the Earldom. It is the same in the rest of Ireland: the evidence of automatic attitudes of hostility comes from these more sheltered areas. The more basic point is that we might be better to look on mediaeval Ireland as a society which had a whole variety of compromises between the two nations involved. We should examine each one as a single system on its own.

These questions hinge in part on the kind of evidence used, whether documentary or physical, historical or archaeological. From this study some of the differences in this period can be seen. The framework of the study must be based on the contemporary documentation, for only this will give the accuracy of dating and the identifications of the people involved that we must have. Archaeological methods will find difficulty, unless they are based on dendrochronological evidence, in assigning an object or building to a narrower bracket than a half-century, or in most cases a century. Few objects actually betray their political origin, and none are confined in their use to a political boundary. No single distribution map of objects from mediaeval Ulster reflects to any degree the boundaries of the Earldom as deduced from the documentary evidence recording the actual ownership or occupation of land. Yet it is this very precision of the documents which can lead us into the oversimplification of drawing hard and fast lines in our story. A clerk has to record the items of income under headings and inevitably he uses terms such as 'manor' which may have other connotations which do not apply to the actual case involved. We must beware of accepting them at face value, as always in history. This provides the role for the physical evidence: to act as a control on the picture we might be led to draw from the historical sources. By focusing our view on individual sites, we are led to ask about the detailed settlement of a particular area. In the realm of social history it can contribute information on such questions as living conditions or housing which we can set against the various categories of land tenure of which we may read. We can see that while the Earl enjoyed a standard of living comparable to an English magnate's, his tenants were living very differently: these tenants seem not to have varied much in housing, whether they held by knight service or by suit of the county court. In economics the distribution of pottery or of grave slabs reveals some of the constraints of marketing and distributions of goods, while their manufacturing details help to betray the English origins of the craftsmen who made them. It is from evidence like this that we may assess some of the socio-economic impact of the Anglo-Normans on the Irish. Yet this evidence would be useless without the chronology of the documents. We would flounder among the confusion of mottes, largely obsolete in Britain by 1177 yet being put up in Ulster apparently until the mid-thirteenth century, while the Earl's castles are completely up to English standards of their day. We could never explain the chain of events which led to John de Courcy calling in northern English Cistercians and so, at Inch, patronising the earliest Gothic in Ireland, if we did not know the dates and persons concerned. We must use all the evidence we have and use it together.

These arguments may seem a far cry from that winter's morning when John de Courcy rode into Downpatrick in 1177, yet in that event much of what we have discussed was prefigured. The Earldom of Ulster was not a typical part of the Anglo-Norman settlement of Ireland as seen from Dublin. In the slenderness of his resources and his dependence on Irish help, his venture in the north was to set the pattern for his successors. Wherever they went in Europe, the Normans were above all energetic and prepared to assimilate themselves to the local conditions of the lands they conquered. Their history in Ulster, at the other end of their more glamorous Mediterranean conquests, was typical: making a profit from Irish agriculture, fighting and building for themselves, and as firmly convinced as any Victorian mill-owner that what they did was right in their own sight and in the sight of God. Because of our historical perspective we must beware of making judgements based on either later events or ideas, like nineteenth century nationalism, or patterns which we have detected in other mediaeval societies, in Ireland or elsewhere. We may, and will, use the Earldom of Ulster to make such comparisons but we may only do so after we have established its history from its own sources.

NOTES

1. *Patent and Close Rolls, Ireland,* (ed. E. Tresham), p. 38; *Clyn's Annals,* 1343.

2. *Patent and Close Rolls, Ireland,* (ed. E. Tresham), pp. 38B, 45; *Calendar of Patent Rolls, 1345-8,* p. 298.

3. *Annals of Ireland,* (ed. J. T. Gilbert), II, pp. 391, 393.

4. Appendix Three.

5. *Clyn's Annals, Annals of Ulster,* 1344.

6. J. Hogan: *Proceedings of the Royal Irish Academy,* XL(C), 1932, p. 226; S. O Ceallaigh: *Gleanings from Ulster history,* p. 62.

7. *Annals of Ulster,* 1354.

8. *Ibid.,* 1359, 1368.

9. *Annals of Ireland* (ed. J. T. Gilbert), II, p. 283.

10. *Ibid.,* p. 283; *Annals of Ulster,* 1374, 1375.

11. *Ibid.,* 1384.

12. A. J. Otway-Ruthven: *A history of medieval Ireland,* pp. 322, 328-9.

13. E. Curtis: *Richard II in Ireland,* pp. 105-7, 144-6.

14. *Patent and Close Rolls, Ireland,* (ed. E. Tresham), p. 146B; G. Hill: *The MacDonnells of Antrim,* pp. 22-3.

15. *Patent and Close Rolls, Ireland,* (ed. E. Tresham), p. 115.

16. *Calendar of Patent Rolls, 1385-8,* p. 438; *1388-92,* p. 405.

17. *Ibid., 1364-7,* p. 190; *Calendar of Close Rolls, 1389-92,* pp. 473, 496; *1392-6,* pp. 6, 20.

18. *Patent and Close Rolls, Ireland,* (ed. E. Tresham), p. 170B.

19. *Calendar of Patent Rolls, 1405-8,* p. 88.

20. A. J. Otway-Ruthven: *A history of medieval Ireland,* p. 360.

21. *Annals of Ulster,* 1425; C. O Ceallaigh: *Gleanings from Ulster history,* p. 63.

22. *Patent and Close Rolls, Ireland,* (ed. E. Tresham), p. 246.

23. *Annals of Ulster,* 1425.

24. *Annals of Ulster,* 1433; *Annals of the Four Masters,* 1433.

25. *Calendar of Patent Rolls, 1467-77,* p. 161.

26. D. E. Flanagan: *Dinnseanchas,* V, 1973, pp. 65-7.

27. Appendix Three.

28. *Annals of Ireland,* (ed. J. T. Gilbert), II, p. 393; *Annals of Ulster,* 1376.

29. *Patent and Close Rolls, Ireland,* (ed. E. Tresham), p. 115.

30. *C.D.S.,* III, No.'s 1279, 1369.

31. *Annals of the Four Masters,* 1442, 1454.

32. *Annals of Ulster,* 1472.

33. R. Nicholson: *Scottish Historical Review,* XLII, 1963, pp. 30-40.

34. *36th Report of the Deputy Keeper, P.R.I.,* p. 54.

35. *National Manuscripts of Ireland,* (ed. J. T. Gilbert), II, plate 73.

36. G. H. Orpen: *J.R.S.A.I.,* XLIII, 1913, pp. 137, 139.

37. R. Nicholson: *Scottish Historical Review,* XLII, 1963, pp. 30-40; British Library, *Add. mss.,* V, 25459.

38. S. Painter: *Studies in the history of the English feudal barony,* Chapter VII.

39. N. Denholm-Young: *Seigneurial administration in England,* pp. 67f.

40. M. Altschul: *A baronial family in medieval England,* chapter IX.

41. *Annals of Ulster,* 1383.

42. J. F. Lydon: *The lordship of Ireland in the middle ages,* p. 183.

43. R. Frame: *English Historical Review,* XC, 1975, pp. 748-77.

44. J. F. Lydon: *The lordship of Ireland in the middle ages,* pp. 241-2.

Appendix 1:
Genealogical Tables of Mediaeval Ulster Families

NONE of these tables is complete in all details: the aim has been to illustrate the main lines of descent and connections of the major families involved. The details of Table 2 are derived from W. E. Wightman: *The Lacy family in England and Normandy*, p. 194f; G. W. S. Barrow: *Feudal Britain*, pp. 245-6; W. Dickinson & A. A. Duncan: *Scotland from the earliest times to 1603*, p. 153; G. H. Orpen: *Ireland under the Normans* III, pp. 286-7, IV, p. 159 (the sources for Table 3). Table 1 is derived from J. Hogan's article in the *Proceedings of the Royal Irish Academy*, XL (C), 1932, plate VI.

Table 1: The O Neills of Cenel Eoghain

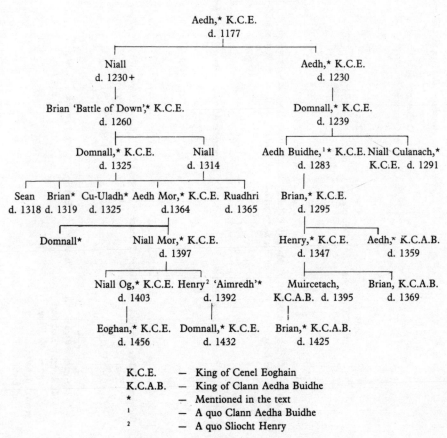

K.C.E.	— King of Cenel Eoghain
K.C.A.B.	— King of Clann Aedha Buidhe
*	— Mentioned in the text
1	— A quo Clann Aedha Buidhe
2	— A quo Sliocht Henry

129

Table 2: The Families of de Lacy, de Galloway and de Burgh

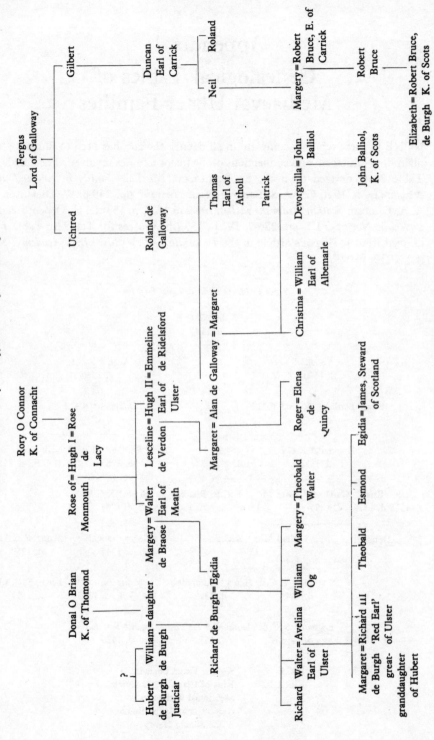

Table 3: The descendants of Richard III de Burgh, Earl of Ulster

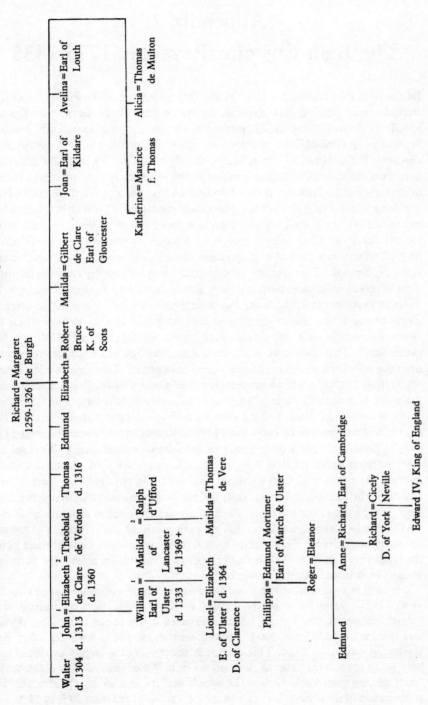

Appendix 2:
The Irish Customs Revenue, 1275-1335

IN the Irish Pipe Rolls calendared by the Deputy Keeper of the Public Records of Ireland, in his 36th to 54th Reports, are the receipts of the Great New Custom levied in Ireland from 1275 intermittently to the mid-fourteenth century. Westropp[1] published lists of them, but they are incomplete and confused in chronology. MacNiocaill[2] has collected the Pipe Roll entries into lists under the ports concerned, but has little discussion of them: similarly Graham[3] has used the totals recorded to rank the ports of Ireland in importance. All these suffer from problems of not taking into account the annual variations in yield or in the details of the records (some ports have more sums entered for them because more years' records survive). What follows here is an attempt to present the figures of the original records as a list and in graph form (fig. 11), the production of which needs some explanation. The problem of converting these accounts, recorded as lump sums received at certain ports between given dates, into figures of receipts for calendar years was met by finding the monthly average for each period concerned. These averages were then re-distributed into the calendar years: in cases where ten or eleven months only of a year were accounted for, the annual figure was extrapolated. Thus gaps may occur both when the figures for a year are missing from the calendars, or where the coverage is only partial. There are two large gaps: one is from 1312 to 1321, which deprives us of a record of the Bruce invasion, and the other between 1324 and 1333, when the receipts from Ross and Cork alone could be calculated. These two gaps are the only ones longer than four years so that the table of receipts can be considered generally complete between 1276 and 1312. On the graph, two ports have been omitted for the sake of clarity: Wexford and Kerry, which contributed 0.15% and 0.30% respectively of the total customs revenue. As a result of these methods, it must be emphasised that there is little chance of the individual annual totals quoted being absolutely accurate, any more than that the sums received at the Exchequer were the same as those levied at each port. It can be claimed, however, that they are relatively accurate, and can be used on a comparative basis. The customs were levied only on wool, wool-fells and hides; the figures are a guide to the pastoral prosperity of the regions around the ports, not to their own manufacturing strength.

It is clear at a glance that there was a serious decline in customs revenue after the years 1291-2 (years for which no figures survive). Before then the average total annual receipt came to about £1,321; afterwards it was about £574. This decline was sudden: in 1293 the total received was about £887, with no other year producing more than £734. This decline is selective, being largely produced by a very sharp drop in the value of the customs from Waterford and New Ross, with a lesser decline from Cork: Dublin, Drogheda and the rest are hardly affected. The contribution of these first two ports to the total received fell from 57% to 37%. Any

132

explanation of this decline in the revenue must, therefore, be based on causes affecting, in particular, the trade of the pastoral hinterlands of Waterford and Ross between 1290 and 1294.

Internal political factors are lacking to explain this pattern of decline and would hardly be so permanent: the 1321 and 1322 figures are surprisingly high in spite of the Bruce invasions. The 1290's saw the start of a period of war for Edward I. The wars occurred in different areas at different times, so all trade need not have been dislocated; piracy was endemic, nor was war total, either to prohibit trade or to last without frequent truces. War should stimulate the consumption, for example, of hides, but royal purchases might not have paid customs. Again the timing of the decline in revenue, before 1294, and its permanence rules out this explanation: even to the Scottish campaigns, the Irish contribution seems largely to have been food; the purchases of hides would have had to be enormous to produce this effect.[4]

There remain several more general points. Firstly it is in the south-east, the hinterlands of Cork, Waterford and Ross, that the main pastoral prosperity of Ireland lay in this period. The figures clearly show the weak economic position of Ulster and the west, represented by Limerick and Galway. The story of the Customs, and in particular their decline, is also a part of the financial problems of the royal administration in Ireland under the last years of Edward I and Edward II.[5] At this time, they were faced by a declining income on the one hand and, on the other, increased expenditure needed for internal security and, above all, excessive demands for money to be sent to England to pay for the Scottish wars. Before 1291-2 the Customs revenue clearly matched the royal estimate of 2,000 marks,[6] and at this figure formed 20% of a (very approximate) annual income of £6,500. Within four years it was yielding only a half of the pre-1291 figure, a serious blow to a precarious position. Whatever the cause of this decline, as defined above, it is clearly a part of the troubles of the royal administration of fourteenth century Ireland.

PORTS	1276 £	s.	1277 £	s.	1278 £	s.	1279 £	s.	1281 £	s.	1282 £	s.	1287 £	s.	1288 £	s.	1290 £	s.	1293 £	s.	1294 £	s.	1295 £	s.	1296 £	s.
Cork	208	16	185	16	101	9	94	10	250	4	288	0	244	6	244	12	321	12	195	8	127	2	120	12	120	12
Drogheda	66	12	101	8	113	17	147	16	146	2	147	2	158	12	123	7	194	16	132	8	160	10	156	0	156	0
Dublin	114	0	106	8	20	15	7	8	153	0	181	17	128	16	157	16	164	2	61	7	76	7			66	0
Galway	11	8	17	2			12	0	35	8			22	0	18	4	16	7	21	8	21	10				
Kerry													13	6	4	14	9	19	5	18	11	6				
Limerick					5	8	7	9	13	6			9	18	9	18	3	6	4	18	15	18	8	8	8	8
Ross	387	3	472	4	529	3	564	4	329	15	699	0	376	16	451	14	493	16	230	16	89	0				
Ulster	12	12	21	4	30	5	39	17	37	1			27	4	28	1	28	10	16	18	8	8	8	8	8	8
Waterford					416	13	388	8	301	16	381	18	322	0	362	15	434	2	203	0	105	18	200	8	200	8
Wexford	5	8	3	8	3	0	3	16					0	14	1	10	2	17	2	12	2	1				
Youghal	48	12	49	16	50	18			82	13	62	8	36	6	38	1	38	14	22	15	17	10	15	0	15	0
TOTALS	854	11	930	6	1271	8	1265	8	1346	5	1760	5	1339	18	1440	12	1707	11	887	8	635	3	508	16	574	16

PORTS	1297 £	s.	1298 £	s.	1302 £	s.	1303 £	s.	1307* £	s.	1308* £	s.	1311 £	s.	1312 £	s.	1321 £	s.	1322 £	s.	1323* £	s.	1324 £	s.	1332* £	s.
Cork	113	15	67	4	148	0	174	12	213	18	151	13	131	8	131	8	120	0			72	12	90	0	120	0
Drogheda	156	16			99	12	117	4	112	17			145	4	145	4	106	13	106	13						
Dublin	94	16			90	16	91	8	126	0			30	0	30	0	79	19	79	19			81	0		
Galway	34	4	34	3	20	0											18	1	18	1						
Kerry					4	0	1	0																		
Limerick	8	8			11	14	14	12			5	8														
Ross			75	0	148	15	217	17					190	16	190	16	90	16	90	16			48	0	40	16
Ulster	8	8			33	6	18	12					29	14	29	14										
Waterford	182	14	78	10	92	11	100	0					130	4	130	4	74	0	74	0	3	0	97	16		
Wexford					2	12	1	0					1	16												
Youghal	15	0	15	0	26	4			22	4			18	12	18	12	15	9	15	9			4	4		
TOTALS	613	5	269	17	677	10	736	5	475	1	157	1	677	14	675	18	484	18	364	18	75	12	321	0	160	16

*Annual totals not included when calculating post-1292 annual average, because of inadequate data.

NOTES

1. T. J. Westropp: *Proceedings of the Royal Irish Academy*, XXX (C) 1913, pp. 361-428.

2. G. MacNiocaill: *Na Burgeisi*, II, pp. 522-8.

3. B. J. Graham, in *The Development of the Irish town* (ed R. A. Butlin), pp. 39-42.

4. I am very grateful to Dr M. Prestwich of St. Andrews University for discussion of these points.

5. H. G. Richardson and G. O. Sayles: *Proceedings of the Royal Irish Academy*, LXII (C), 1962, pp. 87-100; J. F. Lydon: *Irish Historical Studies*, XIV, 1964, pp. 39-57; R. H. M. Dolley: *Proceedings of the Royal Irish Academy*, LXVI (C), 1968, pp. 235-97.

6. *Calendar of Documents relating to Ireland*, II, no. 2329.

K

Appendix 3:

The Account Rolls of the Ministers of Elizabeth de Burgh, 1353-60

SIX documents are published here, referred to for convenience as rolls I to VI, kept in the Public Record Office in London (reference SC6/1239/32 & 33). They consist of, firstly, accounts of three consecutive terms (rolls I-III), respectively covering: from the feast of the purification of the Virgin to St Peter ad vincula, a.r. Edward III 27 (2 February to 1 August 1353); from St Peter ad vincula a.r. Edward III 27 to the purification of the Virgin a.r. Edward III 28 (1 August 1353 to 2 February 1354); the purification of the Virgin a.r. Edward III 28 to St Peter ad vincula a.r. Edward III 28 (2 February to 1 August 1354). Secondly, there are two other consecutive accounts: the first (roll IV) from 1 August a.r. Edward III 31 to 1 August a.r. Edward III 32 (i.e. 1358-59): the second (roll V) runs from St Peter ad vincula a.r. Edward III 32 to the feast of St Michael in the next year (1 August 1359 to 29 September 1360). The first three accounts appear to be complete but roll IV lacks an account of expenses, but has more detail on receipts; roll V only has receipts from the fisheries and expenses. All are the accounts of John of Knaresburgh (Knaresborough in Yorkshire), described as the receiver of Elizabeth de Burgh, as presented to her treasurer. The sixth document, the briefest of all, is simply headed 'Accounts of John of Knaresburgh for the 27 and 28th years': it consists of allowances made to him. In date it overlaps with rolls I-III but the calculations do not fit with the figures, of arrears for example, in them.

The entries of receipts in rolls I to IV are very largely repetitive in both content and order. In order therefore to save space, and also to facilitate comparisons from one roll to another, the receipts of these rolls have been conflated into one list. Such variations − other than the few minor ones of the order of the individual items − as do exist, along with additional information in various individual accounts, have been noted as they occur. This list is followed by the expenses accounted for in each of rolls I to III (there are no expenses on IV) which vary too much to be tabulated together. Rolls V and VI follow individually. The manuscripts are generally neatly written but occasionally closely written emendations or stains make the writing too difficult for this reader.

There are some more general observations to be made. Roll I looks as though it is the start of a run separated by at least a short break from earlier accounts. There are no arrears carried forward on to it, while the entries are fewer and less complete than those of the later rolls: less money is raised. Overall, there is clearly a rising trend to Elizabeth's income from Ulster during the 1350's. Between rolls I and III, which cover the same term, there is a rise of some 15% in receipts (from £45. 6. 4¼ to £52. 10. 1). Between rolls II and III (making up a complete year) and roll IV there is a rise from £121. 7. 4. to £124. 2. 3: this last would have been larger but for the damage caused by Henry Savage at Portros (£3. 1. 0): without this there would have been a rise of about 5%. The fisheries show a steady rise in receipts from £15. 13. 10 (roll II) to £21. 18. 6 (roll IV) to £50. 0. 0 (roll V). More significant as an indicator of increasing stability are the accounts of the mills with repairs bringing more into production in 1360 than there had been in 1353, and to more profit. It is useful to compare the figures with the annual receipts from the same manors in 1259-62, derived from the accounts of Henry de Mandeville (*National manuscripts of Ireland*, ed. J. T. Gilbert, plate 73; E. Curtis: *Proceedings of the Royal Irish Academy*, XXXIX(C), 1929, pp. 10-11).

	1259-62	II/III-1353-54	IV-1359-60
	£ s. d.	£ s. d.	£ s. d.
Culrath	11. 10. 4	11. 7. 0	12. 13. 6
Portros	10. 0. 0	20. 7. 0	17. 9. 4
Portkaman	5. 0. 0	15. 2. 0	15. 4. 8
Stanton*	2. 0. 0	2. 0. 0	2. 0. 0
Dunsomery**	4. 8. 4	18. 10. 4	19. 1. 10
Dundrif**	13. 6. 8	2. 18. 2	4. 6. 8
Mills	84. 15. 0	10. 4. 8	13. 9. 4
Fisheries of Bann & Lyn	20. 16. 8	15. 13. 10	21. 18. 6

*Not a manor in either period.
**Dundrif is part of Dunsomery in 1353-60: a truer comparison is made by comparing the combined receipts. It looks as though receipts entered under Dundrif in 1259-62 were transferred to the Dunsomery account in 1353-60.

ROLLS I-IV – RECEIPTS

	I 2 Feb 1353 to 1 Aug 1353	II 1 Aug 1353 to 1 Feb 1354	III 2 Feb 1354 to 1 Aug 1354	IV 1 Aug 1358 to 1 Aug 1359
Arrears	£ s. d.	£ s. d.	£ s. d.	£ s. d.
From the previous account		3. 2. 9½	69. 15. 5¼	5. 15. 8
Culrath[1]				
Assisia villae	2. 0. 0	2. 0. 0	2. 0. 0	4. 0. 0
Castelnarium	1. 0	1. 0	1. 0	3. 0
Bann Crossing (passagium aquae de Ban)[2]	1. 0	1. 6	1. 6	3. 4
Court	1. 0	1. 0	1. 0	7. 0
Tolls[3]	1. 8	1. 8	1. 8	3. 4
Meadow	1. 0	1. 0	1. 0	2. 0
Assisia de Dondouan[4]	1. 0. 0	1. 0. 0	1. 0. 0	2. 0. 0
Sumpeton/Sumceston[5]	1. 0. 0	1. 0. 0	1. 10. 0	3. 0. 0
Kirketon[6]	10. 0	10. 0	10. 0	1. 6. 8
Ardbegan[7]	6. 8	6. 8	8. 0	16. 8
Pertyland[8]	5. 0	5. 0	5. 0	10. 0
Garden between the castle and the Bann[9]				8
1 acre called Heryngland[9]				4
1 waste acre newly let to John Baret[9]				6
Total	5. 7. 4	5. 7. 10	5. 19. 2	12. 13. 6

ROLLS I-IV – RECEIPTS (Continued)

	I 2 Feb 1353 to 1 Aug 1353			II 1 Aug 1353 to 1 Feb 1354			III 2 Feb 1354 to 1 Aug 1354			IV 1 Aug 1358 to 1 Aug 1359		
	£	s.	d.	£	s.	d.	£	s.	d.	£	s.	d.
Portros												
Assisia tenementorum[10]	10.	0.	0	10.	0.	0	10.	0.	0	8.	15.	0
Assisia tenementorum (Pentecost)										8.	4.	0
Increase from Langiplatum/Langplatum/ Langflat			6			6			6		2.	0
Court		1.	0		1.	0		1.	0		3.	4
Prise of fish		1.	0		1.	0		1.	0		2.	0
Tolls[11]					1.	0		1.	0		3.	0
Total	10.	2.	6	10.	3.	6	10.	3.	6	17.	9.	4
Portkaman[12]												
Assisia tenementorum[13]	4.	10.	0	4.	10.	0	4.	10.	0	9.	0.	0
Assisia of 20 acres at Weston			10			10			10			
1 cottage at Seton			2			2			2			4
Prise of fish at Seton[14]		1.	0									—
Court[15]		1.	0		1.	8		1.	8		6.	8
1 carucate of demesne, let out[16]		10.	0		10.	0		10.	0		5.	0
Assisia Stanton[17]	1.	0.	0	1.	0.	0	1.	0.	0	2.	0.	0
Increase there								3.	4			
80 acres of demesne at Stanton		6.	8		6.	8		6.	8		13.	4
Balybogy[18]	1.	0.	0	1.	0.	0	1.	0.	0	2.	0.	0
Sandleyton[19]	1.	0.	0	1.	0.	0	1.	0.	0			
40 acres at Weston[20]											3.	4
Cottages near the mill at Portkaman[21]											1.	0
Prise of fish on the river Bush (Bos)[22]										1.	0.	0
Fine for having an inquisition[23]											5.	0
Total	8.	9.	8	8.	9.	4	8.	12.	8	17.	4.	8
Dunsomery[24]												
Four 'villatae' of land	8.	13.	4	8.	13.	4						
Dundrift/Dundrif/Dundreft[25]	1.	9.	1	1.	9.	1				4.	6.	8
Five villatae, at 43/4 each[26]							10.	16.	8			
Villae[27] of Aldton[28]										4.	2.	11
Newton										4.	6.	8
Rathrahan & Lechetone										4.	6.	8
Tweth[29]										4.	0.	5
Court at Dunseverick		3.	0		3.	4		3.	4		16.	2
Sale of a cow					2.	0						
Thomas fitz William's chattels									9			
Thomas fitz William's fine[30]											10.	0
Alan Olorkan's fine[31]											10.	0
An Irish widow's heriot – one cow											4.	0
From the sale of a small porpoise found on the shore											5.	0
Totals	10.	5.	5	10.	7.	9	11.	0.	9	23.	8.	6

ROLLS I-IV – RECEIPTS (Continued)

	I 2 Feb 1353 to 1 Aug 1353			II 1 Aug 1353 to 1 Feb 1354			III 2 Feb 1354 to 1 Aug 1354			IV 1 Aug 1358 to 1 Aug 1359		
	£	s.	d.	£	s.	d.	£	s.	d.	£	s.	d.
Mills												
Culrath[32]			—	1.	6.	8	1.	0.	0	4.	13.	4
Milton[33]		5.	0		5.	0		5.	0	1.	0.	0
Balybogy		5.	0		6.	0		6.	0		13.	4
Dunsumery[34]		11.	0		11.	0		11.	0			
Lecheton		18.	0		18.	0		18.	0	2.	0.	0
Ardbauran/Ardberghin/Ardberhan/ Ardbegan[35]			—			—			—		16.	0
Tiberdornan[36]			—			—			—			—
Portkaman[37]	1.	10.	0	2.	0.	0	1.	18.	0	3.	6.	8
Lyn[38]			—			—			—			—
Aldton[39]										1.	0.	0
Total	3.	9.	0	5.	6.	8	4.	18.	0	13.	9.	4
Fisheries[40]												
Bann and Lyn				14.	10.	0						
?[41]					5.	0						
Fisheries court (on the Bann)					3.	4					4.	6
Farm of the boat called 'Kychenbot'[42]										1.	10.	0
Farm of 15 boats on the Bann										15.	0.	0
Farm of Lyn fisheries[43]										4.	0.	0
Farm of 2 boats on the Bann[44]											5.	0
Staksilver[45]											14.	0
Fees for Licences for fishing with one boat[46]												
Farm of fisheries on the ? river[47]					14.	0						
Prise of fish at Seton[48]					1.	6						
Total				15.	13.	10				21.	18.	6
Antrum[49]												
Assisia villae[50]		3.	4	1.	4.	3	1.	5.	0		13.	4
Assisia villae										1.	14.	10
3 burgages[51]		1.	6		3.	0		3.	0		7.	0
Prise of 16 brewers[52]		2.	8			—		12.	8		5.	6
Court		3.	0		9.	10		12.	11	1.	10.	2
Mill[53]	1.	1.	0	1.	3.	4	1.	3.	4	2.	10.	0
Arrears of Patrick Sandal[54]		6.	4			—			—			—
Rent of Hugh de Bornes[55]		3.	4			—			—			—
Rent of Wymondland[56]			6			—			—			—
Rent of Olbertland[57]			7			—			—			—
Four carucates of demesne[58]	3.	6.	8	3.	6.	8	4.	0.	0	8.	0.	0
One carucate at Hantoncotes/ Hontoncotis[59]		10.	0		13.	4		13.	4	1.	6.	8
Carried forward	5.	18.	11	7.	0.	5	8.	10.	3	16.	7.	6

ROLLS I-IV – RECEIPTS (Continued)

	I 2 Feb 1353 to 1 Aug 1353			II 1 Aug 1353 to 1 Feb 1354			III 2 Feb 1354 to 1 Aug 1354			IV 1 Aug 1358 to 1 Aug 1359		
	£	s.	d.	£	s.	d.	£	s.	d.	£	s.	d.
Brought forward	5.	18.	11	7.	0.	5	8.	10.	3	16.	7.	6
80[60] acres of land at Joncastel/Johancastel		5.	0		5.	0		5.	0		13.	4
2 carucates 16½ acres of betaghs' lands[61]	1.	11.	4½	1.	11.	8	1.	13.	11	3.	16.	7
Prise of brewers of Irish Antrim[62]		5.	0			—			—		10.	0
Render of land called Roykanland[63]		1.	8		1.	8		5.	0		10.	0
Render of the hagard outside the castle[64]			2			—			—		1.	0
Render of the orchard[65]			—		4.	0			—		8.	0
Betaghs' work services			—		5.	0		5.	0		13.	4
Tolls of the vill[66]									7		1.	0
Chattels seized[67]				3.	13.	4						
?[68]				7.	2¾							
Fine[69]								5.	0			
One carucate called Thornleyton let to Lord Robert Savage											10.	0
Rent of a new tower[70]											1.	0
Heriot (one cow) sold[71]											4.	6
Total	8.	2.	1½	13.	8.	3¾	11.	4.	9	23.	16.	3

Fines and amercements[72]

	I			II			III			IV		
From William Richard for an inquisition on Culrath mill								3.	4			
From William fitz John for an inquisition on Lechetone mill								1.	8			
From William Hulit, mayor of Portros, arrears of assisia								6.	3			
Total			—			—		11.	3			—

Loganton[73]

	I	II	III	IV		
One carucate let to John Sendal	—	—	—	1.	0.	0

General receipts and horses sold[74]

	I	II	III	IV		
2 horses sold by John of Knaresburgh				1.	5.	1
Fine from Roger Spenser, farmer of Antrum mill					13.	4
Fine from Richard de Castro, rector of Balybony,[75] for fishing with a boat on the Bann in 1354. He did so in the name of the Prior of St Andrew,[76] who used to have a free boat on the river but the Prior's temporalities were in the hands of Lord Roger[77] and the fishery in Elizabeth de Burgh's					13.	4
Total	—	—	—	2.	11.	9

ROLLS I-IV – RECEIPTS (Continued)

	I 2 Feb 1353 to 1 Aug 1353	II 1 Aug 1353 to 1 Feb 1354	III 2 Feb 1354 to 1 Aug 1354	IV 1 Aug 1358 to 1 Aug 1359
	£ s. d.	£ s. d.	£ s. d.	£ s. d.
Connacht Received from Elizabeth de Burgh's receiver there, but 'no-one dared to go because of the war' in roll IV: unmentioned in rolls I and II	—	—	15. 6. 4	—
Overall Totals received	45. 16. 0½	72. 0. 0¼	137. 11. 10¼	129. 18. 1

Roll I – Expenditure

	£ s. d.
Advanced	
Delivered by Richard of Kyngeston in England as is accounted for by William in his roll for the 27th year	27. 5. 0
Total	27. 5. 0

Expenses

Expenses of John of Knaresburgh going from Herdefeld to Ireland on the 1st April, on his passage to Dublin for 23 days	1. 3. 0
For a boat from Carlingford to Greencastle;[78] the boat was broken there	1. 0
To the men of William Makgengus[79] for a safe passage to the castle of Rath[80]	2. 4
For taking letters on Elizabeth de Burgh's business from John of Knaresburgh from Carlingford to Ralph de Burgh	6
Given to Stephen Makhoulyn,[81] clericus, for protection of Elizabeth de Burgh's lands in Ulster	1. 0
Given to the men of MacGilkon for safe conduct through the middle of Ui Tuirtre (per mediam de Turtrye) on the Sunday after the feast of St John Baptist	4
To John Stall, Elizabeth de Burgh's messenger	6
To William Magengus for safe conduct on the said passage returning on the Tuesday after the feast of Mary Magdalene	1. 0
Spent on Elizabeth de Burgh's business on this journey in Ulster	8
To John of Camlyn for custody of the castle and demesne of Antrim from the feast of the Purification to feast of the nativity of St John Baptist	1. 5 0
From the render of the bridge of Coleraine, destroyed by various men before John of Knaresburgh's arrival in those parts	1. 0
Total	2. 16. 4

Gifts and Renders pardoned

From the quota of the tenants at Portros	3. 0. 0
From the quota of the tenants at Portkaman	3. 4
As a gift to John of Knaresburgh for his work in Ulster	5. 0. 0
Total	8. 3. 4

Fees

His fee from 1st April to 31st July	4.	8.	7
Total	4.	8.	7
Total of expenses and advances	42.	13.	3
John of Knaresburgh owes	3.	2.	9½

Roll II – Expenditure

	£	s.	d.
Expenses			
One new mill-stone bought for Ardbehin mill		13.	4
One old mill-stone bought for Donsomery mill		2.	0
Hire of a boat from Carlingford to Cloch[82]		1.	0
Hire of Hugh Dikot and a man, with two horses on Elizabeth de Burgh's business in England and Ireland over 22 days		5.	0
To McGilcon and his men for safe conduct of money from Culrath to Antrum on 3rd April		2.	8
Hire of a boat from Manybillis[83] to Carlingford on 1st April		3.	0
To Thomas Crokeschank, Elizabeth de Burgh's receiver and bailiff in Dwyskard for his work from the feast of Peter and John to the feast of (ms. illegible)		10.	0
To Walter de Say for his help against Okahen and McUlyn[84]		3.	4
To Patrick Sandal, bailiff of the manor of Antrum for his work		3.	4
Spent on Elizabeth de Burgh's business			11
	2.	4.	7
John of Knaresburgh owes	69.	15.	5¼

Roll III – Expenditure

	£	s.	d.
Expenses and Fees			
Hire of a boat from Drogheda to Le Pere[85] for John de Knaresburgh with 2 men and 2 horses on 22nd June		3.	0
For the expenses of Walter de Say and 40 men with 40 horses at Antrum, and for safe conduct through the middle of Ui Tuirtre (per mediam Turtrie) to the town of Culrath[86]		1.	8
For the conduct of Walter and his men back on the same road and to the men of McCarran on the Tuesday after the feast of St Peter ad vinculas		1.	0
To Thomas Crokschank, Elizabeth de Burgh's receiver in Gwyskard[87] and bailiff, for his work		10.	0
To Patrick Sandal receiver and bailiff of the manor of Antrum		3.	4
To Walter de Say, vicar of Culrath for his help in collecting Elizabeth de Burgh's rents		3.	4
Fee to John de Armis of Camlyn for custody of the castle and demesne of Antrim, from the feast of St Peter ad vinculas in the 27th year to the feast of the apostles Philip and James in the 28th year three quarters of one year's salary of 50/-			
To Richard Port, carpenter and his men for repairing the mill of Lyn	2.	4.	0
For expenses on the way			10
Total	5.	4.	8

Expenses in returning to London

Hire of a boat for John of Knaresburgh with 2 men and 4 horses from			
Manybillis to Liverpool (Lyverpol)	1.	2.	0
For food for the men and horses		3.	3
For their expenses, with one man and one horse, from Liverpool to London, 9 days	1.	0.	0
Total	2.	5.	3

Fees

John of Knaresburgh's fee for one year	13.	6.	8

Advance

Received from William de Manton, Elizabeth de Burgh's treasurer	105.	9. ·	3

And he is quit

Roll V

Account of John de Knaresburgh, attorney and receiver of Lady Elizabeth de Burgo, Lady of Clare from the feast of St Peter ad vinculas in the 32nd year of King Edward III to the feast of St Michael in the next year.

	£	s.	d.
Arrears	85.	13.	3

Fisheries of Bann and Lyn

Farm of one boat called 'Kychenboot' let to John Baret in this year	2.	6.	8
Farm of 18 boats let to various men	25.	6.	8
Farm of one boat let to Henry, son of Lord Robert Savage for 26/8, which cannot			
be collected			nil
From Alan for 3 boats, which he has for the office of bailiff		16.	0
From staksilver		14.	0
From the court		16.	8
From Lyn fisheries	20.	0.	0
Total	50.	0.	0

Total of arrears and receipts	135.	13.	3

Fees

The receivers' fees were not paid during the time of this account

Expenses

To one man going from Kilkenny to Ulster to provide various things for making			
Elizabeth de Burgh's hospital at the Bann and Lyn in the month of May.			
One penny given to the clerk Stapill Kristall. To Roger Hulle of Culrath			
2d per day		4.	10

Advances

From Lord William de Manton, treasurer, on 2nd September in 32nd year	120.	0.	0
From the same Lord William, in payment for 14 lampreys bought in Ireland		9.	0
Total	120.	9.	0

Total of expenses and advances	120.	13.	10
John de Knaresburgh owes	14.	19.	5

	£	s.	d.
He is allowed 30/7 for renders of 2 carucates at Antrum, owed by John son of Robert Savage which cannot be collected	1.	10.	7
He is allowed 43/4 of Lord Edward de Burgo's arrears in Connacht, which cannot be collected	2.	3.	4
He is allowed 20/- which Henry Savage owes from last year for a boat on the Bann fisheries which cannot be collected	1.	0.	0
He is allowed 17/3, arrears from Smalbone which cannot be collected		17.	3
Total of allowances	5.	11.	2
Against the account of John of Knaresburgh	9.	8.	3

And he is pardoned this sum for his work
And he is quit

Memorandum: It is decided that the accounts of the fisheries of the Bann and Lyn shall be drawn up from the feast of St Michael to the feast of St Michael.

Roll VI

Ulster

Account of John of Knaresburgh receiver there for the 27th and 28th year.[88]

	£	s.	d.
Total of expenses and advances as allowed below	126.	6.	2
John owes	11.	5.	8¼
He is allowed 2/7 for various items struck off this debt		2.	7
And so he owes	11.	3.	1¼
And he is allowed from the arrears of 2 carucates in Antrum let to John son of Robert Savage for the terms of St Martin and Pentecost in the 27th year, because they cannot be collected he says until the next account	1.	10.	7
From the farm of Portkaman mill, given to Richard de Castro for Elizabeth de Burgh's work before John went to those parts		3.	0
From the dues of Edward de Burgo of Connacht which cannot be collected in time for this account: to be carried to the next account	2.	3.	4
From the dues of Raymond de Burgo for the Easter term in the 28th year which he cannot collect in time for this account	2.	8.	7
For a horse which John has in his keeping	4.	0.	0
Total[89]	6.	5.	6
And there is against John de Knaresburgh's account	4.	17.	7¼

NOTES

1. Culrath/Coulrath: Coleraine. G. H. Orpen: *Ireland under the Normans*, III, p. 289.

2. 'Farmed' in rolls II and III; let to Richard Miles in roll IV.

3. In roll IV, let to Roger Tollere.

4. Dondouan: Dundooan (C8535) c. two miles north of Coleraine: G. H. Orpen: *J.R.S.A.I.*, XLV 1915, p. 128.

5. Sumpeton: unidentified.

6. Kirketon: Kirkistown – G. H. Orpen: *J.R.S.A.I.*, XV, 1915, p. 139.

7. Ardbegan: unidentified but part of the possessions of Coleraine Dominican Friary in the sixteenth century (G. H. Orpen: *Ireland under the Normans*, III, p. 289).

8. Pertyland: unidentified. In Elizabeth de Burgh's hands through escheat, rolls I-IV.

9. Three entries in roll IV only: for John Baret roll V; his acre was let at 1/- per year.

10. The entry for Portros (Portrush) is fuller in roll IV. John of Knaresburgh accounts for £8. 15. 0 received from Henry Thoules, mayor of Portrush, for St Martin's term: 25/- are missing for some reason (the ms. is illegible). He received £8. 4. 0 from Thomas Brokeschankes (or Crokeshankes – see mills and expenditure, roll III), mayor for Pentecost term: he owed 26/4 because he could not raise it as a result of the poverty and devastation in the land of Smalburn, caused by Henry Savage. 9/8 are allowed to him because the land called Elie is let to farm to Robert de Burnes and John de Hossey.

11. Not mentioned in roll I; in roll IV 'let to farm to William'.

12. Portkaman: Bushmills – W. Reeves: *Ecclesiastical Antiquities*, p. 77.

13. In roll IV, 9 carucates.

14. Transferred to the accounts of fisheries in rolls II and III. In roll IV, nothing is rendered, although it is valued at 3/4, because it was in the hands of Nicholas Halewood, who has nothing to be distrained to pay the debt. Possibly Port Ballintrae.

15. In roll IV, the court has been let to farm to Hugh Slyper.

16. In roll IV let for St Martin's term only.

17. Stanton: To be identified with 'villa que vocatur La Pere' – G. H. Orpen: *Ireland under the Normans*, III, p. 288. This becomes in Irish Ballyclogh, probably the townlands of that name between one and two miles south of Bushmills on the left bank of the R. Bush. In roll III the assises of Stanton render 3/4 more than in rolls I and II because property was in Elizabeth de Burgh's hands because of the minority of the heirs of William and John de Arma of Camlyn.

18. Cf. Balybough – G. H. Orpen: *J.R.S.A.I.*, XLV, 1915, p. 128. Identifiable with Ballybogy townland, c. five miles east of Coleraine (C9232). The Ballybogy between Clough and Cloughmills, suggested by Orpen, seems too far from Bushmills for this context.

19. Sandleyton: unidentified. In roll IV, it rendered nothing because waste for St Martin's term: he accounts for £1. 0. 0 for Pentecost term, for it is let to Thomas fitz Robert at £2. 0. 0 per year.

20. Appears, along with the next four entries, in roll IV only: it presumably includes the 20 acres at Weston accounted for in the previous three rolls (it is described as 'incrementum').

21. In Elizabeth de Burgh's hands in roll IV, because of an inquisition into its possession.

22. Cf. entry made under Fisheries in roll II.

23. Paid by Richard Kerra of Balybogy. The inquisition, over the cottage by Portkaman mill (see above, n. 21), was held before Lord Robert Savage, seneschal of Ulster, and John of Knaresborough: it said that the cottage had come into the hands of Richard, lately Earl of Ulster (i.e. Richard III de Burgh the Red Earl), through escheat and that Richard Kerra was the true heir.

24. Dunsomery: Dunseverick – G. H. Orpen, *Ireland under the Normans*, III, p. 288.

25. Dundrif: Dunluce – *Ibid.*, p. 288. Renders no more in rolls I and II because of a lack of tenants.

26. These five townships in roll III are presumably the four of rolls I and II, with Dunluce.

27. These four villae are presumably the four of rolls I and II.

28. Renders 3/9 less than its previous valuation because 15 acres were waste in St Martin's term. It was to render the old valuation of £4. 6. 8 in future.

29. Renders less 6/3 because 25 acres were waste in St Martin's term. It was to render at the old valuation of £4. 6. 8 in future.

30. Fined for the death of Gilbert the Galloglas (Galloglaghi).

31. Fined for the death of Mac Stoker, an Irishman of Elizabeth de Clare.

32. Ruined in roll I, in Elizabeth de Clare's hands in roll II, renders less in III, because William fitz Henry spent 6/8 on repairing the axle (axella) and two wheels. Combined with Lyn in roll IV.

33. Farmed by Thomas Crokeshank (of Portrush) in this year for a term of ten years: Milton perhaps is to be identified with Ballywillin about one mile south of Portrush (W. Reeves: *Ecclesiastical Antiquities*, p. 76).

34. Is omitted from roll IV: repaired in roll II (expenditure).

35. Waste in rolls I and II (though a mill-stone is bought – *vid.* expenditure); newly repaired and let to Thomas fitz Hugh in roll III.

36. Tiberdornan: Toberdornan td. c. four miles south-east of Portrush (C8937). Waste in rolls I-III: newly repaired in roll IV but the farmer Adam fitz William had been released from three years' farm.

37. 2/- allowed from the farm in roll III, to offset repairs.

38. Lyn: the Cutts of Coleraine (two miles up the Bann from the town) – G. H. Orpen: *Ireland under the Normans*, III, p. 290. Not noted in rolls I and III, waste in roll II, combined with Coleraine in roll IV.

39. Only mentioned in roll IV.

40. No fisheries, except that at Portros, appear in roll I. In roll III it is recorded that the renders are collected in St Martin's term (1 August to 2 February). Salmon spawn in the late summer and early autumn, which presumably explains this pattern: the fisheries are on the north Antrim salmon rivers. In roll IV, the entry is headed 'Fisheries of Bann and Lyn' – the Bush renders under Portkaman.

41. Ms. illegible except for the sum received (checked with total).

42. Let to William fitz Richard.

43. Let to Lord Robert Savage.

44. No more was received because of the war.

45. Presumably a toll on fixed nets or weirs.

46. Issued to Robert Vang, William fitz Henry and others, for fishing after 24th June (nativity of St John Baptist).

47. Ms. illegible. Presumably the Bush – the entry is in roll II only while the Bush fisheries render £1 under Portkaman in roll IV.

48. Renders 1/- in roll I, and nil in roll IV, under Portkaman.

49. Manor of Antrum, roll III; manor of Antrum at Irisantrum in roll IV. Antrim town.

50. 'No more because a great part of the town was destroyed by war and part in Elizabeth de Burgh's hands through escheat' (roll I). Ms. illegible for the first entry in roll II but in the other rolls this is the first. In roll III, the £1. 5. 0 is stated to include rents from free tenants. In roll IV, the 13/4 is received from 80 burgages at 2d per burgage per year: 34/10 is received from free tenants.

51. In Elizabeth de Burgh's hands through escheat.

52. Not mentioned in roll II; the entry in roll III presumably includes the brewers accounted for separately under Irish Antrim of rolls I and IV.

53. The mill let to Roger Spenser on a term of ten years in roll IV.

54. This, and the next three entries, appear only in roll I.

55. For Richard Land.

56. Unidentified.

57. Unidentified.

58. In roll I, this and the next seven entries are accounted for under a separate head, 'Antrim demesne': the previous entries are totalled to £2. 2. 3; the demesne entries to £5. 19. 10¼. The other rolls do not observe the division and their entries do not follow a single order.

59. Unidentified: ms. illegible for the sum rendered in roll I; from the total it was deduced to be 10/-. In Elizabeth de Burgh's hands for lack of tenants in roll III.

60. 40 acres in roll I: acreage not stated in roll IV.

61. 'in hibernica villa de Antrum' (rolls I, II and III); 'de redditu betagiorum videlicet nativorum de Irisantrum' (roll IV); 3 carucates, 20 acres in roll II; area not stated in rolls III and IV.

62. Three brewers in roll I; number illegible in roll IV (from the render presumably also 3): not mentioned in rolls II and III.

63. Thus rolls I and IV; roll III has Croynkanland; II Cronkanland: described as 40 acres in roll IV.

64. 'One acre called Le Hagard' in roll IV; not mentioned in rolls II and III. The last entry of roll I.

65. 'Below Antrim castle' in roll IV; not mentioned in rolls I and IV.

66. Tolls do not appear in rolls I and II. Let to Robert (ms. illegible) in roll IV.

67. From John (ms. illegible): the remaining items occur only in the one roll as listed.

68. Ms. illegible.

69. From the heir of Simon Mcquiltan (killed by John McQuany).

70. Let for 2/- per annum to Patrick Sendal and Adam Hosey. Built on Elizabeth de Burgh's land.

71. Heriot of William Kerd.

72. These items appear only in roll III.

73. Loganton: cf. G. H. Orpen: *J.R.S.A.I.*, XV, 1915, p. 127; Ballylagan, c.six miles upstream from Coleraine on the west bank of the Bann. This item appears only in roll IV, where it is entered between Portros and Portkaman.

74. This item also appears only in roll IV.

75. Balybony: Ballymoney parish − W. Reeves: *Ecclesiastical Antiquities*, p. 80.

76. Either the Priory of St Andrew in Ards (Black Abbey), which had been in trouble as an alien priory before 1361 (*Calendar of Patent Rolls 1358-61*, p. 561), and so liable to give confusion, or else a mistake (by Richard de Castro?) for St Patrick's Down, granted one free boat on the Bann by Hugh de Lacy (W. Dugdale: *Monasticon Anglicanum*, VI (2), p. 1125).

77. This man is unknown. The obvious person to take the temporalities would have been Robert Savage seneschal of Ulster in the name of Lionel of Clarence, husband of the heiress of the Earldom.

78. 'Grenecastell': Greencastle, Co. Down.

79. I.e. Maginnis; he was custos pasagii de Inisdulian: cf. Imberdoilan (the Newry pass) − *C.D.I.*, II no. 1918.

80. Rath: Dundrum, Co. Down.

81. Makhoulyn: MacQuillan.

82. A port named Cloch is unknown, unless Dundrum bay, Co. Down.

83. Manybillis: Maynbillis: Movilla, Co. Down.

84. A John de Say stood surety for the de Mandevilles in 1282 (*C.D.I.*, II, no. 1918): three de Says shared 10 carucates at Dromert (near Ballymoney) with Sir Robert and John Savage in 1333 (G. H. Orpen: *J.R.S.A.I.*, XLV, 1915, p. 129). OKahen: O Cahan; McUlyn: McQuillan.

85. Le Pere: this must be the same as the Cloch of note 82.

86. This confirms the position of Ui Tuirtre in mid-Antrim.

87. Twescard.

88. Written, reversed, at the foot of the roll.

89. The horse is not included.

Bibliography

Addyman, P. V., Coney Island, Lough Neagh; Prehistoric Settlement, Anglo-Norman castle and Elizabethan Native fortress, in *U.J.A.*, XVIII, 1965, pp. 78-101.

-----, Excavations at Ludgershall castle, Wiltshire, in *Medieval Archaeology*, XII, 1968, pp. 179-80; XVI, 1972, pp. 113-4.

Alcock, L., Castle Tower, Penmaen, a Norman ring-work in Glamorgan, in *Antiquaries' Journal*, XLVI, 1966, pp. 178-210.

Altschul, M., *A baronial family in medieval England*, Baltimore, 1965.

Analecta Hibernica, Irish Manuscripts Commission, Dublin, 1930-

Annals of Ireland (ed. J. T. Gilbert), *Chartularies of St. Mary's Abbey, Dublin*, vol. II, London (Rolls series), 1884.

The Annals of Ireland by Friar John Clyn and Thady Dowling, (ed. R. Butler), Irish Archaeological Society, 1849.

Annals of the Kingdom of Ireland by the Four Masters, (ed. J. O'Donovan), 7 vols., Dublin, 1848-51.

The Annals of Loch Cé, (ed. W. M. Hennessy), Rolls Series, 1871.

The Annals of Ulster, (ed. W. M. Hennessy and B. MacCarthy), 4 vols., Dublin, 1887-1901.

An Archaeological Survey of County Down, (ed. E. M. Jope), H.M.S.O., Belfast, 1966.

Baillie, M. G. L., A horizontal mill of the eighth century A.D. at Drumard, County Derry, in *U.J.A.*, XXXVIII, 1975, pp. 25-32.

Barrow, G. W. S., *Feudal Britain*, London, 1971.

Barton, K., A Medieval pottery kiln at Ham Green, Bristol, in *Transactions of the Bristol and Gloucester Archaeological Society*, LXXXIII, 1963, pp. 95-126.

Bateson, D. B., Roman material from Ireland: a reconsideration, in *Proceedings of the Royal Irish Academy*, LXXIII(C), 1973, pp. 21-98.

Bateson, M., The Laws of Breteuil, in *English Historical Review*, XV, 1900, pp. 73-78, 302-18, 496-523, 754-7; XVI, 1901, pp. 92-110, 332-45.

Bilson, J., The Architecture of the Cistercians with special reference to some of their earlier churches in England, in *Archaeological Journal*, LXVI, 1909, pp. 185-280.

Butler, L. A. S., Some early Northern grave covers; a re-assessment, in *Archaeologia Aeliana*, 4th series XXXVI, 1958, pp. 207-20.

Bryant, G. F., Experimental kiln firings at Barton-on-Humber, in *Medieval Archaeology*, XXI, 1977, pp. 106-23.

Byrne, F. J., *Irish Kings and high Kings*, London, 1973.

Calendar of Close Rolls, London, 1892-   .

Calendar of Documents relating to Ireland, (ed. H. S. Sweetman), 5 vols., London, 1875-86.

Calendar of Documents relating to Scotland, (ed. J. Bain), 4 vols., Edinburgh, 1881-88.

Calendar of Justiciary Rolls, Ireland, 3 vols., Dublin, 1905-56.

Calendar of Liberate Rolls, London, 1916-   .

Calendar of Patent Rolls, London, 1891-   .

Carthcart King, D., The field archaeology of mottes in England and Wales, in *Château Gaillard*, V, 1970, pp. 101-10.

Collins, A. E. P., Settlement in Ulster, 0-1100 A.D., in *U.J.A.*, XXXI, 1968, pp. 53-8.

Colvin, H. M., (ed) *The history of the King's works*, London, 1963.

Costello, M. A., *De Annatis Hiberniae*, vol. I (Ulster), Dublin, 1912.

Curtis, E., *Richard II in Ireland*, Oxford, 1927.

-----, The Sheriff's accounts of the Honor of Dungarvan, County Wexford, Twescard in Ulster, and of County Waterford, in *Proceedings of the Royal Irish Academy*, XXXIX (C), 1929, pp. 1-17.

-----, The Dower Charter of Affreca de Courcy, in *Proceedings of the Belfast Natural History and Philosophical Society*, session for 1928-29, pp. 2-10.

-----, The 'Bonnaght' of Ulster, in *Hermathena*, XXI, 1931, pp. 87-105.

Curtis, E., Rental of the manor of Lisronagh, in *Proceedings of the Royal Irish Academy*, XLIII (C), 1935-37 pp. 41-73.

-----, The MacQuillan or Mandeville Lords of the Route, in *Proceedings of the Royal Irish Academy*, XLIV C, 1938, pp. 99-113.

----- & McDowell, R. B., *Irish Historical Documents, 1172-1922*, 1943.

Davey, P. J. (ed.), *Medieval pottery from excavations in the North-West*, Liverpool, 1977.

Davies, O. & George, A. H., Norman graveslabs from County Down, in *U.J.A.*, IX, 1946, pp. 37-44.

----- & Quinn, D. B., The Irish Pipe Roll of 14 John, in *U.J.A.*, IV, 1941, supplement.

Davison, B. K., Excavations at Ballynarry, County Down, in *U.J.A.*, XXIV/XXV, 1961-62, pp. 39-87.

Denholm-Young, N., *Seignorial administration in England*, London, 1937.

Department of the Environment, *Official guides* to individual Ancient Monuments.

Dickinson, C. W. & Waterman, D. M., Excavation of a Rath with Motte at Castleskreen, County Down, in *U.J.A.*, XXII, 1959, pp. 67-82.

The Dictionary of National Biography (compact edition), Oxford, 1975.

Documents illustrative of English history in the 13th and 14th centuries, (ed. H. Cole), London, 1844.

Dolley, R. H. M., The Irish mints of Edward I, in *Proceedings of the Royal Irish Academy*, LXVI (C), 1968, pp. 235-97.

-----, *Medieval Anglo-Irish coins*, London, 1972.

----- & Seaby, W. A., *Anglo-Irish coins, John – Edward III, in the Ulster Museum*, Oxford, 1968.

Dugdale, W., *Monasticon Anglicanum*, (ed. J. Caley, H. Ellis & B. Bandinel), 8 vols., London, 1846.

Excavations, Annual Bulletin of Excavations in Ireland, Association of Young Irish Archaeologists, Belfast, 1970-

Faulkner, P. A., Domestic Planning from the 12th to 14th centuries, in *Archaeological Journal*, CXV, 1958, pp. 150-3.

Flanagan, D. E., Moylinny, in *U.J.A.*, XXXII, 1969, pp. 98-9.

-----, The names of Downpatrick, in *Dinnseanchas*, IV, 1971, pp. 89-112.

-----, Three settlement names in County Down, in *Dinnseanchas*, V, 1973, pp. 65-71.

Frame, R., English officials and Irish chiefs in the fourteenth century, in *English Historical Review*, XC, 1975, pp. 748-77.

Fyson, D. R., Some early Northern grave covers, in *Archaeologia Aeliana*, fourth series, XXXIV, 1956, pp. 213-8.

Giraldus Cambrensis, *Expugnatio Hibernica* (ed. B. Scott & F. X. Martin), Dublin, Royal Irish Academy, 1978.

Glasscock, R. E., Moated sites and Deserted Boroughs and Villages, in *Irish Geographical Studies; Essays presented to E. Estyn Evans*, (ed. N. Stephens and R. E. Glasscock), Belfast, 1970, pp. 162-77.

-----, Mottes in Ireland, in *Château Gaillard*, VII, 1974, pp. 95-110.

Goddard, A., Studies in the vegetational changes associated with the introduction of blanket peat accumulation in north-east Ireland, unpublished Ph.D. thesis, Queen's University, Belfast, 1971.

Gwynn, A., Nicholas MacMaol Iosa, in *Feilsgribhin Eoin Mhic Neill*, (ed. J. Ryan), Dublin, 1940.

----- & Hadcock, R. N., *Medieval Religious Houses: Ireland*, London, 1970.

Hayes-McCoy, G. A., *Scots Mercenary Forces in Ireland*, Dublin and London, 1937.

Hill, G., *The Macdonnells of Antrim*, Belfast, 1873.

Hogan, J., The Irish Law of Kingship, in *Proceedings of the Royal Irish Academy*, XL, (C), 1932, pp. 186-254.

-----, The Ui Briain kingship in Telach Oc, in *Feilsgribhin Eoin Mhic Neill* (ed. J. Ryan), Dublin, 1940, pp. 406-44.

Hogg, R., Jarrett, M. G. & Edwards, B. N. J., Excavations at Tullie House, Carlisle, 1954-56, in *Transactions of the Cumberland and Westmorland Archaeological and Antiquarian Society*, LXIV, 1964, pp. 14-62.

Hore, H. F., Marshal Bagenal's Description of Ulster, in *U.J.A.* (1st series), II, 1852, pp. 137-60.

Johnstone, H., *Edward of Carnarvon*, Manchester, 1946.

Jope, E. M., Moyry, Charlemont, Castleraw and Richhill; fortification to architecture in the North of Ireland, in *U.J.A.*, XXIII, 1960, pp. 97-128.

Jope, E. M., Jope H. M. & Johnson, E. A., Harry Avery's Castle, Newtonstewart, County Tyrone; excavations in 1950, in *U.J.A.*, XIII, 1950, pp. 81-92.

-----, Hogg, R. & Hodges, H. W. M., Excavations in Carlisle, 1953, in *Transactions of the Cumberland and Westmorland Archaeological and Antiquarian Society*, LV, 1956, pp. 59-107.

-----, Dunning, G. C. & Hodges, H. W. M., Kirkcudbright Castle, its pottery and ironwork, in *Proceedings of the Society of Antiquaries of Scotland*, XCI, 1957, pp. 117-38.

----- & Seaby, W. A., A square earthwork in North Belfast; the site of the Ekenhead early 14th Century coin-hoard, in *U.J.A.*, XXII, 1959, pp. 112-5.

Leask, H. G., *Irish Castles and Castellated Houses*, Dundalk, 1944.

-----, *Irish Churches and Monastic Buildings*, Dundalk, 3 vols., 1955-60.

Liber Munerum publicorum Hiberniae, (ed. R. Lascelles), vol. I (parts I-V), London, 1829.

Lydon, J. F., An Irish Army in Scotland, in *Irish Sword*, V, 1962, pp. 184-90.

-----, Irish levies in the Scottish Wars, in *Irish Sword*, V, 1962, pp. 207-17.

-----, *The Lordship of Ireland in the Middle Ages*, Dublin, 1972.

Lynn, C. J., Excavation in the Franciscan Friary Church, Armagh, in *U.J.A.*, XXXVIII, 1975, pp. 61-80.

-----, Greencastle, County Down, In *U.J.A.*, XXXIX, 1976, p. 52.

McKeown, L., The Abbey of Muckamore, in *Journal of the Down and Connor Historical Society*, IX, 1938, pp. 63-70.

McNeill, T. E., Ulster mottes, a checklist, in *U.J.A.*, XXXVIII, 1975, pp. 49-56.

-----, Excavations at Doonbought fort, County Antrim, in *U.J.A.*, XL, 1977, pp. 63-84.

Newstead, R., Medieval pottery and kiln at Ashton, near Chester, in *Liverpool Annals of Archaeology and Anthropology*, XXI, 1934, pp. 5-27.

Nicholls, K. W., Rectory, vicarage and parish in the Western Irish dioceses, in *J.R.S.A.I.*, CI, 1971, pp. 53-84.

Nicholson, R., A sequel to Edward Bruce's invasion of Ireland, in *Scottish Historical Review*, XLII, 1963, pp. 30-40.

O Ceallaigh, S., *Gleanings from Ulster history*, Cork, 1951.

Orpen, G. H., *Ireland under the Normans*, 4 vols., Oxford, 1911 and 1920 (reprinted 1968).

-----, The Earldom of Ulster, in *J.R.S.A.I.*, XLIII, 1913, pp. 30-46 and 133-43; XLIV, 1914, pp. 51-66; XLV, 1915, pp. 123-42.

Otway-Ruthven, A. J., The Dower Charter of John de Courcy's wife, in *U.J.A.*, XII, 1949, pp. 77-81.

-----, The organisation of Anglo-Irish agriculture in the Middle Ages, in *J.R.S.A.I.*, LXXXI, 1951, pp. 1-13.

-----, Knight Service in Ireland, in *J.R.S.A.I.*, LXXXIX, 1959, pp. 1-15.

-----, Parochial Development in the Rural Deanery of Skreen, in *J.R.S.A.I.*, XCIV, 1964, pp. 111-22.

-----, *A history of Medieval Ireland*, London, 1968.

Painter, S., *Studies in the history of the English feudal barony*, Baltimore, 1943.

De Paor, L., Cormac's Chapel; the beginings of the Irish Romanesque, in *North Munster Studies*, (ed. E. Rynne), Limerick, 1967.

Pilcher, J., Archaeology, Palaeoecology and 14^C Dating of the Beaghmore Stone Circle site, in *U.J.A.*, XXXII, 1969, pp. 73-91.

Platt, C. & Coleman-Smith, R., *Excavations in medieval Southampton*, Leicester, 1975.

Pollock, A. J. & Waterman, D. M., A Medieval Pottery Kiln at Downpatrick, in *U.J.A.*, XXVI, 1963, pp. 79-104.

Ponsford, M. *et al.*, Medieval kiln wasters from St. Peter's church, Bristol, in *Transactions of the Bristol and Gloucestershire Archaeological Society*, XCI, 1972, pp. 1-9.

Rees-Jones, S. G. & Waterman, D. M., Recent work at Harry Avery's Castle, County Tyrone, in *U.J.A.*, XXX, 1967, pp. 76-82.

Reeves, W., *Ecclesiastical Antiquities of Down, Connor and Dromore*, Dublin, 1847.

Renn, D. F., *Norman Castles in Britain*, London, 1968.

Reports of the Commissioners respecting the Public Records of Ireland, 1810-15.

Reports of the Deputy Keepers of the Public Records of Ireland.

Richardson, J. G., Some Norman Monastic foundations in Ireland, in Watt *et al.*, 1961, pp. 29-43.

Rotuli de Liberate et Misis et Praestitis, regnante Johanne (ed. T. D. Hardy), London, 1844.

Rotulcrum patentium et clausarum cancellariae Hiberniae calendarium (ed. E. Tresham), Irish Record Commission, 1828.

Royal Commission on Ancient Monuments (Scotland): *Inventories.*

Royal Commission on Ancient Monuments (Wales): *Inventories.*

Royal Commission on Historical Manuscripts: *Report on the papers of Lord de L'Isle and Dudley*, 5 vols., London, 1925-61.

Royal Commission on Historical Monuments (England): *Inventories.*

Ryan, J., *Feilsgribhin Eoin Mhic Neill*, Dublin, 1940.

Ryan, M., Native pottery in early historic Ireland, in *Proceedings of the Royal Irish Academy*, LXXIII (C), 1973, pp. 619-45.

St. John, E., The grant of Castleknock to Hugh Tyrel, in *J.R.S.A.I.*, LXII, 1933, pp. 206-20.

Stalley, R. A., *Architecture and Sculpture in Ireland 1150-1350*, Dublin, 1971.

-----, Mellifont abbey; some observations on its architectural history, in *Studies*, Winter 1975, pp. 347-67.

-----, William of Prene and the royal works in Ireland, *Journal of the British Archaeological Association*, CXXXI, 1978, pp. 30-49.

Stenton, F. M., *The first century of English feudalism*, Oxford, 1961.

Tabraham, C., Norman settlement in Upper Clydesdale, in *Transactions of the Dumfries and Galloway Natural History and Antiquarian Society*, LIII, (3rd series) 1977-78, pp. 114-28.

Waterman, D. M., Excavations at Dundrum Castle, 1950, in *U.J.A.*, XIV, 1951, pp. 15-29.

-----, Excavations at the Entrance to Carrickfergus Castle, 1950, in *U.J.A.*, XV, 1952, pp. 103-18.

-----, Excavations at Clough Castle, County Down, in *U.J.A.*, XVII, 1954, pp. 103-63.

-----, Excavations at Dromore Motte, County Down, in *U.J.A.*, XVII, 1954, pp. 164-8.

-----, Excavations at Seafin Castle and Ballyroney Motte and Bailey, in *U.J.A.*, XVIII, 1955, pp. 83-104.

-----, Greencastle, County Donegal, in *U.J.A.*, XXI, 1958, pp. 74-88.

-----, Excavations at Lismahon, County Down, in *Medieval Archaeology*, III, 1959, pp. 139-76.

-----, Piper's Fort, Farranfad, County Down, in *U.J.A.*, XXII, 1959, pp. 83-7.

-----, Excavations at Duneight, County Down, in *U.J.A.*, XXVI, 1963, pp. 55-78.

-----, Notes on Transitional Architectural Fragments in County Donegal, in *U.J.A.*, XXVII, 1964, pp. 133-6.

-----, Somersetshire and other foreign building stone in Medieval Ireland, c. 1175-1400, in *U.J.A.*, XXXIII, 1970, pp. 63-75.

-----, Romanesque stone-carving from Killyleagh, County Down, in *U.J.A.*, XXXIV, 1971, p. 110.

----- & Collins, A. E. P., Excavations at Greencastle, County Down, 1951, in *U.J.A.*, XV, 1952, pp. 87-102.

Watt, J. A., *The Church and the two nations in Medieval Ireland*, Cambridge, 1970.

-----, *The Church in Medieval Ireland*, Dublin, 1972.

-----, Morrall, J. B. & Martin, F. X., *Medieval Studies presented to Aubrey Gwynn, S. J.*, Dublin, 1961.

Webster, G. & Dunning, G. C., A Medieval pottery kiln at Audlem, Cheshire, in *Medieval Archaeology*, IV, 1960, pp. 109-25.

Wilcox, R. J., Timber reinforcement in medieval castles, in *Château Gaillard*, V, 1972, pp. 193-202.

-----, Timber and iron reinforcement in medieval churches, unpublished Ph.D. thesis, Queen's University, Belfast.

Wood-Martin, W. G., *The Lake-dwellings of Ireland*, Dublin, 1886.

Index